Kid Gloves

ADAM MARS-JONES

PENGUIN BOOKS

PENGUIN BOOKS

UK | USA | Canada | Ireland | Australia
India | New Zealand | South Africa

Penguin Books is part of the Penguin Random House group of companies
whose addresses can be found at global.penguinrandomhouse.com.

First published by Particular Books 2015
Published in Penguin Books 2016

001

Copyright © Adam Mars-Jones, 2015

The moral right of the author has been asserted

Set in 12.5 / 15pt Garamond MT Std by
Palimpsest Book Production Ltd, Falkirk, Stirlingshire
Printed in Great Britain by Clays Ltd, St Ives plc

A CIP catalogue record for this book is available from the British Library

978-1-846-14877-4

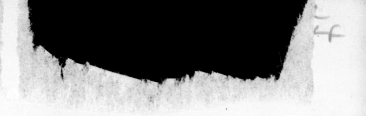

'Moving, lucid and frequently hilarious'
Robert McCrum, *Guardian*, Books of the Year

'A glorious memoir – funny and poignant in equal measure'
Brian Viner, *Daily Mail*

'Portrays painful moments with humour and grace. He brings out the
comic absurdity of his father employing lawyer's arguments to refute
his son's sexuality . . . *Kid Gloves* is full of truth about the ironies of
family life, of the ways that we define ourselves through our parents
and against them' Bee Wilson, *Sunday Times*

'The writing sings with cleverness and wit'
Claudia FitzHerbert, *Sunday Telegraph*

'Deeply engaging . . . a feat of rhetoric, control and, one may say,
devotion' Paul Griffiths, *The Times Literary Supplement*

'Funny and subtle . . . the book's special chemistry derives from
the disparity between the painful facts described and the
affection with which they are recounted'
Gaby Wood, *Daily Telegraph*, Books of the Year

'The account of caring for his father is especially touching . . . an
entertaining, tricky, nuanced portrait' Kate Kellaway, *Observer*

'Mars-Jones's relationship with Sir William, a contradictory character,
was highly complicated and this candid funny and occasionally vexed
memoir charts its highs and lows' *Mail on Sunday*, Books of the Year

'Beautiful, fresh, vivid prose . . . The book brims with humour
and each sentence is a delight to read. It also contains – courtesy
of an extended metaphor drawn from Jane Grigson's recipe for
cooking salmon in a court-bouillon – one of the best descriptions
of sibling rivalry in contemporary literature. Above all, it is a
celebration of language, a love shared by father and son alike'
Andrew Wilson, *Independent*

'Ingeniously constructed and full of insight'
Leo Robson, *The Times Literary Supplement*, Books of the Year

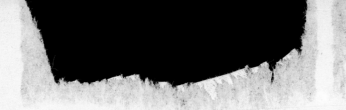

ABOUT THE AUTHOR

Adam Mars-Jones is the author of three novels, *The Waters of Thirst*, *Pilcrow* and *Cedilla*, and two collections of short stories, *Lantern Lecture* and *Monopolies of Loss*. He is also the author of *Blind Bitter Happiness*, a book of essays, and *Noriko Smiling*, a book about Ozu's film *Late Spring*. He lives in London.

Guy Holborn was kind enough to send me a transcript of the appeal hearing in *O'Sullivan & Another v. Management Agency & Music Ltd & Others*. Jill Evans gently pointed out that my ignorance of the law was greater even than I knew.

Parts of this book have appeared in different form in the *London Review of Books*.

For Ebn, Chloe, Holly and Ella

This may be a memoir of my father but I didn't set out to write one, more of an account of a particular time, though necessarily having shreds and slabs of the man scattered across it. I informally moved in with my parents while my mother was dying of lung cancer, something she did with self-effacing briskness in little more than a month. After she was dead, in January 1998, it made sense for me to stay in place to look after the survivor.

My father had been casually described by medical authority as demented, though not officially diagnosed. He was likely to lose his bearings if he had to adjust to a new environment. In fact this was never really something I considered. As an under-employed freelance I had time to spare. Dad had a good pension and his rent for a large flat in Gray's Inn Square was low, thanks to the oligarchic machinery of the Ancient and Honourable Society of Gray's Inn. As a retired High Court judge, ex-Treasurer and bencher his status in its rankings was high. There was money to pay for a certain amount of care, so that I could continue to be present from Tuesday to Friday at the school gates in Dulwich Village when my daughter Holly, six, finished her proto-academic day.

I didn't feel I had a duty to look after Dad, or if I did I preferred to hide it behind a more libertarian formula. I had a right to look after him. I had first dibs, I could play bagsie. It wasn't that I was bounden, merely entitled. My brothers might play a part, but Tim (the older) lived in Gloucestershire and was tied to Dad mainly by the bonds of rejection – a phrase I found in Richard Sennett's book *Authority* and tried to persuade Tim was a productive way of describing his experience. Matthew (the younger), though based in North London, had a fuller workload than I did. I was free to look after Dad and no-one could override my claim. If I was going to end up doing it anyway, it was sensible to surround myself with the most selfish possible arguments. Then I could never make out I had somehow been railroaded into filial duty.

Dad's mental state seemed, to us laymen, closer to withdrawal than any lamentable state of confusion, delusion, vacancy. He could follow conversations without taking an active part, in the time-honoured, head-swivelling fashion of the tennis spectator, happy to watch the interplay with no presumptuous thought of raising a racket himself.

There had been a time when he would smash back everything that came over the net towards him, but he must have forgotten it. Dad had retired as a judge at seventy-five, and in the five years-plus since then he had done nothing remotely active, unless you count listening to Rachmaninov's symphonies. He was a half-serious Celtic fundamentalist who would adopt anyone or anything he admired into the ranks of the faithful, and even lugubrious Rachmaninov (described by Stravinsky as a six-and-a-half-foot scowl, and hardly an obvious candidate for recruitment to the ranks of undersized charmers) could be made over as an honorary Welshman.

Dad wasn't professionally Welsh, if that means any sort of caricature, but he was serious about his Welshness. His English intonation was standard, perhaps modelled on the radio voices he heard in his childhood, before regionalism was a virtue rather than an obstacle to progress. It's true that he deviated from the received pronunciation to say 'sandwich' as 'sangwidge', making it sound like 'language', but that was his only deformation of spoken English. When he spoke Welsh, though, there was an extra vitality detectable, almost a roguish-ness, as if the character that expressed itself in his first language was less thoroughly moralized than the public figure and even the family man.

Welsh people were better – or maybe they just had better names. Osian Ellis the harpist. Caradoc Evans the writer. William Mathias the composer. Clough Williams-Ellis the architect of Portmeirion. Kyffin Williams the painter (rhymes with Puffin). Every sound was firmly enunciated by Welsh speakers, taken care of at both ends, launched and landed.

Welsh tongues held on to every part of the word, even in the case of a straightforward place name like Bangor, separ-ating the syllables but somehow leaving the *g* on both sides of the chasm, rolling the final *r*. Welsh speakers didn't posi-tively give it two stressed syllables, they just couldn't bear to cheat either part of the emphasis that was its birthright. It was as if the natives, unable to defeat the *saesneg* invader on his own appropriated turf, him with his second homes and his gleaming Range Rovers, became interior emigrants, find-ing a refuge in the living rock of the language, and clung to every craggy inch.

Even when speaking English Welsh speakers pronounced words lingeringly. Dad remembered a preacher from his youth whose version of the word 'phenomenon' was like a four-gun salute. 'A cow in a field,' he said, 'is not a phe-no-men-on, and nor is the moon in the sky. But when the cow jumps over the moon . . . *that* is a phe-no-men-on.'

In retirement Dad could seem vague because his attention tended to be de-centred. His hearing was very acute, and even his vision (despite alleged macular degeneration) could be dis-concertingly sharp, picking out window-cleaners at work on the far side of Gray's Inn Square when he wasn't near the window himself.

3

He might comment on something on the radio that no-one else was listening to, which could give an impression of disconnection. A couple of years earlier, when he had been mildly feverish with a kidney infection, I had slept in his room for a couple of nights so as to help with the management of the pee bottle in the long watches of the night. Once I was drifting off to sleep, with the World Service dimly on the radio in the background. The programme was about mountain climbing. I was woken by his voice softly calling out to me. 'Adam?'

'Yes Dad, what is it?'

'Have you ever worn . . . crampons?'

If I hadn't made the connection with what was on the radio, I would have thought he was away with the fairies, not up on the peaks with the alpinists of the airwaves.

It hadn't even seemed certain that he'd be able to take in the fact of Mum's death. His routine the morning after she had died was standard, with a carer arranged by the council helping him along the corridor to the bathroom, but from that moment on the day's routine would be taken apart. I had the feeling, hearing the splash of water in the bathroom and the chatty coaxing, that he was being prepared for execution.

I didn't know what I would do if at some point he asked, 'Where's Sheila?' once he'd been told. Would I have to keep on breaking the news, or would it be better to come up with a story about her being out shopping – away on holiday, even – and hope he wouldn't ask again?

In fact, once he was installed in his bedroom chair and the carer had left, he took in the information fully and cleanly. He said, 'Oh God,' but then after a deep intake of breath turned the exclamation into the beginning of a hymn, singing, 'Our help in ages past, our hope in years to come.' He wept and I held his hand. He never lost sight of the fact of her death, never deluded himself. When, weeks later, I apologized for the fact that he had been given no warning, he seemed surprised, as if it was the most natural thing in the world for his wife of fifty years to slip away without a word.

Sheila had said that she didn't want him to know what was happening. I had just finished telling her that her dying belonged to her and that she shouldn't consider anyone else's wishes, so I could hardly overrule this decision even though I disagreed with it. She said that she could cope with everything except the thought of his life without her, and so we kept him in the dark.

They had stopped sharing a bed when he came home after his stay in hospital with the kidney infection, and his lack of mobility meant that they wouldn't run into each other. They would each call out, 'Good morning, darling,' when the carer was helping him along the corridor to the bathroom. Sheila did her dying only a few yards away from him, but towards the end their connection had dwindled to this ritual exchange. She had uncoupled the marital train and left her husband behind in a siding.

Her last public appearance had been on my birthday, in late October. We had gone to the ENO to see Janáček's *From The House Of The Dead*. It's an uplifting piece of work, if you like your uplift very bleak indeed. My taste rather than hers, though she seemed to enjoy the evening. Her illness hadn't shown itself, still wore the mask of health. She had a cough, but nothing out of the way in a late-October audience. In fact her discreet style of coughing, never disrupting the music, was more like the stylized enactment of symptoms the heroine gives on stage, in an opera of a lusher type, to give formal notice that she is mortally ill. Sheila, on the other hand, had enough energy to walk most of the way home, up St Martin's Lane and then Monmouth Street to where we intersected with the bus routes running along New Oxford Street in the direction of our homes.

Dad took in the fact of Sheila's death cleanly, but didn't ask for details. He may not have realized that her body was still in the flat at the time. When the undertakers came to collect it later in the day there was a potentially awkward moment. His bedroom (not the marital bedroom but what had once been his study) lay immediately inside the flat's front door, and it wasn't usual for his door to be closed. But it wasn't too artificial a piece of behaviour for me to slip into his room and distract him with chat, keeping the door closed behind me, while the undertaker's men passed in through the hall and then back out with their load.

Dad's days were more or less the same before and after his widowering (if that word exists). After his assisted shower he would be based in his room for the morning, with the radio on. Towards lunchtime he would move to the sitting-room and watch television. There was a convention in force that Dad was strongly interested in the news, a fan of rugby no matter who was playing and involved almost on a cellular level when a Welsh squad was on the pitch, but in practice the gaze he turned on the screen was neutral, if not slightly mystified.

I could leave Dad on his own for a couple of hours with a clear conscience, long enough to go to the gym or meet a friend for coffee. I'd tell him when I'd be back, and he was never anxious. I don't know that he actually remembered when I'd be back on such occasions, or even who it was that would be returning. Dad's egotism was deep, though not cold, and he didn't need an acute short-term memory to know that he was Sir William Mars-Jones, and therefore the sort of person who would in the natural order of things be looked after. It would never have occurred to him that he might be restricting my life, and this was as it should be. If family history had played out differently and I had been looking after my mother, things would have been much more difficult, although her personality was much more open and tender, in fact for that very reason. She would have worried obsessively that there were other things I would rather be doing, actually should be doing, and would automatically have characterized herself as a burden. Dad could never be a burden, in his own mind, which was a factor in allowing him not to be one. He didn't obsessively enter other people's thoughts.

It's part of my psychology, not perhaps the deepest part but part of what I work up and perform, to take things in my stride, to make out that nothing slows me down or drags me off course. I tell people that as long as I have ten minutes to myself at some stage, the day feels as if it belongs to me, and saying so makes it more likely. Nevertheless there are hazards to behaving in this way. Like any other policy of believing your own publicity, it can invite the collapse it refuses to consider.

On the other hand, I gave up remarkably little. There was for instance a piano in the flat, an upright Monington & Weston, lacquered in a Chinese style, which my parents had seen on the pavement outside a music shop and decided they had to have. This was the instrument I had learned on, and Dad had learned to blot out the sounds I made in my earliest, most ham-fisted years. I remember him inspecting the sheet music, when I was about thirteen, and asking politely what the marking '*pp*' meant. 'It means very quiet indeed,' I explained. 'Fancy that,' he said neutrally, but I was slow to take the hint. I was having a Debussy phase at the time, but the *Cathédrale Engloutie* from his first book of Preludes wasn't going to stay submerged for long while I was on hand to pump it up.

Now that I was in the full flower of semi-competence, he was tolerant and even appreciative of my playing, though in a rather codified way. He would wait for the end of the first piece and then applaud heartily from wherever he was stationed in the flat, expressing warm approval for a job well done and a hope that the recital was now over. This hint I understood. My taste in music was not his.

It seemed to me that an electronic keyboard would, with its headphone option, enable me to spare Dad any disturbance. I would also be able to play in the late or early hours if I couldn't sleep. I don't know why I didn't ask Dad if he minded me using his money for this purpose. He wasn't likely to refuse. Perhaps I wanted to spice up my virtuous persona with a little high-minded embezzling. What sort of person abuses his power of attorney to steal from his helpless father? I bought an ex-demonstration Clavinova from Chappell's, its price reduced by a third but still amounting to a couple of thousand pounds. It enormously increased my sense of psychological space. It was like having an extra room built onto the flat, where nobody went but me.

I also had access to the organ in Gray's Inn Chapel, by triple permission of Dean, Preacher and Organist. The organist, Christopher Bowers-Broadbent, had actively encouraged me, giving me my only actual piece of advice on how to manage the instrument, though it sounded like something from an old manual of etiquette for lady travellers. *Keep your knees together, and don't look down.*

My sleeping quarters were upstairs in a converted attic. There were small skylights of clouded glass but no windows, and no plumbing. The ceilings were a lot lower than the ones downstairs, and sometimes I hit my head on the lintels despite my long familiarity with the spaces. The flat was built after the war to replace what had been bombed, approximating to the Georgian pattern but making no claim to elegance. My parents had been the first tenants, moving in at about the time I was born, and they had converted the flat ahead of time by installing a spiral staircase to the attic, which would more normally be accessed from a trap door above the shared landing outside the front door.

My love life wasn't hampered by my new role as carer. Dad knew my partner, Keith, well enough, though he had never felt it necessary to remember the name. It certainly wasn't hard to have Keith over for a meal on a Saturday, for instance, and then to say, 'Dad, Keith's going home now,' while in fact running him a bath.

Many of Dad's old friends lived nearby. Emlyn Hooson lived across the landing, Henrietta Wilson was next door at number 5, the formidable Edith Wellwood lived at number 1 (a building dating from 1695 that had dodged the bombs responsible for so much damage to the Inn). The Lewises, Esyr and Elizabeth, lived in South Square a hundred yards or so away. Anything beyond that, the distant purlieus of Raymond and Verulam Buildings, qualified in Edith's eyes as the 'suburbs' of Gray's Inn, though she had the demanding and unstable perspective of the socialist snob, embarrassed that the address given on her birth certificate was Caledonian Road and painfully conscious of being the poorest resident. When she had first seen Gray's Inn in the 1930s, looking down into its gardens from the top deck of a bus, she had wondered what this place could possibly be. A posh lunatic asylum seemed to be the likeliest answer, and now she was an inmate of it.

Gray's Inn was a little legal parish, though increasingly a plutocratic monoculture, much less diverse than it had been in my childhood, when such bohemians as architects and accountants might have their homes there. Earlier in the twentieth century it accommodated without apparent effort an even more wayward, literary type of inhabitant, as exemplified by Edward Marsh and Maurice Baring. Successive Rent Acts have weakened the position of residents, so that only the longest-established can feel themselves secure. Newcomers can hope for nothing better than an assured shorthold tenancy, and must accept that widows have no right to remain. Even in the late 1990s, Gray's Inn was mainly deserted at weekends and outside legal term. The flats are mainly on the top floors of the buildings (the third), with offices on the lower levels. Outside the working week most of those upper windows were dark.

It felt entirely natural to invite Dad's friends to dinner since they were my friends too. And not just dinner: a couple of times I took on the duty, which had been part of my mother's routine, of giving 'the gentlemen' breakfast on a Sunday. The gentlemen in question were the Preacher of the Inn, the Revd Roger Holloway, and the Dean of Chapel, Master (Tony) Butcher. I apologize for a form of words which makes him sound like a card from a Happy Families pack, but this is correct usage within the Inn when referring to benchers.

Roger Holloway was a man whose faith co-existed with a formidable worldliness – while living in Hong Kong in the 1980s he had appeared every day on each of the colony's two television channels, in the morning contributing the equivalent of *Thought for the Day*, presenting a claret-tasting programme on the other channel in the evenings. There can't be many preachers who have used Lady Diana Cooper as an authority for a point of doctrine (the impossibility of repentance as an act of will), quoting her as saying that when she met her Maker she would only be able to say, 'Dear God, I'm sorry I'm not sorry.'

Roger claimed to have a list of names that were guaranteed to kick-start Dad's dormant desire to hold the floor. The one I remember is 'Goronwy Rees' (not a name I knew). Accusations of Cold War-era betrayal and double-dealing would follow. A Welshman who turned his coat was not to be forgiven, even if there was no proof of his treachery. I can't say I ever tried my luck with this Open Sesame. I accepted the new Dad, who was so different from the old one that any flashback would be jarring. He became exasperated from time to time but there were no outbursts.

Dad didn't seem to have religious faith so much as religious confidence. Every morning he woke with the expectation of having fine things shown to him by life or its executive officers. It seemed obvious that God would turn out to (i) exist and (ii) put in a good word. Round His omnipresent neck he might wear a Garrick Club tie.

It was strange to see Dad take so little interest in food after Sheila's death, and even in drink. Gray's Inn was, and perhaps is, very male socially, certainly at the higher levels. Students eat a certain number of dinners in the Hall, while benchers like Dad are well looked after at table. The cellars of the Inn are grandly stocked. When I made arrangements for a reception after Sheila's funeral service in the Chapel, it was proposed that we serve the Inn's 'quaffing wine'. I agreed to this without asking for more detail, though it would have been interesting to know how many grades there were below this, and how many above.

There's a gesture people make in social settings like weddings where drink flows freely, and glasses are discreetly topped up without an enquiry, so as not to interrupt conversation. The gesture involves placing the hand palm down over the glass, symbolically blocking access to the vessel. It's not an elaborate gesture, not a difficult thing to get right, but I never saw Dad make it.

Dad's background in Congregationalist Denbighshire was teetotalitarian – his own father drank only one alcoholic drink in his life, and that was (fair play) a glass of champagne at Dad's wedding reception. I imagine him choking it down as if it was sparkling rat poison. The early prohibition left traces: not having a taste for beer, Dad rather disapproved of pubs, but had no objection to drinking at home or on classier premises.

He had joined the RNVR (Royal Naval Volunteer Reserve) before the War and served on a number of ships, having particularly fond memories of HMS *Euryalus*. The custom of 'splicing the mainbrace', the distribution of a tot of rum daily, was still in force. This Nelsonian beverage was not just a ritualized perk but a form of currency. Favours could be secured or acknowledged by pledging all or part of one's tot.

The smallest possible subdivision of the ration was 'sippers'. When you were taking sippers, everyone would be watching your Adam's apple to make sure it didn't move. The spirit was admitted to the mouth by a subtle suction amounting to osmosis. A larger share was 'gulpers'. When it came to gulpers the Adam's apple was allowed a single movement. When the whole tot was being offered up, the cry was 'Sandy bottoms!'.

Not much remained in Dad's vocabulary of naval lingo, though he did hang on to the expression 'belay the last pipe', used to indicate that an order has been countermanded. I absorbed it unthinkingly, so that it has become my normal way of saying 'Forget what I just said' or 'Ignore my last e-mail' – but then I have to explain what the phrase means, and its advantages as a piece of shorthand disappear.

It doesn't seem likely that Dad got another of his standard phrases – 'Rally buffaloes!' – from his time at sea. It was the very unwelcome phrase he used in our teenage years to tell us to get out of bed.

The staple adult drink that I remember from my childhood was gin and bitter lemon. No-one has been able to explain to me the vogue for this mixer, with a taste both caustic and insipid. Was tonic water rationed in some way?

Sometimes I wonder how anyone of that generation got home safe after a party, at a time when refusing an alcoholic drink was bad manners and the breathalyser didn't exist. Of course the roads were emptier then.

One of Dad's early cases, and one of his favourite anecdotes, involved a charge of drink-driving from that ancient time, the period in a barrister's early professional life when he borrows briefs from his fellows in chambers in advance of a conference with a client, piling them up on his desk to give the necessary impression of a thriving practice.

Dad's client had been charged on the basis of his poor performance walking a straight line. This was the period's low-tech guide to intoxication, a white line drawn on the floor at police stations. Urine tests? Blood tests? Not relevant to the story as he told it.

The client's defence was that he suffered from Ménière's disease, a problem of the inner ear which affects hearing and balance. His was a severe case, making it impossible for him to walk a straight line. Dad marshalled an expert witness to testify to his medical condition. The Crown did the same. The outcome of the case depended, as it so often does, on which of these carried more weight, whether Tweedledum or Tweedledee excelled in authority and gravitas. The expert witness called by Dad gave evidence that the accused did indeed suffer from Ménière's disease, and could not therefore be expected to walk a straight line. The Crown's counterpart testified that he did not in fact suffer from the disease. His inability to walk a straight line amounted only to a confession by the legs that unlawful quantities of alcohol had been admitted to the mouth.

The verdict went in favour of Tweedledum, with Dad's client acquitted. His driving licence was safe – but then it was officially rescinded, on the basis that his severe Ménière's disease rendered him unfit to drive. This was the aspect of the story I liked best, the irony of the trump card turning into the joker. The law is not mocked! Except that Dad's client asked if there was a mechanism for getting his licence back. Yes there was – but he would need to get a medical expert to certify that he didn't have Ménière's disease. A phone call to Tweedledee, and Dad's client was on his way to the swift reissue of a driving licence. The law is mocked on a regular basis, perhaps most heartily by those who make a living from it.

In his free-drinking social circle Dad rarely came up against abstainers, but the parents of Peter Rundell, a schoolfriend of mine when I was ten or eleven, turned out to be fierce advocates of Moral Rearmament. Dad learned this at an evening event that turned out to be governed by the statutes of Prohibition. The discovery gave him a hunted look, and his small talk was unusually small. Though the deprivation hit Dad hard I didn't much care how adults carried on, and I even enjoyed being the Rundells' guest at plays put on at the Westminster Theatre, then a stronghold of Moral Rearmament. I was theatrically naive, but sophisticated enough, even so, to feel uneasy when we in the audience were issued with white sticks during the interval of a play called *Blindsight*. I tapped my way across the lobby with my eyes shut, making broad gestures with my free hand, hoping it would close round an ice cream.

Dad the raconteur, in full flow at the dinner-table, was a very different creature from Dad the solemn upholder of his profession, though he was always confident of his own consistency. I don't think he noticed that the view of the law as an amoral game, which he could pass on with such relish while telling a story such as the one about the alleged Ménière's disease, was the same one that he so violently objected to in the event that other people advanced it and he wasn't in the mood to laugh along.

When he was a beginner at the Bar Dad was able to acquire a wig second-hand, and so was spared the effort of ageing a new one, by dusting it with ash or soaking it in tea. Heavy smokers have an inbuilt advantage when it comes to achieving the yellow tint desired, but the effect isn't immediate.

Those who go shopping for barristers' wigs in long-established shops on or near Chancery Lane, such as Ede & Ravenscroft or Stanley Ley, are offered two tiers of quality, but they aren't all that far apart. They don't correspond to the economy and luxury own-brand lines in a supermarket, since the price differential is hardly more than 10 per cent. If you ask what the difference is, you'll be told that although both are made from horsehair, the more expensive ones are made from the tail hair, the marginally thriftier ones from the mane.

And is tail hair so much better as wig material than mane (which would seem to grow in smaller quantities)? Does that account for the difference in price? If you ask these supplementary questions, and are alone in the shop, and have happened on the right sales assistant, you may be told: 'To put it bluntly, sir, we need to wash the shit out of it.'

After the gin-and-bitter-lemon years, in the 1970s, Dad took to drinking whisky and ginger ale, which he described as a 'whisky sour' though it bears no real relation to the drink of that name.

Alcohol amplified something Dad also felt in full sobriety, a sense of disappointment with the way his sons were developing. This was especially true in the mid-1970s, when we were all coming to the end of our education. Where was our drive, our ambition? We seemed to be coasting at best. He wasn't so much disappointed as incredulous. We seemed to think the world owed us a living!

There was some truth in this, of course, though it could hardly be otherwise. Our circumstances were so different from his. He had tunnelled through rock to make his way in the world, while we had been accustomed from an early age to using the tube, with Chancery Lane station just round the corner from our childhood home.

Dad's ideal was that we would all become lawyers, which would be following his footsteps in one sense, except that his drive and ambition had taken him very far from the paths trodden by his farming ancestors. To follow him would be very different from being like him, would mean in fact that we were very unlike him. The more we were like him the less we would follow him. All this tangle needs to be kept distinct from the common-sense awareness that we would most likely never emerge from his shadow and be assumed, even if we went on to 'great things', to have got our start thanks to his eminence. It was understandable that he wanted us to soar, but how could we do that if we used him as a launch-pad?

We confidently diagnosed Dad in the popular-science terms of the day as a 'Type A personality', unable to relax, likely to suffer from strokes, heart attacks and other forms of stress-related condition, the self-inflicted wounds of an oppressive character. When he developed a stomach ulcer it seemed to prove us right, though that particular line of punitive pseudo-medical reasoning has since been discredited and retired.

Dad always called sherry 'sherry wine' with a slightly lah-di-dah pronunciation, though I didn't know what nuance of pretension was being identified. Sherry wasn't classified by Dad as a women's drink – it was associated with the young man who had saved my parents' lives in Spain the year after they were married, when they had got themselves into difficulties swimming. On special occasions we might toast his name. ¡Xavier Cremades!

When the time came, Sheila organized a retirement party for him at the Garrick. She decided to serve champagne cocktails, the only such drink she herself liked. She also decided to do things properly, improving on the standard catering protocol whereby the drink is topped up with champagne but the other ingredients (a little brandy, a few drops of angostura, a sugar lump) are not reinforced. On this special occasion, there would be no mere top-up but the provision (expense be damned) of a whole new drink.

Surely she knew she was playing with firewater? Even the angostura raises the alcohol content. Only the sugar can enter a plea of not guilty, and even then can be suspected of aiding and abetting by disguising the potency of the drink with sweetness. Dad had a strong head for alcohol in those days, which is only a way of saying that it distorted him less on the surface than in the depths. In the second hour of the party a woman of my generation, known to him since her birth, exercising perhaps unconsciously the double privilege of good looks and long intimacy, made some mild enquiries about the ideological assumptions of the judiciary – the sort of thing that might be aired on *Start the Week* without setting the switchboard alight. She asked Bill (as she called him, having graduated to that intimacy from Uncle Bill) if he thought judges as a group had really taken on board the recent upheavals in society, such as multiculturalism and the transformed position of women.

This was never the sort of speculation that Dad welcomed, but perhaps the champagne cocktails played a part in making him so grandly cold, coldly grand. He told her that she had spoiled his party and must leave immediately. She was horrified and did what she could to make amends, saying that casting any sort of shadow on his special day had been the furthest thing from her mind. She was terribly sorry if she had given offence. Again it may have been the influence of the cocktail, multicultural in its own right, combining champagne and brandy from the Old World, sugar and bitters from the New, which gave Dad's verdict its austere force. 'That,' he said, 'is something you will have to live with for the rest of your life.'

This was a dismal own goal, to send a guest away, taking all the shine off the occasion, and a warning that some of Dad's less appealing behaviour patterns were still some way from retirement.

There were times after he retired when Dad would have to be helped the two hundred yards home from Hall, more or less to the point of being carried by Inn staff or fellow benchers. This was hideously embarrassing, for my mother having to receive this stumbling procession of dignitaries, for me if I happened to run into them as they tried to negotiate the steps outside number 3 Gray's Inn Square, but it was nowhere as bad as it might have been if he had felt any shame himself. Hangdog wasn't his style, or it wasn't until the next morning. He was serene, as if this was the way he always came home, or as if these nice fellows had wanted to give him a treat and he hadn't liked to say no. The whole charade made it surprisingly easy to play along.

Sometimes he would remain roughly vertical until he reached the bedroom, then topple slowly sideways without distress to the floor, perhaps pulling some bedclothes with him in what was more a slide than a fall, a controlled descent with a touch of the maladroit grace of the performers he most admired, Max Wall, Tommy Cooper, Ralph Richardson.

Moderation didn't come naturally to Dad, and self-discipline needed reinforcement from outside. At various points in later life Dad went to a luxurious health farm, his favoured being called Champneys, to lose a few pounds. The regime also required abstinence from alcohol. These expensive bouts of self-denial could be redeemed if he happened to coincide with a woman who shared his taste and talent for flirting. Flirtation without possibility made the hours speed by. Age didn't disqualify such compatible women, but nor certainly did youth. The word he used of them was 'sparklers'.

Flirtation as he practised it wasn't any sort of rehearsal for infidelity but a formal vocal display, lyrical rather than heroic, little Wigmore Hall recitals rather than opera house *tours de force*. When a woman friend of mine paid a visit to the Gray's Inn flat, Dad called her 'darling'. My mother was only marginally piqued, but decided to patrol the marital perimeter by asking sweetly, 'If Frances is Darling, what then am I?'

In general Dad imposed himself on company by force of personality rather than brute quickness of wit. His preferred style was the polished story ('Did I ever tell you about the time . . . ?'), not the dazzling improvisation. It helped that from his perch among the higher ranks of a hierarchical profession he didn't often meet the Challenge Direct. But now he had to exert steady pressure on the charm pedal if he was to accelerate safely out of danger. 'Sheila is Darling One,' he said, 'Frances is Darling Two.' This formula not only smoothed any ruffled wifely feathers but passed into currency. If Frances was visiting, or if Dad answered the phone to her, he would greet her as Darling Two, and be rewarded, as we all hoped to be, by her throaty smoker's laugh.

In the absence of sparklers Champneys could be a bit of a martyrdom, forcing his thoughts inward. Once I received a postcard from him at that address, saying: 'No sparklers here this time. You have always been a rewarding son.' The lack of a logical connection only added to the touchingness of the message. Except when in exile from bibulous normality, this was a vein of intimate introspection that he preferred to leave alone.

From quite early on in his career, perhaps even before he became a judge, Dad had told us about how he was looking forward to retirement, to all the things he would set his hand to when he only had the time, although he undertook hobbies (such as painting in oils or french-polishing) only in brief unrestful spasms. As a family we had once built a Mirror dinghy, and this was a hobby he organized and delegated. The Mirror dinghy was a kit, though of a full-sized craft, a flat-pack yacht, ordered through the *Daily Mirror*. There were red sails to match the *Mirror*'s masthead, though I'm not sure I had seen the newspaper then (ours was a *Times* and *Express* household). We were all dragooned into doing some of the work in the garage of our holiday house, attaching the prefabricated pieces to each other with twists of copper wire before waterproofing the seams (caulking them, even, in an amateurish way) with a strong-smelling resin paste. His actual hobby wasn't building a boat, more being the clerk of works, project manager of a small family boat-building business.

After about a week of supervised labour it was time to join the assembled parts into something close to the finished shape, except that it turned out we had been making, with our different teams working on different sides of the garage, two starboard sides instead of mirrored twins. Our Mirror dinghy failed the mirror test. The two halves might snuggle up to each other, nestling together like spoons, but they would never mate. We had proved the advertisers wrong when they had claimed the instructions to be foolproof.

Dad paid a local handyman to unbodge our bodging and put the dinghy together properly, though it would probably have been cheaper to buy another kit and make two port sides this time. Then we could have had the beginning of a fleet. But the holiday was already almost over, and there was a factor of humiliation involved. It can never feel good to hire a third party to do your DIY. The finished dinghy – finished by other hands – was seaworthy and serviceable but never quite smelled of success, and that was perhaps Dad's real addiction, the resinous perfume he needed to have in his nostrils.

Still, he was positive that there would be memoirs and radio plays, there would be songs – he was handy with a guitar, not practising much but reliably energized by an audience.

Even after I had been published he was confident he would put me in the shade. He had no doubt that he would be able to blast his own work over the makeshift crossbar of my slight success as effortlessly as Barry John converting a try in front of roaring crowds. He seemed to think that my psychology was robust enough to cope with being superseded when his own books started appearing, but he did worry about how Matthew, whose business was music and recording, would handle the blow to his confidence when Dad's first single stormed all the way to Number One.

If he had doubts he kept them to himself. Anxiety wasn't for public consumption, and if he worried then he did it on his own time. Yet he held on tight to his job and didn't retire before he had to, in 1990, at seventy-five. Not so long before, retirement had been something for judges to choose for themselves without an imposed schedule, but that system too had its drawbacks, and even Lord Denning, influential Master of the Rolls and Dad's hero as a prose stylist, was immortal a little too long.

Dad continued to work part-time after technically retiring, presiding over the elaborate arguments of a litigant-in-person named Petch, who was suing his employers in the civil service. Amateurs in court require careful steering. They're likely to be long-winded, often nervous, sometimes even truculent, and they aren't attuned, the way professional counsel are, to shifts in a judge's body language, the little signals meaning that a line of argument is finding favour or should instantly be abandoned. Dad was patient and generous with such solo pilots of litigation, though his brother judges tended to have less respect for their erratic though predictable manoeuvres.

He always called them that, his brother judges, often adding the name, 'my brother Elwyn' for instance, as if this was a blood relation. Mightily he was teased by his sons for this, as they pretended to believe these were new discoveries on the Mars-Jones family tree, a job lot of stuffy uncles emerging from the woodwork.

In the case of Petch, though, the proceedings meandered on to the point where Dad lost confidence in his ability to pull everything together with a lucid summing-up. He lost some sleep over that. Then the case was finally settled before he was called upon to give judgment. He was probably as pleased as the plaintiff.

In retirement Dad was presumably not under as much stress as he was used to, but he could still come up with the odd explosion, so perhaps stress wasn't a factor in the first place. One detonation was on a birthday of mine, which I had decided to have in the Gray's Inn flat. This was a calculated risk, and it might seem as if I was asking for trouble, but there were reasons: a family friend had embarked on her travels but cut them short after dysentery, and was recovering in the flat – I didn't want her to miss out on the event. My parents were out that evening themselves, so there seemed no reason not to celebrate demurely on the premises. In the end the convalescing friend went home to Brighton, though by then the arrangements had been made, so she missed an event that turned out to be memorable.

My parents came home from their party in time to overlap with mine. Sheila socialized for a little while, then started making preparations for bed. At first Dad was genial. Then he took offence at an innocent remark made by one of the guests, and told him to leave. I pointed out that he could only logically order out people he had himself invited, and that my guests were welcome until such time as I expelled them – but the mood was no longer festive, and we beat a massed retreat. As I was gathering together the presents I had been given, Dad came up to me and poked me in the chest. I could have dropped the presents and stayed upright, but like a game-show contestant I was determined to hang on to my trophies. I knew there was a sofa behind me and chose to topple backwards onto that.

This was not the birthday present I would have hoped for from Dad. As we trooped out of the flat and made our way downstairs, Sheila appeared on the landing above us in her nightie, wringing her creamed hands and saying in social agony, 'It's all right for you lot – you can leave. I have to live with it.' She had left the sitting-room for ten minutes, the way people do in films about poltergeists, and the next thing she knew her furniture was arranged on the ceiling. 'It' was Dad's bad behaviour, his short fuse, unless it was actually a wick that drew rage from his glass by capillary action.

The birthday assault was so out of proportion as not even to be properly upsetting. I decided to make an experiment in apology studies. Better in the circumstances to steer clear of any non-apology, un-apology, anti-apology. If demanding redress from Dad never seemed to work, perhaps I should try a new approach, to see if he was vulnerable from a different angle. The best rhetorical move (against a master of rhetoric) might be to say that I didn't need an apology. Dad knew the martial arts of argument supremely well, and could turn almost any throw against an opponent, but if I stepped smoothly away he might topple backwards in his turn, from sheer surprise.

The day after my birthday I went round to Gray's Inn and explained that I wasn't expecting an apology. I explained that this was because Dad was a loose cannon when he had drink inside him. If I put him and my friends together in the same space then I had to accept the risk and not bleat when things went wrong.

I knew from long experience that Dad's apologies weren't worth having anyway. In our teenaged years we were incensed by the forms of words that Dad would come up with after family rows. They seemed designed to wind up the tension rather than soothe it in any way. They were strange cocktails of amnesia, shoulder-shrugging and indirect accusation. If I had to name a specific cocktail I'd nominate the boilermaker, with its bright and murky liquor floating in layers. An example might be: *Sheila tells me that you were upset by something I said last night . . . I don't remember what it was, but all I can say is . . . you can be very annoying.*

Perhaps this was what is known as professional deformation, as much as individual difficulty with the idea of being at fault. Lawyers will never be in a hurry to admit liability. For them it must always be a last resort. A. P. Herbert makes a semi-serious point along these lines in one of his *Misleading Cases*. A describes B as lacking even the manners of a pig. B demands an apology. A capitulates to the demand, saying that B does in fact have the manners of a pig. Does this count as an apology or as an aggravation of slander?

In this case Dad didn't exactly topple. He was outraged at my patronizing and manipulative manoeuvre, and responded with one of his own. He told me to leave at once, and when I didn't move he made to pick up the phone, saying he would call the police and have me thrown out. This was low-grade bluster by his standards, as was the demand that I should surrender my keys and pay no further visits to the parental home. Sheila overruled him the moment he said so. I stayed long enough to establish as a matter of record that I wasn't being thrown out, then left him to simmer.

24

I hoped that my destabilizing tactics would enable Sheila, who didn't enjoy the rooted place, even the ascendancy, of alcohol in the household, to make some demands of her own. This was a lot to hope for, given that she hated any kind of 'atmosphere' and had never made much headway when it came to influencing Dad's behaviour. The morning of a hangover was one of the few opportunities she was able to turn to her advantage, reinforcing the self-disgust of Dad's every lurching cell with a little tender chiding. At other times Dad had a blithe resistance to the virtues he had married, something that I've seen in other men of his generation.

For a week or so I paid visits only when she would be alone. Did I wear him down? Not quite. I got a letter that combined different elements of his most characteristic manner: rueful charm and now-look-here-laddie-enough-is-enough. The letter was much closer to an apology than anything I could remember, in speech let alone in writing. It broke precedent in that respect, which is never a step a lawyer takes lightly. In fact precedent was holy to him, but now, unprecedentedly, fault was being admitted.

The rueful charm emanated from the address given at the top of the page: *The Doghouse, Gray's Inn*. The note of enough-is-enough was struck by a passage which made clear that Dad did not accept there was a pattern of behaviour attributable to drink. I could have a specific apology but no general admission. It was a lawyerly way of proceeding after all, an apology 'without prejudice', as if he was agreeing to make a payment to an injured party without technically admitting liability. He would accept chastisement as long as he wasn't expected to abase himself. It was the most favourable settlement I was going to get.

Dad the widower wasn't much tempted by alcohol, though he still liked champagne as an idea, essence of spontaneity and celebration. He enjoyed orange juice as part of breakfast, and this was one of the few deeply rooted pleasures that I could continue to administer. Though the kitchen of the flat was relatively short on labour-saving devices we could boast a small electric squeezer, whose ageing engine ground away not very effectively when the halved fruit was pushed down on it, its automatic-reverse mechanism cutting in from time to time with disconcerting abruptness.

At a certain point I changed Dad's routine, and my own, preferring to see Keith on Mondays at the Highbury flat and letting Matthew take charge of Dad. Shopping on a Monday I saw a wide variety of types of orange on display in a super-market, and bought large quantities. I thought it might be fun to have a taste test, to establish which variety Dad liked best. Matthew was happy to be master of ceremonies for a blind tasting.

In fact Dad derailed the format with his response to the first sample. He gave it 10 out of 10, making it unlikely that even the most gifted statistician could extract meaningful infor-mation from his subsequent scores. In any case he gave full marks to all the other juices he was offered.

Had he detected the patronizing children's-activity-time element in the evening planned for him? I'd actually like to think so, though I imagine he was just in an appreciative mood. Maybe he enjoyed seeing two sons in one day, even if his pet name for Matthew in this period was Nogood Boyo, a Dylan Thomas reference which Matthew took in good part but which nettled me on his behalf.

During this late phase of his life the drink which meant most to him, more even than orange juice, was buttermilk, a taste from his childhood which could be catered to by visiting any large branch of Sainsbury's. Despite his sweet tooth in other areas he would drink it as it was, straight from the glass.

In his Denbighshire childhood, on his way to school, he would dip his finger into the milk churn waiting for collection at the side of the road. His finger would break into the creamiest layer of the top of the milk, and convey its unique flavour to his mouth. This was a taste that was beyond Sainsbury's power to reproduce – Taste the Difference 1920s Denbighshire Farm Top-of-the-Milk Fresh from the Churn – even at the chain's largest and most cosmopolitan branches.

A book came out that year called *The Justice Game*, by Geoffrey Robertson, with a very favourable mention of Dad. Sir William Mars-Jones was offered as proof (though this was the only example given) of the argument that civil rights and press freedom are safe in the hands of the judiciary, on the basis of his handling of the ABC trial of the late 1970s, in which two journalists and their source were charged under the Official Secrets Act.

Dad was still living at the heart of the legal community, and sometimes colleagues would call in on him. I left Robertson's book on display by Dad's chair, having inscribed it *For Dad on Father's Day 1998 / see pages 128–32, whenever you need a lift*. The idea was that distinguished legal visitors would pick up the volume and be led to the relevant passage by this inscription, though of course they might resort directly to the index, in search most urgently of their own names and then their host's. Dad had never been uncomfortable with applause, and now he could receive the book's accolade any number of times, with a wondering pleasure that could never go stale. I imagined him after a visitor had left, ringing like a lightly struck bell with the reverberation of recent praise, unsure whether he had really only dreamed it.

When we were children Dad would tell us that the noblest profession was the preacher's, the second noblest the teacher's and third the lawyer's. I don't know why doctors didn't get a look in, but it was obviously important for Dad's chosen profession to make the top three. When someone once quoted the maxim 'suffer any injustice rather than go to law' in his hearing, he was greatly offended. This cynical notion struck at the roots of his vocation. Perhaps he realized, as I have only just done, that it was a worldly paraphrase of 1 Corinthians 6:7 – 'Now therefore there is utterly a fault among you, because ye go to law one with another. Why do ye not rather take wrong? why do ye not rather suffer yourselves to be defrauded?' In his capacity as preacher St Paul might have the luxury of pulling rank over teachers and lawyers, but he could certainly be a pain in the neck.

As Dad explained it to his young family, it was his job to decide who was telling the truth. This sounds rather more like the jury's job, but Dad always held on to the idea of a necessary connection between law and the truth of things. He would never have agreed that a barrister is someone who wins arguments for a living, though that might be an outsider's way of putting it.

There were trophies from successful cases on display in the Gray's Inn flat which fascinated me as a child, since they occupied an intermediate state between toy and self-sufficient adult object. One was a model of the internal workings of a steam locomotive's engine, made of wood in muted shades of green, yellow and red. There was a sheet of perspex over the assembly, but a wheel on the side could be turned to demonstrate the action of the piston. Children's toys of the period, the late 1950s or early '60s, didn't do a great deal, but they could do a bit more than that, and this object was somehow more precious than a toy although less satisfying.

It was of course an exhibit from a case of Dad's, used by him in court to demonstrate how a careless train driver, leaving the cab and for some reason venturing onto the rails, could be run over by a locomotive he had confidently assumed was stationary and would remain so. I don't know who it was that retained Dad's services, possibly an individual railway line or else the British Transport Commission – the National Railways Board if it was after 1962. Presumably, too, Dad had been hired to argue against compensation, or at least to limit it.

As a sensitive child (is there any other kind?) I should by rights have been haunted by the image of this terrible event, with its resonance of the heartless rhymes I found so hard to get out of my head (*Lucy met a train / the train met Lucy / the rails were juicy / the juice was Lucy*).

In those days my sympathies went most readily to animals or to suffering mothers. In any case sorrow reached me most reliably through books. I haunted the Holborn Public Library and soon graduated from the children's shelves in the basement to the adult holdings. My mind wanted to grow up as soon as possible, though there were areas of experience that I shrank from.

The nearest bookshop to Gray's Inn was Her Majesty's Stationery Office on High Holborn, whose stock in trade puzzled me since it contained nothing remotely readable. Her Majesty's interests seemed very specialized. I was determined to find something worthy of my book token just the same, and eventually found a small volume with an enticing cover, illustrated with colourful birds. There were no pictures inside, but that was a challenge I was used to. It wasn't easy to become emotionally involved with a book about Scottish game bird populations, statistically analysed, but I managed to break my heart over the inexorable decline of *Tetrao urogallus urogallus*, the capercaillie.

Precociously reading a Balzac novel (I was perhaps thirteen by this stage), I came across a passage where the hero borrowed his mother's life savings so as to launch himself in the world. I couldn't bear to read any further, knowing that he was going to ruin her. I could imagine nothing worse. A steam locomotive would have weighed lightly on me compared to the dreadfulness of impoverishing a mother.

Connected with the model of the locomotive's inner workings was another trophy, more obviously dazzling but equally far from the possibility of play – a locomotive name plate, with raised gold lettering against red, mounted at an angle on a stand and given pride of place on the room divider that lived inside the front door, breaking up the space of the hall (a piece of furniture that has since outlived its own naffness and become not only evocative but collectable). The name on the plate was MARS. The locomotive in Dad's successfully argued case had been in the same class (the Planet class). Having done well by his employers, he had asked to be notified if the time came for MARS to be scrapped and in due course had been presented with its name plate. It too is collectable, though unfortunately the value of locomotive name plates is assessed according to the number of letters, and MARS is about as skimpy a plate as exists. There's no equivalent of the scoring system in Scrabble. There are no triple word scores, nor even extra points for rarer letters (in which case the M would push the total up a little). So what you want to find in your shed is the SIR TRAFFORD LEIGH MALLORY. The value of the MARS plate shrinks still further when a prospective buyer discovers it was only ever attached to a goods train. It's a blue-collar plate, not worth much more than the metal it was cast from.

Dad was christened William Lloyd Jones, with the second barrel added to the surname only at his father's urging when he was on dangerous duty (Russian convoys) during the War. The thinking seemed to be that the enhancement of his name would protect him in some way. It was a life raft launched by deed poll. Dad was proud of the distinctive compound form that resulted, and I've mildly enjoyed inheriting it, though I can't say I would go to war to defend my hyphen. The last of my film reviews to be published by the *Independent*, in 1997, appeared under a version of my name with the hyphen inserted in the only other place that is anatomically possible without rupturing tissue (Adam-Mars), which seemed a low blow, after the hundreds of pieces I had filed over the previous decade, but the injury, though curiously literal, was only symbolic. The component letters seem intractable for anagram-making purposes but can be persuaded to yield the pleasing nonsense of As Modern As Jam.

Though in two parts, the surname isn't cumbersome, hardly taking any longer to pronounce than (say) Markham or Johnson. The schoolboy nicknames it made possible (Mars Bar, Marzipan) carried no great sting. Names can function as shields in a school setting, protecting the bearer from the more personal assaults of Fatty, Spotty, Speccy.

Dad himself experienced a little public teasing on the basis of the name, when his great friend Peter Thomas appeared against him in a case of sheep-stealing, and had fun with the formal introduction of counsel by saying, 'My Lord, in this case I represent the Crown, while my learned friend Mr Ma-a-a-a-s-Jones . . . appears for the defence.' Meh-eh-eh-ehs-Jones? I don't know which transcription best conveys the fondly jeering bleat. It's the massing of syllables that counts against Hedgepinshot-Mandeville-Pickwort (a minor character in *The Apes of God*) and even against Christopher Bowers-Broadbent, the organist of Gray's Inn. When I read my first *Guinness Book of Records* as a child – I was slow to understand that reference books don't have to be read from cover to cover – my eyes filled with tears when I imagined the schoolboy teasing that must have been meted out to the bearer of the longest surname in history: Tollemache-Tollemache de

Orellana Plantagenet Tollemache-Tollemache. Yes, that was all surname, every bit of it, according to the *Guinness Book of Records*, and I wouldn't have dreamed of questioning any such authority (in fact any book, at that time). It seemed a pity, though, that the name lacked the full complement of hyphens to give its freight-train length a proper set of couplings.

It bothered me that the British record was always smaller than the world record, less impressive, unless of course they happened to be the same thing. To my mind, over-instructed and under-informed as it was, pickled in the jingoism of ignorance, the British record should always be bigger than the world record, or what was the point of being British? My dogmatism would have made me a good little Red Guard, though in practice I didn't join the Scouts or even the Wolf Cubs.

I should have kept firm mental hold of the British billion with its dozen zeroes, a thousand times larger than what the Americans had to offer. Our billion was the biggest in the world until 1975.

A year or two after the steam-engine cutaway another supertoy arrived, a meticulous balsa-wood model of a railway bridge, about four feet long. It must have been built as a visual aid for another case of Dad's, but if I was ever told about the human disaster that led to the litigation I soon forgot it. This mighty piece of engineering did eventually find its place in our world. The model railway layout in the attic, mounted on trestle tables, had reached its maximum size until someone realized that it could extend beyond the awkward area (too narrow for a table) that limited it, by the installation of the providential bridge, which happened to be to scale, more or less. The model railway was already rather elaborate, so that the gala displays we gave for other Inn children required typed programmes and a lot of choreography if all our gadgets were to be properly shown off. After some bravura shunting to get the audience warmed up, a mailbag would be magically collected by a train that didn't need to stop to pick it up, the giraffe sticking out above the carriage marked ZOO would lower its head in obedience to a concealed magnet inches before striking a low bridge, and (when pop culture had started to colonize and contaminate the Tri-ang Hornby arcadia) rockets fired from one train triggered the destruction of a carriage on another, the panels leaping apart from the impact of a spring-loaded arm whose final act was to detonate a cap, leaving a little wisp of acrid smoke to hang in the air of the attic. Applause.

Dad always told us when we were little that he could tell when someone was lying. With children this is a safe, self-fulfilling prophecy, and it certainly worked with us up to a certain age. But he also made out that his divination was just as effective outside the immediate context of family.

Dad was proud of having sized up a potential client called Kevin McClory as being honest, though McClory's narrative had the odds stacked against it. He had taken it to a number of lawyers already, according to Dad, and none of them had thought there was any substance in his claims. This was the early 1960s. Kevin McClory's story was that Ian Fleming had stolen work he had done for a James Bond screenplay and incorporated it without payment or credit into a James Bond novel, *Thunderball*. It wasn't an easy claim to believe. Successful authors attract allegations of plagiarism as fine wool sings to the moth.

Was it likely that a writer with a reputation and a following would stoop to stealing another man's ideas? Much more probable, surely, for a nonentity to be searching for a payoff in return for not making any more trouble. Nevertheless Dad looked him in the eyes, decided Kevin McClory was telling the truth and agreed to represent him.

In the fantasy I somehow absorbed of what happened in court Dad cross-examined the snooty Fleming, who of course drawled through his cigarette holder throughout, then finally broke down and admitted iniquity. The patient intellectual abrasion of cross-examination is the forensic equivalent of those mills of God which grind slow but grind exceeding fine. It was Dad's special skill, thanks in part to a subtly aggressive instinct and in part to the hundreds of hours he put into mastering the material in all its aspects, and this was a complicated case, heard in front of Mr Justice Ungoed-Thomas, whose magnificent name makes him seem half Welshman and half mushroom.

In fact the case was settled, on humiliating terms for Fleming, without his going under Dad's forensic dentist's drill. McClory received damages and also the film rights to the contested story, which meant he could now make his own James Bond film, although he didn't own film rights to the character of 'James Bond' outside a narrowly defined context.

Even so it was a tremendous result. Kevin McClory had suits made on Savile Row with '007' embroidered on the inside breast pockets, now that he had a licence to make a killing. It must have been quite a payday for Dad too. A colleague of his remembered his fee for the case as being £10,000, not in today's money but in 1963 pounds. And not in fact in pounds but guineas – the extra shilling over each twenty would go to his clerk. Dad loved to pronounce the abbreviation for guineas that appeared on chambers invoices ('Guas') the way it was written, as 'gwahs', and no wonder.

If the sum is accurate, then its vast size must reflect both the importance of the case and the fact that this was a client with deep pockets and access to his wealthy wife's capacious handbag.

Dad was proud of the result he had achieved for his client and took the family to a gala preview of *Thunderball*. At ten, I was not yet at the age when boys long to see the films from which their parents want to protect them. I was at an age when I longed to be protected from the film my parents wanted me to see. The underwater battle which provides the film with its climax (very much Kevin McClory's idea, as was established in court) horrified me with the grimness of its violence. I kept my eyes closed as much as I could while the harpoon-guns did their worst, and managed not to develop any overwhelming fetish for scuba gear.

Courtroom advocacy is just as much a performing art as dance or theatre. A courtroom is routinely described as being a sort of theatre itself, but it's a small one – closer to a rehearsal studio than a stadium – and the performance is never repeated. You have to be there. It leaves no traces except written ones, though we're so used to seeing court cases on film and television that the evanescence of the real thing gets forgotten. It's easier to form a direct impression of Anna Pavlova's skills than F. E. Smith's. Even if Dad had been given his chance to flay Ian Fleming in the witness box there would only be circumstantial evidence to show how he went about it.

The closest thing I can get to a display of Dad's expertise as a barrister in the *Thunderball* year of 1963, when he must have been at his most formidable, is the cross-examining of witnesses he did during the Vassall tribunal, as transcribed in the eventual report. Even so it's like looking at a musical score that lacks expression marks, tempo indications, dynamics. I suppose it's obvious that the spoken word is elusive even when it has the power to win or lose people money – or freedom – but I had never really thought about it.

John Vassall was a civil servant who had been sent to prison for eighteen years in 1962 after being convicted of passing secrets on to the Soviets. While working at the British embassy in Moscow during the 1950s he had been invited to a party, drugged and photographed in compromising positions with a number of men. The question for the tribunal to decide was whether he had been shielded by his superiors during his miserable career of espionage, the implied motive being a shared sexual secret if not necessarily ideological common ground, though the two were generally thought to converge. Was there in fact (as press coverage of the case had broadly hinted) a nest of perverted traitors at the Admiralty? Why had T. G. D. (Tam) Galbraith, a Conservative Party politician and Civil Lord of the Admiralty, sent letters to a junior civil servant, one who was apparently known in his department as 'Aunty', and had even visited him in the Dolphin Square flat that was so obviously too luxurious for a junior's income such as his?

I remember Dad referring to Vassall at the time, and my confusion about whether this was a name of a person or a role. I knew that to be a vassal was to be an underling, though I don't know how I knew. Perhaps despite my imperviousness to history I had learned something about feudalism at school, though it was too early for the celebrated Jackdaw series put out by Jonathan Cape, reinforced folders of documents in facsimile that made the past come alive, to my myopic eyes, by making it shine on the level of stationery. From Dad's grim tone when he said the word 'Vassall' I knew not to ask questions, and osmotically absorbed the message that submissiveness was always culpable, though for some people an inescapable destiny.

The Vassall tribunal was Britain's mirror-image of the Stalin-era show trial, not a charade of manufactured guilt but a masque of questionable innocence. Some sort of whitewash took place under floodlights. If there had been actual evidence against Galbraith, his resignation would long since have been offered and accepted. Instead the ranks had closed behind him, and being examined in public on the eleventh day of the tribunal, Thursday, 31 January 1963, was an ordeal for him but not a hanging matter. It was his job to get through the day somehow, and Dad's job was to trip him up.

It wasn't likely that an experienced politician like Galbraith would be broken down by cross-examination, assuming that such breakdowns are anything more than a convention of courtroom scenes in films and plays. Mars-Jones QC wasn't going to land a knockout blow, nor was it his job to, but he could do something entirely appropriate for counsel retained by the Beaverbrook press, by inflicting paper cuts.

Mars-Jones QC puts it to Galbraith that he is conceding some degree of friendship with Vassall. Galbraith ties himself in knots trying to resist that impossible formula 'some degree of friendship'.

'I tried to be friendly with everybody,' he says, 'but it is not the same thing as being a friend of anybody's . . . It is impossible to say one is an enemy. I think one is therefore presumably a friend.'

Mars-Jones QC presses the point: '. . . there was no degree of friendship between you and Vassall at any time?' 'If friendship implies affection, no. I do not know what friendship means, you see, it is such a wide word.'

He claimed to see no difference between *Dear Vassall* and *My dear Vassall* as forms of address in correspondence. (How glad he must have been not have written *Dear John* or *My Dear John*, leaving the smoking gun of a Christian name in Vassall's possession.) Under pressure from Mars-Jones QC he says, 'I am therefore going to eliminate the word "my" from my vocabulary.' Any impossibility of retrieving Dad's tone applies equally to Galbraith. The last sentence could be delivered with an attempt at dismissive lightness or with real exasperation.

It was being formally established at a public hearing that

37

Beaverbrook's papers had printed only responsible innuendo, a nod and a wink in the public interest. From the transcript I get an impression of chilly sparring, a needling cross-examination with an undertone of disrespect.

At some point Galbraith complains about there being no mention in the newspaper coverage of visits paid to Vassall's Dolphin Square flat of his wife being present. Mars-Jones QC suggests that if he wanted the fact mentioned he should have brought it up himself. Galbraith maintains that it was up to the journalists to ask him. He wasn't obliged to volunteer the information. This seems rather contorted logic, and Mars-Jones QC points out that journalists asking such a question would seem to be making an indelicate suggestion (never mind that the whole coverage in the press had been suggestively indelicate).

At one point in the cross-examination Mars-Jones QC says, 'But you still have not answered my question. I have asked it twice.' 'Perhaps you will be third time lucky.' 'I will try.' After another bit of skirmishing Dad says, 'That is not an answer to my question, Mr Galbraith, but I am not going to ask it again.' This seems more or less rude, in that more deferent era, when speaking to a government minister not charged with any offence.

Mars-Jones QC argues that the edition of the *Express* that circulated in Galbraith's Glasgow constituency omitted material printed in the first edition that he later objected to, so that there could be no question of the paper conducting any sort of campaign against him. A major part of Galbraith's objection attached to the headline, and Dad points out that sub-editors make those decisions. He replies, 'I am really very ignorant on the make-up of newspaper work. So far as I can see, everybody is able to shuffle off his responsibility to somebody else.'

Dad begins to treat him like a child. 'Is that a fair answer to give, when you do not know anything about it?' 'No, I said that is what it appeared to me, but I do not know.' The slight slippage of grammar in this answer may indicate flusterment.

Dad continues to strike the infantilizing note. 'But you do not know who is responsible for the format of the front page or for the headlines?'

'No.'

'Do you know why headlines are prepared? Do you know what the function of a headline is?' Dad could hardly go further in this line of calculated humiliation if he told Galbraith to stand up straight or to take the chewing-gum out of his mouth.

A little later, seeming to take advantage of his psychological ascendancy, Dad asks, 'And the answer to my question is a simple "No", is it not?'

'Will you repeat your question?' Not an unreasonable request in the circumstances, since there has been a fair amount of intervening by-play. Dad is almost toying with him by this time, saying, 'No. I am sorry, Mr Galbraith, but I will not,' before returning to a crucial point. *'Do you now agree that reasonable persons of goodwill might quite properly take the view that the relationship between you and Mr Vassall was one which was too familiar between a minister and a junior civil servant?'*

'I certainly do not.'

This exchange by itself may have earned Dad his fee, with Galbraith showing the soft white underbelly of any future libel case, and Mars-Jones QC refraining for the moment from sinking forensic teeth into it.

Galbraith sometimes made some odd choices in his correspondence – something in which the tribunal took a keen interest, in fact, since he had sent John Vassall a chatty postcard while on a family holiday in Belgium. But it seems safe to assume he sent no Christmas card that year to W. L. Mars-Jones QC.

Kevin McClory, though, kept in touch with Dad. They were on good terms, as was only right if McClory had benefited in a strong material way from Dad's taking the case. If I don't remember Dad going to a preview of *Never Say Never Again* when it was released in 1983, it doesn't mean he didn't go. Kevin McClory was executive producer, and Sean Connery returned to the role of James Bond after twelve years. Film critics found it disappointing that the film was so clearly a new version of *Thunderball*, not realizing that it couldn't be a fresh story without exceeding the rights McClory had won in 1963 and rendering him liable to be sued in his turn.

When my first book was published McClory passed on an invitation through Dad for me to spend some time with him in the Bahamas and to write the real story of the *Thunderball* affair. I wasn't really tempted. There might be a wetsuit waiting with my name on it, but there might also be a harpoon-gun whose bolt had the same inscription. 'The real story' I was supposed to tell wouldn't be an independent account but Kevin McClory's version. Mars-Jones *père* had helped bring him prosperity, and now Mars-Jones *fils* would add a little polish to his reputation. McClory wasn't known for being open-handed – perhaps the idea was to pay me in daiquiris and sun cream.

Ian Fleming was in poor health during the court case and died the next year, but the *Thunderball* affair rolled on. Jonathan Cape, publishers of the novel, and having every reason to know that Kevin McClory watched fiercely over his interests, brought out a biography of Fleming by John Pearson. McClory wasn't satisfied with the account it gave of the legal action and its findings, so once again the lawyers were whipped out of their kennels and sent across the fields baying for redress.

Pearson's tone had been misleadingly breezy:

As [Fleming] sat in court day after day, swallowing the nitro-glycerine pills prescribed to prevent another heart attack and listening to all those old arguments again, he must have told himself how unnecessary it all was, how easily it could all have been avoided. A little thoughtlessness, a great deal of impatience, a lifetime's habit of taking too much on trust – they were all to blame.

Again McClory won the point, so that the first edition of Pearson's book had to have a statement from the publisher bound in (with the promise that the alterations would be included in subsequent editions and reprints), setting the record straight and apologizing for inaccuracy. 'Since these pages were written,' went the statement from Jonathan Cape,

> certain facts have come to the notice of ourselves and the author which enable us to amplify passages in Chapters 24 and 25 which, whilst published by us in good faith, do not fully reflect the events leading to the High Court action in which Ian Fleming was concerned . . .

If you have an aversion, as I do, to the prissy form 'whilst', feeling that it carries a note of insincerity wherever it goes, then the word will seem perfectly at home in a passage of forced apology.

After two such successes, it was always likely that Kevin McClory would overreach himself. In the 1990s he proposed a second remake of *Thunderball*, to be called *Warhead 2000 A.D.* and possibly starring the Bond *du jour* Timothy Dalton. He then joined forces with Sony with plans to open up a whole rival franchise, having at this late date decided that he had been shortchanged by what had been thought in 1963 a highly advantageous settlement. Now he put in a claim for a proportion of the total profit from the whole roster of Bond films, on the basis that the work he had done on that early script had provided a template for the entire catalogue. He didn't get his way in court this time. It seems pretty clear that his ownership of rights to the one film was easier to establish than any claim to the whole series. If he had scaled down his demands, instead of trying to go nuclear, he might have got his way with *Warhead 2000 A.D.*

Kevin McClory died in 2006, to muted mourning, but the disputes didn't die with him. In 2007 there appeared a book called *The Battle for Bond* by Robert Sellers, not from Cape but from Tomahawk Press, which reproduced court documents from the *Thunderball* trial. This time it was the Fleming forces on the attack, with the Ian Fleming Will Trust contesting that these documents were not a matter of public record and therefore an infringement of copyright. Tomahawk's position was that the documents were indeed public – but a small publisher must think twice before taking on a rich estate. Unsold copies of the first edition were surrendered, presumably to be pulped, and the second edition, though bearing the traditional defiant slogan 'The Book They Tried to Ban', leaves out the disputed material.

In compensation it has a foreword by Len Deighton, who felt confident that he knew Fleming well enough to speak in his name in opposition to the Fleming Will Trust. He writes: 'How Ian Fleming would have hated to know that this book had been censored . . . As a gentleman he would have felt that harassing a fellow author to be the ultimate demonstration of bad taste.' I don't know much about cricket but I can recognize a sticky wicket when it swallows the batsman whole. Fleming's gentlemanliness has to be assessed as part-time, and when he was off the clock he wasn't above appropriating another writer's work and passing it off as his. If Ian Fleming's gentlemanliness had been uninterrupted, there could have been no book for him to rise up in hypothetical righteousness to defend.

The dispute over *Thunderball*, with lawsuits erupting over so many years, resembles a small volcano in its alternation of activity and periods of dormancy, or perhaps a cold sore brewing up every few years a fresh batch of litigant virus. Dad stuck around for one cycle of infection and then moved on.

Perhaps even now the dispute isn't dead and buried but merely dozing. I imagine the McClory Estate and the Ian Fleming Will Trust as the last organisms to survive on a ravaged and blistered planet, periodically serving writs on each other.

The instructing solicitor in the 1963 case, Peter Carter-Ruck, attributed the successful outcome of the case to Dad's performance, though it was also clearly important (and perhaps not expected by the other side) that Kevin McClory stood firm in the witness box. There were complications, with two plaintiffs initiating the proceedings (though McClory's business partner, Jack Whittingham, withdrew, in poor health and worried about the financial risk involved) and two defendants throughout, Fleming and Ivar Bryce, which makes it harder to separate out individual motives from the swirl of courtroom manoeuvres.

Apart from Whittingham the three principals were well funded. McClory had recently married an heiress, Fleming's earnings from the Bond books were colossal and Bryce was not only a rich man but had married an heiress of his own. According to *The Battle for Bond* it was Bryce who decided to settle the case, but logically it was Fleming who was vulnerable. It would be a huge blow to his standing if he was found by the court to have plagiarized McClory's screenplay, and it was strongly in his interest to accept any terms before such a judgment was given.

The settlement allowed him to say, after the hearing, 'I am glad that the whole expensive misunderstanding has now been disposed of', though this was just the sort of blurring of the issue which got Jonathan Cape and John Pearson into trouble with the Fleming biography three years later.

There were those who said that Bill Mars-Jones loved the sound of his own voice (this group occasionally included members of his immediate family), that he talked for the pleasure of hearing himself speak. On this occasion his vocal performance was close to heroic. His laying out of the case against Ian Fleming lasted twenty-eight hours and eight minutes. As court time is measured out, Dad spoke for more than a week.

A full performance of *Der Ring Des Nibelungen* lasts fifteen hours, just over half the length of Dad's opening speech in the *Thunderball* case, and even Wagnerian roles aren't continuous. It's true that Dad didn't need to hit specific notes, but he will have needed to pay attention to vocal variety. Vital to avoid the sing-song intonations which can tug a judge's eyelids downward in the long watches of the afternoon.

What was the point of so extended an opening? It can be a way of dramatizing confidence, indicating the wealth of evidence on offer, by saying in effect: 'My client's case is not made of straw, My Lord, nor of sticks, nor even of stoutly bonded bricks, bricks so well laid and soundly mortared that no huffing and puffing on the part of Mr Fleming's advocates (my learned friends) could make the slightest impression on its solidity of structure, but of concrete. Reinforced concrete.' Putting pressure, hour by endless hour, on the defendant. This sounds like overkill, but Dad was well known for the obsessiveness of his preparation, insisting on seeing every piece of paperwork rather than relying on someone else's selection of what was important. I wonder if he hadn't been scarred by an early case, caught out when he hadn't been quite so meticulous and getting a nasty surprise in court. In any case the combination of flair and attention to detail amounts to a formidable armoury for a courtroom lawyer.

It's conventional to blame the case for the deterioration in Fleming's condition, though his health problems were of long standing. Only Ann Fleming, Ian's wife, seemed to feel that the trial had a beneficial effect on his physical well-being. 'Goodness I miss the Old Bailey,' she wrote in a letter to Evelyn Waugh in December 1963, though in fact the case was heard in the Royal Courts of Justice, 'the case did Ian a power of good, no smoking in court and one hour for a simple lunch.'

Of course anyone writing to Waugh did well to keep the entertainment level high and to point up any possible irony, but perhaps she really did feel that the Chancery Division of the High Court stood in for a health club of a particularly exclusive kind, a judicial Champneys whose mortificatory element (sitting on hard wooden benches hour after hour to hear yourself characterized as profiteer and cad) was only an aspect of its efficacy and its prestige.

I don't know why Dad felt the need to dress up his involvement in the *Thunderball* case with the fairy story about his inbuilt lie detector. It's obvious that Kevin McClory didn't come to Dad direct, and that Peter Carter-Ruck took McClory on as a client not because success was guaranteed but because payment was assured either way. Dad was the right man for the job, with a methodical approach that ran no risk of being dry, thanks to the whiff of danger he gave off in court. Why be embarrassed about that? But perhaps he disliked any idea of being a hired gun, and cried up the moral standing of his line of work accordingly. The traditional costume of the barrister – wig, gown and bands – is designed to produce the same effect, lending to a mercenary some of the dignity of a priest. Stylized battledress and a bandolier, even one made of horsehair, would attract the wrong sort of client.

Dad didn't have anything as coherent as a philosophy of the law, and his personal principles could be strongly polarized without adding up to a standard opinion-poll profile. He was against capital punishment, for instance, and strongly opposed to pornography. These are common attitudes individually but the combination is mildly anomalous. Displayed as a Venn diagram, the two relevant circles would show little overlap. Admittedly the overlap between those in favour of capital punishment and those opposed to censorship would be smaller still, but Dad still has to count as something of a free-thinker.

This was very much the point made by Geoffrey Robertson in *The Justice Game*: that when the first ABC trial (the nickname came from the surnames of the defendants, two journalists and their source being prosecuted under the Official Secrets Act) was abandoned due to the ill-health of the judge, and Mr Justice Mars-Jones was named to preside over a new one, Robertson – representing the three – did not have high hopes of his fair-mindedness in court. Knowing that Mars-Jones J (this is how judges are styled in law reports) was a great upholder of law and order, and moreover that juries 'ate out of his hand', he told his clients they could expect to spend their Christmas in prison.

Instead Mars-Jones J dismissed the charges, saying that the Official Secrets Act had never been intended to be used in such a way. When told that the Attorney General had authorized the prosecution, he said (I must go to slow-motion here, it's such a wonderful moment, a Clint Eastwood moment), 'Then he can un-authorize it.' Is that a cheroot clenched between Dad's teeth, or possibly a toothpick? He has slung a dusty poncho over the ceremonial scarlet. To throw out a case in this way is a permanent possibility of judicial procedure, but it takes a strong judge to make it happen, particularly if the result will be to nullify a case that the government has set its heart on. The jingle of spurs is rarely heard in the courtroom these days.

His independence of mind was partly protected by the fact he didn't want to rise any higher in the law. He was content to be a judge of first instance. Occasional stints in the Court of Appeal, sitting with two judges who seemed to gravitate towards points of law with a mystical certainty, convinced him that he lacked the rapid analytical processing required to excel in that arena.

I was studying in the States at the time of the ABC case, and heard only the vaguest rumblings about it. I didn't need to know more, as I thought then, since it was so obvious that Dad would be on the wrong side. If no man is a hero to his valet, then certainly no judge is a libertarian to his son. In the ABC affair I had the excuse of geographical distance, but even when I was much closer to his professional life I ignored its possible element of idealism. There was a case in 1982, for instance, presided over by Dad, in which a Jamaican couple sued the police for assault, wrongful arrest and malicious prosecution. Dad seemed to find it mildly amusing that a black couple should have the surname White. He gave a wouldn't-you-just-know-it shrug when he mentioned it, though he would never have thought it strange that a white couple should have the surname Black. There was nothing odder about a black person being called White than for a person called Smith not to work in a forge, or for someone called Mars to be living right here on Earth. He would have given the same sort of shrug and raised his eyebrows, mock-indulgence, mock-exasperation, if the couple in his case had been surnamed Black, though if a third party had pulled a wry face at a white person being called White he would have been puzzled about where the element of humour lay.

Of course my friendship group wasn't the delirious funky mix my attitudes implied. Even so, I could take up anti-racist attitudes with a suavity that left Dad in the dust – it's just that it wasn't me who awarded David and Lucille White £51,392, describing police conduct as 'monstrous, wicked and shameful' and giving the plaintiffs some assurance, finally, that not every part of the system was contemptuous of their rights.

Fifty thousand pounds was a substantial sum in 1982. I had a friend who started work at Faber that year on a salary of £2,000 odd, in an economy and a publishing climate that seems in retrospect lustily, even obstreperously vital. (Admittedly that sort of job was always close to being an internship with pocket money thrown in, and was a respectable work environment for educated young women before they got married, even perhaps actively in search of a husband.)

There were less newsworthy cases that Dad mentioned with quiet satisfaction. One was a case of arson in the 1970s, proved by an unusual exhibit. The malefactor, against whom there was no other evidence, and who denied ever being on the premises, had eaten an apple before setting the fire, and had foolishly left the core in a desk drawer before he left. The apple core survived the blaze, and a conviction was obtained on the basis of the arsonist's bite matching the marks that had been left on it. Almost a biblical incident – he had eaten of the fruit of the tree of the knowledge of good and evil, whereof his legal representatives would certainly have advised him not to eat. Or, if he did, to dispose of the core.

By *CSI* standards this was fairly elementary forensic science, but it got the job done and the criminal put away. Not a case with very wide implications, admittedly. Even a handbook of *Arson for Dummies* might not feel the need to warn its readers against writing their names in wet cement before torching a factory, or leaving behind photographs of themselves – in the act of striking the relevant match – locked in a fireproof safe.

Dad's non-standard convictions were strongly engaged by one of the most famous cases of his career, the trial of Ian Brady and Myra Hindley in 1966. He was only junior counsel for the prosecution, with the Attorney General, Elwyn Jones, leading, but Dad made the opening speech (in a cleared courtroom, as requested by the defence) at the hearing in front of magistrates at Hyde in Cheshire the previous December. Technically he spoke the first words in the proceedings against Brady, twenty-seven, a stock clerk, and Hindley, twenty-three, typist, of Wardle Brook Avenue.

The death penalty for murder had only been abolished the previous year, and for many people this case with its specific horrors (sexually charged cruelty, a woman delivering children up to torture) annihilated the arguments for liberalization. Myra Hindley must have driven quite a few supporters of the reform back into the hangman's arms. It didn't take Dad that way, even though he was presumably in court when the tape-recording Brady and Hindley made of Lesley Ann Downey being killed was played. He never mentioned it.

I remember him forbidding us to read about the trial in the papers. From an eleven-year-old's point of view, this was being warned off something that wouldn't have occurred to me in the first place, and the prohibition didn't breed curiosity as it might have done in someone older or more rebellious.

The trial had its effect on me, but not in any direct way. I was a studious boy, though there were some subjects for which I felt no affinity (history and geography). I'd always enjoyed maths. I remember when I realized how many zeroes were needed to represent a billion (an old-guard British billion of a million million) and how this thrilled me. I was sitting on the lavatory at the time that the realization struck, but this was not an earthbound moment.

Now I was having trouble, not so much with maths as with a maths teacher who had taken against me. In some way this was tied in with Dad and his frequent appearances in the press. In class I became 'Mars-Jones, whose clever father is never out of the papers'. I didn't understand why this was shameful. I doubt if my classmates did either, though they had no difficulty in understanding the invitation to laugh along.

I had already noticed that some of my classmates, the rough boys, talked to Mr Waller out of lessons in a way I thought was somehow disturbing. Since this was Westminster Under School in Eccleston Square, London SW1, my viewing some of my fellow pupils as 'rough boys' indicates that I was in a class of my own as a milksop.

At lunch one day Mr Waller had charge of our table. The chief 'rough boy' took a drink of water, pretended to notice something at the bottom of his glass and said, 'Sir? Do you see what's written on the bottom of these glasses?'

We all looked. All I could see was a word written there (well, stamped really), the name of the manufacturer. *Duralex*. The boy went on, 'Funny that they make glasses as well, eh, sir?'

I knew that something dirty was being insinuated, but not what it was. O happy days before Internet porn, when an eleven-year-old could be so much in the dark. The trade name Durex meant nothing to me. I had a vague knowledge of the existence of the contraceptive sheath, though I knew it under the name of the 'rubber johnny'. I had also acquired some spectacular misinformation on the subject along the way. Was my unworldliness so obvious that other boys got a kick out of telling me fibs? I knew, or thought I knew, that there was a hole in a rubber johnny and that sometimes the man's 'stuff' (another vagueness, but made authoritative by Nicholas Monsarrat's *The Cruel Sea*, which was a true book about the War) took a whole day to pass through it. Perhaps I had been told the old myth about the government insisting on a pinhole being made in one protective in a hundred, to safeguard the birth rate, and had got it turned round. I had only the vaguest idea of what the man and the woman did, and none at all about why they would want to. I seem to have thought there was some sort of filtration involved, or a slow drip process as with coffee made by the Cona method, a feature of dinner parties at the Gray's Inn flat.

How did Mr Waller react to this transgressive and smutty line of chat? Clearly his professional response should have been to kill the conversation without making too much of a fuss. Instead he gave a complicit snigger.

He had his favourites and his unfavourites, and it was no mystery where I fitted in. At one point I was unwell and missed a few days of school, and when I went back it felt as if maths lessons had been purposefully accelerated so as to leave me behind. The equations had turned ugly. The numbers were no longer on my side.

Mr Waller didn't seem to want me to catch up. I wasn't used to academic failure, and went to Dad for help. I don't remember confiding in my mother, but I expect that's because I so often did. Sharing my worries with Dad was the memorable event, though I'm sure she smoothed my way to him.

He took action, not making the fuss I had feared but tracking down a suitably diligent classmate and having the relevant pages of his exercise book photocopied. In those days domestic photocopying was an exotic venture, and he emphasized its fantastic cost. I'm sure his surprise was genuine, but it can't really have been a significant drain on the family budget, so perhaps he was guarding against the possibility that I would come to expect the mechanical reproduction of schoolwork as a matter of course.

In fact the photocopied pages were only a limited help. The results of the process were far from crisp, with dark lines superimposed, and I couldn't reliably make out the handwriting. Dad asked me if I was on my way to recovering my rightful place at the top of the class, and I recognized this from Latin lessons as the type of question that expects the answer Yes. I tried to make out that it was only a matter of time.

However much Dad tried to help me with my maths problem, he was part of it himself. His appearances in the papers, associated with a shocking court case, seemed to inflame my teacher. Mr Waller would ask me a difficult question, already grasping the piece of chalk he would throw at me if I got it wrong. The pressure he applied made it more likely that I would fail, and I duly acquired an incompetence when faced with mathematical operations. I don't think Mr Waller explicitly aimed at this effect. A week or two of cringing would have satisfied him. Of course I didn't know the exact source of his resentment and badgering, but it seems obvious that I was really only a stand-in for Dad, unlucky enough to be within range of flung chalk.

I was fitfully aware of Dad's public status. At one stage we went on a family holiday to Ireland, taking the ferry to Dun Laoghaire and hiring a car for further exploring. The tune I pounded out on the piano in any hotel unwise enough to leave one unlocked was 'A Walk In The Black Forest'. I did my best to duplicate the ersatz bounce of that exemplary, laboratory-designed earworm. Horst Jankowski's instrumental was a big hit worldwide in 1965, which suggests (unless I was criminally behind the times) a time roughly contemporary with the trial of Brady and Hindley. I remember us getting as far as Galway.

We went fishing and caught some pollack, though Mum said we wouldn't be asking the hotel kitchen to cook them for us, since (as everyone knew) pollack tasted of blotting paper. If I'd been able to make the leap from precociousness to actual prescience, I would have sung out, 'But Mum, they're *sustainable!*'

At the hotel there was a swimming pool with a tricky name, the Fuchsia Pool. The word had to be said very carefully to avoid embarrassment, though it turned out that 'fuchsia' was only the name of the pinky-red ballerina-like flowers that grew round the pool. The book in which I eventually saw the word 'fuck' in print for the first time, Mark Rascovich's *The Bedford Incident*, was already in existence (published 1963) but I hadn't come across it yet.

The Bedford Incident is a Cold War reworking of *Moby-Dick*, ending with the mutual destruction by warhead of a Russian submarine and a US destroyer. I couldn't altogether blame the American sailors for their use of foul language. They were about to be blown to atoms, by an atom bomb no less, and as I understood it 'fuck' was the equivalent of the nuclear option in conversation.

I had assumed, though, that this supremely taboo four-letter word was so beyond the pale as to resist the normal conventions of English spelling. I imagined specialized characters being necessary to transcribe it, lead-lined ones perhaps. Even so it might cause mutations in neighbouring words.

In the Welsh language, of course, mutation is a fact of consonantal daily life, and doesn't indicate the presence of background radiation, though it certainly helps to deter visitors.

It was disappointing that 'fuck' was spelled no differently than 'buck', 'duck', 'luck'. Even 'fuch' would be some sort of homage, however half-hearted.

The Fuchsia Pool itself was shaped like a stylized fish, with the tail section being a shallow area safe for toddlers. I was a confident swimmer and nervous diver, but the hotel pool had, instead of a diving board, a white metal slide. I climbed up the ladder to the top of it and then became paralysed. After a while Dad came over and suggested that I hold on tight to the edges of the slide on my first ride down, so as to control my descent. There was a bucket of water next to me at the top of the ladder, and he volunteered to slosh it liberally over the slide so as to make it easier for me to hold on. Not bothering to examine the logic of the proposition, I agreed to it.

Only when I had committed my body weight to the slippery metal, and the world slid out of control, did I understand that I had been betrayed, lied to by someone who maintained that only the truth would set you free. It was wonderful, not the betrayal as such but the accelerating joy it forced me to feel. I didn't bother him with protests, in fact I hardly noticed him as I rushed back to the bottom of the white metal ladder. Dad had found a way to nudge me brusquely free from the deadlock of my milksop psychology.

I remember we travelled under assumed names. It was felt unwise for Dad to visit the Irish Republic after having sent so many of its irregular affiliates down. That's what I remember, but of course it makes no sense. In 1965 Dad wasn't yet a judge, and even if he had been, no Troubles had arisen for him to get the wrong side of. I hope at least that the confusion in my memory doesn't mean I was, say, sixteen and trembling at the top of the slide beside a hotel swimming pool, rather than eleven.

I must be mixing up two holidays – except that we only went to Ireland the once, and no other destination would call for precautions of even this rudimentary kind. I don't have a memory, not even a false one, of the name we travelled under, though I find it hard to imagine not being interested.

Perhaps I was reading a book. I've always been able to read without queasiness in cars, on trains, in planes, on roller-coasters. Nice to think we might have gone under some name rich in associations, travelling perhaps as the Melmoths. Did we have false passports, even? The existence of the Common Travel Area may have made such elaborate preparations unnecessary, but the whole business of travelling incognito suggests the murder mysteries played out in country hotels off season.

Later on, in the 1970s and '80s, there were definite security concerns. Dad had some firearms training and was even issued with a gun, though it was kept locked up in the safe of the Gray's Inn Treasury Office where there was no risk of its being useful. Certainly if the weapon had lived in the flat, I would have wanted to see it and Dad would have wanted to wave it about with all due solemnity.

Before terrorism put judges at risk, there was the old-school underworld. The High Court Judge Edmund Davies, who lived at number 1 Gray's Inn Square, received threats after he passed controversially severe sentences on those responsible for the 'great' train robbery of 1963. Precautions were put in place. Cynthia Terry, wife of the Under-Treasurer (and also my god-mother, 'Aunty See-See' as we called her), was asked to give up her normal seat in the Chapel and position herself upstairs in the gallery. There she would be well placed to deter, by screaming or lobbing a hymn book, any intruder devious enough to walk into the Inn from High Holborn and enter the Chapel during morning service.

I feel sure that if Aunty See-See was combat-ready in any marked way she would have mentioned it.

Dad was certainly advised, once terrorism was a real force, to check the underside of his car for explosive devices. I didn't ever see him do it. In fact my mind's eye shows me him very much not doing it: leaning over to one side a little way from the car, as if that would give him the necessary visual access. By this time his Jaguar days were over and he drove sensible estate cars with automatic transmissions. Then I see him going halfway down on his knees for a better view before realizing he would risk sullying the excellence of his suiting with dirt if he allowed his knees to touch down on the road surface. He considers the use of newspaper to protect the cherished cloth and then understands that ink-smudges are at least as much of a threat to his turn-out as tarmac-scuffs . . . of course none of this amounts to a memory. On a television screen these images would be accompanied by a caption warning of RECONSTRUCTION, though why anybody but me would want to watch I couldn't say.

If the national shock delivered by the Moors Murders had led to the restoration of the death penalty, Dad might have found himself in difficulties. He not only disapproved of the death penalty, implicitly on religious grounds, but said, after the event, that he would not have accepted appointment as a judge if he was required to pronounce it. Technically capital punishment was retained for a few specialized offences, such as treason, piracy with violence, and arson in naval shipyards, but it would be a scruple too far to expect him to decline preferment in case these virtually hypothetical crimes materialized in his court.

His principle wasn't tested, since the black cap remained a historical item (he became a judge in 1969), but that doesn't make his moral position unreal. It's true that I never saw Dad undergo a real crisis of conscience, and his ambition seemed to lie close to the core of him, though I saw enough discrepancy of temperament in the last phase of his life not to be so sure. What's the appropriately judicial phrase? To reserve judgment.

What Dad felt he learned from the Moors Murders case was that pornography was an actively corrosive force. The books Ian Brady read, the images he saw, inflamed and released an underlying inhumanity. It's doubtful that even before 1966 he was in favour of sexual material being made freely available – I can't see him approving of a world in which copies of *Reveille* and *Titbits* were brazenly displayed where minors could see them – but after that case his opposition became definite.

If conversation turned in that direction he would maintain that the last word on the subject had been spoken by Pamela Hansford Johnson in her book *On Iniquity*, which describes her change of heart on this issue from a liberal to a conservative stance, the catalyst being Ian Brady.

There was a sort of troubled open-mindedness in our household, the product I suppose of slightly different attitudes between my parents. I remember one evening when the BBC broadcast some footage of *Oh! Calcutta!* There was debate over whether we should watch it. We did. The images were of naked bodies frozen every few frames and allowed to overlap, producing an effect that soon became abstract (particularly on a black-and-white television) and we uneasily agreed they were beautiful.

I never got around to reading Hansford Johnson's book in Dad's lifetime. Perhaps he was only using it as a sort of barricade, to keep dissension at a distance. If I had read it and taken issue with its arguments, he might only have withdrawn behind another obstacle, though his withdrawals were usually feints and it was never safe to assume a lasting retreat.

The tone of *On Iniquity* is sometimes impossibly quaint:

Not so long ago, I raised a little storm by suggesting, in a letter to the *Guardian*, that it was not desirable for Krafft-Ebing

[who wrote *Psychopathia Sexualis*, intended as a serious study]
to be available in relatively cheap paperback edition on the
bookstalls of English railway-stations . . .

Class seems to dog the discussion of censorship, just as it had
at the *Lady Chatterley* trial in 1960, with Mervyn Griffith-Jones
QC asking the jury: 'Is it a book that you would even wish
your wife or servants to read?' The cheapness of a book, and
consequently its availability to the lower orders, seems to be
an important element in discussion of the issue.

As Hansford Johnson visualized it, 'The walls of the police
storerooms are almost bulging outwards with the pressure of
tons upon tons of dirty books.' Dad had a similar mental
picture, but at least there were buttresses in place to keep those
storerooms from exploding. Dirty books were being kept out
of circulation by the proper authorities.

Everyone assumed that the smut was safe in its silos, the
general public screened from contamination by thick bulkheads
of probity. It was because Dad had such a high opinion of
the police force in general that he regarded corruption there
as the ultimate betrayal of trust.

In 1964 he had been commissioned to write a report inves-
tigating a particular set of allegations, that confessions had
been extracted under duress. He found there to be some substance to the allegations. Dad was particularly proud of his
report, in which he had tried to match the terse clarity of Lord
Denning's prose style, and felt vindicated when it was held up
as a model of its kind. One newspaper suggested he would
make a good candidate for Ombudsman, defender of the
individual against the injustice of institutions. That office didn't
actually exist, but he was on some sort of spectral short list.

His 1964 report is another example of a publication that I
didn't read in his lifetime, and I have to admit I was disappointed

when I did. It's not impressive as a piece of writing, the language flat without being particularly correct ('fortuitous coincidence' turns up twice), but that's hardly the problem. The whole thing seems an elaborate exercise in fence-sitting, stating that 'allegations of violence, threats of violence and the "planting" of offensive weapons are not established beyond reasonable doubt', before conceding that 'the bulk of the evidence so disclosed tends to support' the allegations made by the men in the case 'and points to their innocence'. Perhaps because I heard Dad talk with such pride about his report, at a time when he loomed large over my world, I expected great things from it. I wanted to think he had laid down some definitive glory to mature over time, like the cellared 'pipe of port' he referred to from time to time, supposedly waiting for our twenty-first birthdays but never materializing. It may be that in historical context he was relatively open-minded about the possibility of the police going wrong. I feel a bit flat, that's all.

It's just the opposite of what went on in the ABC trial, where Dad, far from knuckling under, took a tough independent line. His report seems all too tepid and cautious. But why am I bothered? I passed from childish worship through disillusionment to fixed prejudice, and nothing could be more normal. It shouldn't be hard at this stage to unearth a bit more nuance, except that the states of mind date from different epochs and exist on different scales. They don't want to work together. It's only in cop films that the clueless rookie and the hardbitten old-timer turn out to make a good team.

As a judge Dad became known, rightly or wrongly, for 'hammering bent coppers', a phrase whose separate parts come together to form a harmonious visual image. It was inevitable that his emotions would be deeply engaged when he was called upon to preside over the trial of members of London's Obscene Publications Squad on corruption charges in November 1976. He found it appalling that those whose only function was to root out filth might choose to wallow in it.

As he described it, a newcomer to the squad would find an envelope full of money on his desk in the first week. When he asked what it was for, he would be told it was for moving expenses. The next week there was another envelope, after the contents of the first had been spent, and there was no longer any pretence about what it was for.

It happened that I was in the Gray's Inn flat on the day after the trial ended. Commander Wallace Virgo and Detective Chief Superintendent William Moody had been convicted, and Dad was jubilant, in a mood to celebrate. He produced his wallet and slid out a ten-pound note. For a moment it looked as if he was about to give me some pocket money, except that I was twenty-two and receiving a small allowance from the Department of Education and Science (I remember that the postal address of my benefactors was Honeypot Lane) to pursue a PhD that I never caught up with.

The ten-pound note wasn't for me. Instead Dad handed it to Sheila, saying, 'Darling, I want you to go down to Soho and buy some pornography.' She looked a little dazed as she took the money.

'What is it exactly you want me to do, Bill?' she asked.

'Go to Soho and buy some pornography.'

'But why?'

'Because you won't be able to get any,' he told us. Then he took the tenner back and returned it to his wallet. As perhaps Sheila had suspected from the start, if only because the scene was played out in my presence, it was just a piece of theatre. I don't know if she was surprised that Dad should imagine such a direct connection between a decision in law and the life of the streets, but I certainly was.

Virgo appealed against his conviction, and won. I don't remember Dad making any comment on this setback, but years later I found an unfamiliar cassette recorder with a tape in it. Might this be the famous memoir, which Dad had found impossibly difficult in the end to get started on, so that he decided that speaking aloud was the solution, with a stenographer typing up the material for him to tidy later? I pressed the Play button. It was Dad's voice all right, but he was singing rather than speaking, and accompanying himself on the guitar. 'Virgo – *Virgo*,' he crooned, 'I'll follow you . . . just an old sweet song keeps Virgo on my mind.' He was casting a spell of voodoo justice on the villain who had escaped him, to the tune of Hoagy Carmichael's 'Georgia on My Mind'.

Having a master of argument in the family doesn't necessarily make for a quiet life, particularly if he sees himself not as a user of rhetoric but as someone who speaks his mind. In family arguments Dad was like a professional tennis player who doesn't even realize how much spin he's putting on the ball, going for devastating shots even in what is nominally a knock-up. Except that a tennis pro will admit to having a racket in his hand.

It was part of Dad's constitution that he wanted to win, but I'm not sure he ever realized how much he wanted it. He could be relentless, though he could also be wily in a way that was endlessly frustrating. He could improvise.

This was particularly maddening when I was old enough to feel that I could mount an argument myself on a reasonably sophisticated basis. After I had changed my Cambridge course from Classics to English, a change he reluctantly supported, he asked me at the end of one particular term what I'd been studying. American literature, I told him (an option that hadn't been on the syllabus for long), with special reference to Melville, Hawthorne, Pynchon and Nabokov. 'Nabokov?' he asked. 'The man who wrote that dirty book *Lolita*? The one who likes little girls?'

I could see there was no point in arguing that Humbert's entanglement with Lolita recreated Nabokov's love affair with America, or that it was an allegory of beauty, or even a novel that refused to address the moral issues it seemed to insist on raising. Dad had watched the last ten minutes of the film and hadn't read so much as a page, while I knew both book and film fairly well. He might hate to be underprepared in court, but now, somehow, lack of knowledge gave him a crushing advantage.

I made the decision to keep things extra-literary, shifting my ground to face an adversary who wouldn't be drawn into skirmishes over aesthetics or formal questions but would keep pounding away with the big guns of traditional morality. I pointed out that Mrs Nabokov, Véra, had rescued the manuscript of *Lolita* when her husband was trying to burn it, and that the book, like all the others he published, was dedicated to her.

Dad answered by reflex. I'd love to have an MRI of his brain at that moment, to see which parts were being used, and (almost more fascinating) which were not. A tiny flare of combative instinct in the limbic system, a few neurones firing in the linguistic cortex. I dare say that was all it took. 'And I think she's a wonderful woman . . .' he said, leaving a pause long enough for me to wonder if I was losing my wits – did Dad know Véra Nabokov? How had this come about? Had they shared quaffing wine in Gray's Inn Hall? – before he delivered the judo throw that used my weight against me, '. . . to accept the dedication of a book which proves that her husband really likes little girls.' Part of the frustration of the moment was my sense that Dad could never have riffed so freely if he was really engaged in a question of morals. He was showing off, he just didn't know it.

If Dad was a driven athlete in argument, he was also a chess grandmaster. Sometimes, like a resourceful player, he would establish a gambit over the course of several games and then vary it in a way that was completely destabilizing. I had become used to one form of non-apology, which ran along the lines of 'I'm not a young man . . . I'm getting to be an old man . . . we must try to get along better.' This was in theory a no-fault approach to the family peace process, but one which made clear just the same where the faults lay. Then one day, shortly before his retirement, he successfully ambushed me with a variation: 'I'm not a young man . . . I'm getting to be an old man . . . you have only so much time to make it up to me.'

Over the years he had changed his spots, from the man who had stood as a Labour candidate after the War, even if he succeeded only in splitting the vote and letting the Tory in. He never actually admitted helping the Tory cause more directly, by voting for Mrs Thatcher in the years when it was possible to do so, but I'd be surprised to learn that he never did.

His support for liberal causes may have started and finished with the abolition of the death penalty in 1965. He certainly hadn't approved of the Sexual Offences Act 1967, which decriminalized homosexuality, and by the 1970s had become alarmed by a general culture of permissiveness and the particular anomie of his sons.

In soft cultural terms, as distinct from actual politics, he could boast of having an open mind, or certainly open ears. Dad had been an unlikely but fervent first-generation Beatlemaniac. This was a shared taste in the household, though I have to admit when I first heard 'She Loves You' on the car radio in 1962 I thought in my infant élitism that it was a bad joke. Oh dear oh dear, I thought, have we really come to this? I was eight. A little later, when Tim and I were given record tokens by our grandfather (Sheila's father, the only grandparent we knew) we made highbrow choices of EP, at least partly, I'm sure, to impress each other, with him choosing *Finlandia* while I cast my vote for Gieseking playing the 'Moonlight' Sonata. I wonder who won, and how we knew.

Dad worked out the chords of 'Michelle' on the guitar, and Sheila acquired the sheet music for 'Eleanor Rigby' for trying out on the piano. She had the advantage of being able to read music, though from his Chapel childhood Dad was at home with tonic sol-fa notation for hymns, and could with a little effort decode the little grids studded with black dots, like wiring diagrams for transistors, which represented guitar chords in the tablature used for popular sheet music. On songs without a piano part Sheila might find herself relegated to that unglamorous not-quite-instrument made from a comb and pieces of tissue paper.

Dad bought us The Beatles' albums when they came out, as far as *The White Album*, anyway, whose experimentation displeased him (and many others) so that the capital for *Abbey Road* had to be raised by private subscription.

There was always a worry, since records could only be played in the public spaces of the flat (we were too young to have our own record players), that Dad would find something objectionable coming out of the grand Decca television-cum-radiogram. It was a relief, for instance, when he pronounced 'Lady Madonna' essentially reverent in its appropriation of biblical imagery, though he must have expressed himself less pompously. He could be touchy about anything that mocked holy subjects, though he did enjoy telling one high-class joke with just a touch of blasphemy about it:

Jesus (addressing the crowd gathered round the woman taken in adultery): Let he who is without sin cast the first stone.

(A stone flung with great force strikes the woman on the forehead. Shocked silence.)

Jesus: Really, mother, sometimes you can be *impossible*.

The White Album, which came out shortly after my fourteenth birthday, was a particular embarrassment. I was extremely prudish at this stage, though my prudishness was of a particular kind. It was a matter of social context. I could listen to dubious lyrics on the *White Album* perfectly calmly, though with disapproval, as long as neither parent was around. My mother's presence, even if she was moving in and out of the sitting-room with other things on her mind, would make me nervous, and Dad's presence brought on a much more intense agitation. So it was only the conjunction of all three elements that was unbearable: the offensive record, the paternal presence and the confused son. I had eaten the fruit of the tree of the knowledge of good and evil but it stuck in my throat. I could no longer be a child and had little idea of how to be an adult, but adolescence was the role, of the three, that I found hardest to inhabit. I disliked surliness as a characteristic, and it repelled me just as much when it was my own. All this had little to do with puberty as a physical fact, news of which reached my body rather later.

My solution was as desperate as I felt the problem to be. As the offending moment of the *White Album* approached, I would walk casually over to the radiogram and either turn the volume dial all the way down or lift the needle from the record. Turning the volume down worked well enough for scandalous individual moments, such as the cursing of Sir Walter Raleigh ('he was such a stupid git') on 'I'm So Tired', but lifting the stylus out of the compromising groove was called for when the outrage lasted for longer than a few seconds, as it did for instance on 'Why Don't We Do It in the Road?'. I cursed the

Beatles in my turn (without using bad language) for their dis-obligingness in leaving no visible division between tracks, selfishly advancing their credentials as makers of a unified artwork and ignoring the needs of those who might want to skip the needle lightly across a trench of filth. It was difficult to guess exactly where to put down the needle again. It might happen that the upsetting lyrics sounded out all over again, if I'd underestimated the distance, so it was better to play safe.

The result was that I'd end up skipping whole tracks that had done nothing wrong, so it seemed better to revert to the volume-down method of censorship. I would sit on a patchwork leather pouffe (for yes, we followed trends) near the radiogram until I could hear, from the tiny unamplified sound made by the needle, that we had safely come to the end of 'Why Don't We Do It In The Road?' or 'Sexy Sadie'. Would I have been less vigilant if I had known that 'Sexy Sadie' was originally called 'Maharishi', and was Lennon's bitter farewell to the guru he'd outgrown, Maharishi Mahesh Yogi? Probably not.

I hate to think what my parents felt about my purity campaign focussed on the *White Album*, my attempt to make the two-LP set live up to its name (a name that didn't appear anywhere on the cover or label). No-one ever said anything about it, which was probably for the best. I don't think I was making a cry for help but something a little more contradictory, a cry to be left alone, not to be required to think about certain things.

Early and mid-period Beatles were genuinely things the whole family could enjoy, a category that seems stable until one day it's gone. Late Beatles were already divisive, opening up a rift between us or perhaps just a rift in me. Then there came a point when we would have lost face if Dad liked any of our chosen music, though he was always waiting for us to come around to his choices, just as he assumed that in due course we would abandon *Monty Python* and join him in front of *Dad's Army*.

If we didn't want to share the experience of music then it followed that we needed our own means of mechanical reproduction.

By the time the Mothers of Invention released *Over-Nite Sensation* in 1973, my brothers and I had a record player of our own and could shut ourselves safely away in our bedrooms to be dazzled by the toxic jewels of the counterculture. In the years between 1960 and 1981 there was a holiday home by the seaside on Anglesey, and it was there that Tim and I listened in shock and wonder to the album, which I had bought in Bangor's only forward-looking record shop.

My hands went instinctively in such premises to the racks labelled New Wave & Progressive (that's the old New Wave, of course, not the one that succeeded punk). I was an anti-connoisseur of most popular music. Dance music, in particular, I didn't understand at all. Music was to be listened to in stillness, with a little tapping of the foot if there was no avoiding it. Both feet might be called on in the case of polyrhythms.

It seems very plausible that we kept Matthew out of the room, theoretically to protect his innocence but really to reinforce our feeling of being a corrupt secret society. Almost every lyric on the album was filthy in a way that left the Beatles in the dust. Sometimes the words were witty, like these from 'Camarillo Brillo': 'She stripped away / her rancid poncho / An' laid out naked by the door / We did it till we were un-concho / An' it was useless any more . . .' But usually not.

The doors in the house had 1930s-style locks which only worked from the inside, little depressed recesses about the size of a thumb that could be slid across to engage a catch. We were safely locked in. Dad tried the door and when it failed to yield he gave the knob a theatrical rattling. 'Tim? Adam? What are you doing in there?' We weren't doing anything – we weren't smoking cigarettes, for instance, let alone dope. We were giggling at smut. But by great good fortune Dad entered the room just at the point when Frank Zappa's relentless campaign of obscenity was taking a break. It was the long fade-out on a disgraceful song called 'Dinah-Moe Humm', in which the song's narrator – which doesn't seem the right word – accepts a bet of forty dollars from a defiantly unresponsive woman that he won't be able to give her an orgasm. She (the Dinah-Moe Humm of the title) has in turn bet her sister, also present, an unspecified number of dollars that she (D-M H) can prove that men are scum. The whole song glories in its woeful crassness. The only lyric I could make any sort of claim for is 'Kiss my aura, Dora – it's real angora'. Not Cole Porter, to be sure, but creditable in the cultural context.

The song winds down at last from its disgraceful efforts, with Zappa crooning smugly 'Dinah-Moe . . . and a Dinah-Moe' on a long fade-out. This was the point at which Dad entered the room. The air must have been awash with late-adolescent relief, as well as a trace of our disappointment that no showdown had taken place. Matter and anti-matter had come within a micron of achieving each other's destruction. Our buried hunger for confrontation had been thwarted, and the puritan had entered the room just as the smut-hound was leaving. They hadn't recognized each other.

Even Dad's canny forensic nose couldn't reconstruct the outrage he had just missed. He joined in with the song on its slow fade-out, murmuring 'Dinah-Moe . . . Dinah-Moe' in his turn and nodding his head in time. As the track finished he conceded that the song had 'got something', then left without fuss.

It's a shame he didn't stay for the next track, 'Montana', the last on the album, with its daffy lyrics about making a fortune from raising dental floss. (It added to the song's amusement value that in 1973, along with most of our compatriots, we had no idea what dental floss was, what benefits it was supposed to confer.) This at last was filth-free, close to family entertainment – if it hadn't been, of course, some instinct would have led Dad to stay and we would have had that longed-for, long-avoided barney after all.

Would we have listened to *Over-Nite Sensation* so much if Dad's values hadn't been there in the background, begging to be affronted? Yes, probably, since in those days an album was quite an investment. A new record was something to be listened to intensively. The lurking suspicion that you had wasted your money was no excuse for tucking it away behind something you liked better. A new album must have pride of place on the turntable, played over and over again until it wore a groove in your mind whether you liked it or not.

Now I'm going to pull back and take a broader view of this theme of differences of musical taste, somehow sexually charged, between the generations in the 1960s and '70s. Putting it another way, I'm going to lean on this theme until it suddenly gives way, rather as engineers test a structural element for tensile and compressive strength by subjecting it to increasingly powerful forces. The pioneer in this field is the Kirkaldy Testing Works, now a museum on Central Street, Southwark (it opens to the public on the first Sunday of the month). The main testing machine at the museum is close to fifty feet long and weighs more than a hundred tons, so massive in fact that it was installed first, with the works then built round it. I'll be working on a smaller scale.

The backing vocals on *Over-Nite Sensation* were by Zappa's standards both elaborate and well-sung. Normally such vocal tracks on Mothers of Invention records were done in-house, with band members contributing cheerfully raucous falsetto. This was the equivalent in sound of the matter-of-fact dowdy cross-dressing of the Monty Python troupe, hardly intended to convince or confuse.

Even when Zappa recruited a pair of vocalists who had previously sung mellifluously enough with The Turtles, Howard Kaylan and Mark Volman, the results were on the scrappy side. Since Zappa was such a perfectionist about other aspects of performance, this must have been the way he liked it. The pair of ex-Turtles were billed as 'The Phlorescent Leech & Eddie' (later 'Flo & Eddie'), not so much a musical development as a legal requirement, since they had signed away the right to put their real names on marquees or album covers. It was legitimate for them to be credited in the small print.

If Dad and I had unstable layers in our sexual ideology at this time, areas of painful inconsistency, which we may not have admitted to ourselves, then perhaps the same was true of Frank Zappa also, however fierce his commitment to a cynicism as rancid as the lady's poncho in 'Camarillo Brillo'. The Mothers of Invention catalogue is defiantly short on the love song, so much a staple of popular music that popular music could hardly exist without it. Even song titles – 'My Guitar Wants to Kill Your Mama', 'Penis Dimension', 'Uncle Meat', 'Penguin in Bondage' – seem to jeer or snarl.

Zappa includes wholesome feelings only to travesty them, and yet he can't seem to leave them alone. There comes a time when even the most sympathetic listener must start to doubt his bad faith. A year or two before *Over-Nite Sensation* the Mothers released, and I bought, a live album called *Fillmore East – June 1971*. I was baffled by the grubby artwork, not re-alizing (never having seen a bootleg disc) that this authorized recording was pretending to be one. It's the last record I remember having to listen to on the sitting-room stereogram at Gray's Inn, before the first tentative step towards the privatization of music represented by the record player in the bedroom. Up to this point music had been social and shared, for better or worse, but now it became individual, or conspiratorial, as a matter of course, and any overlap between listening groups became problematic.

The only music of mine that I remember Dad being unable to stand, even when played at low volume as far away from him as the small size of the Anglesey house would allow, was Steve Reich's *Drumming*. He said he couldn't think or do any work while it was playing. It disrupted analytical brain function at an almost neurological level. It's possible that Reich would be pleased with this experimental result.

Much of the material on *Fillmore East – June 1971* is continuous with its predecessor *200 Motels*, meaning that the obscenity is wearing and relentless, but Zappa is too much of a showman to stake everything on the sourly grubby. So to balance 'Bwana Dik' (sample lines: 'My dick is a Harley / You kick it to start') comes the Turtles' 'Happy Together', played for laughs by the original vocalists, Kaylan and Volman, but still offering the sweetness of a pop tune and a couple of choruses sung *a cappella*. The album ends with a Zappa original, 'Tears Began To Fall', whose up-tempo jauntiness is at odds with the self-pitying lyrics: 'Tears began to fall and fall and fall / Down the shirt / 'Cause I feel so hurt / Since my baby drove away . . .'

One version of the lyrics available on the Internet gives the trajectory of those tears as 'down the church', but although being left at the altar is a hardy trope of the heartbroken ballad, I go with 'shirt', which makes better sense and even rhymes. The poor sap is so pole-axed by sorrow that he doesn't have the nous to wipe his eyes.

71

How many times can you parody sentiment before you admit that it affects you? A whole lot of times, if you're Frank Zappa. In 1968 he released an entire album of doo-wop, *Cruisin' with Ruben and the Jets*, which may have been poking fun (at a genre long out of fashion, and what's the point of that?) but also committed to vinyl some of the earliest songs he had written. On *Chunga's Revenge* the most attractive music is the instrumental 'Twenty Small Cigars', but the most beguiling song is certainly 'Sharleena', expressing the emotions of another goofy dude amazed to be deserted by a woman, asking her friends for news of her and crooning in pre-feminist cluelessness that he would be 'so delighted' if they 'sent her back' to him. Just as *Fillmore East* was a pseudo-bootleg, 'Sharleena' is a pseudo-parody, really just a homage in denial about its own sincerity.

I realize that conversations between Dad and Frank Zappa, who never met, were never likely to be intimate or sparkling, but knowing what I know now I feel I could have steered them onto safe territory. Dad may not have been a fan of doo-wop as such, but he was mad keen on the Ink Spots and the Mills Brothers, vocal groups of the previous period who had a certain amount of influence on the genre.

Male vocals are one of the genre requirements of doo-wop (along with nonsense lyrics, close harmony and the prominence of falsetto), so it could be taken as a step away from the disputed territory of parody and pastiche for Zappa to hire women to sing on *Over-Nite Sensation*. But I'm not sure it worked out that way.

The singers booked weren't exactly small time. They were the Ikettes, Ike Turner's backing singers, and Tina Turner was part of the package. The vocal parts were tricky and took time to master. She may not have been the quickest learner (compared to Linda Sims and Debbie Wilson), but

Tina was proud of her work on these tracks and wanted Ike to hear them.

He wasn't impressed, asking 'What is this shit?', and took the Ikettes' name off the album credits. Ike Turner's reputation hasn't exactly soared over the years, and it seems uncontroversial to say he was not the helpmeet and business manager most people would choose.

His negotiating position when approached by Zappa was strange in itself, since he didn't want the singers paid more than $25 a track. Most negotiators with their eye on profit stipulate a floor rather than a ceiling to the auction, but he clearly considered it important to keep Tina's status in the marketplace low, throwing her in as a bonus with the backing singers who were presumably recruited in the first place to back her. The deal between Turner and Zappa, Ike and Frank, was a strange confluence of negativity. A businessman who didn't want his wife to know her true worth was signing a contract with another who prided himself on his cheapness in everything. Zappa aimed with the help of a world-class vocalist, her services acquired well below market rates, to give vocal depth and lustre to songs about the low inherent value of women, though this was not of course what I heard in 1973.

Danger! The heavy rhetorical superstructure is bringing this conceit close to collapse. It's all going a bit Tay Bridge. Time to underpin the whole ramshackle edifice with stanchions of properly reinforced personal material.

If Dad had confronted me, or us, with this scatological wallowing, pointing out how sickening it was, with its reliance on our complicity in its degradation of women, what would I, or we, have said? Never mind that he lacked a feminist vocabulary. He was by generation a sexist but hardly misogynistic. Family life didn't require him to show his ideological colours more clearly by calling on him to shape the future of a female child – there are adjustments that fathers without daughters don't have to make. The sensible thing would have been to play for time, pointing out that the two of the Mothers' albums from the previous year, *Waka/Jawaka* and *The Grand Wazoo*, came as close to big-band revivalism as avant-garde progressive rock could reasonably be expected to get.

Then I would probably have said, 'You just don't get it,' delivered with an attempt at scornful finality – so much easier to pronounce, as a sentence, than its more truthful cousins, *I just don't get it. I don't get how free speech and censorship can both be so . . . nasty.* If I didn't want to be protected, then it was a mystery how I was going to avoid being degraded myself.

When arguments of this sort loomed with Dad I held tight to my trump card, which was probably why relatively few of them were fully played out. Dad had an acute tactical sense of when an opponent had a secret weapon, so that it might be wise to hold his fire. And what was my secret weapon? Only that Dad had a copy of *The Godfather* on the bookshelves in his study, which fell open at a grotesquely sexual passage on page 26. Cheap paperbacks blab, they spill every secret. Only a respectable quality of binding keeps its counsel, discreet about which pages have been most urgently consulted, exactly where the reader's lowest self has been worked on. I was armed against any attack from Dad. Let him who is without smut cast the first stone.

I could imagine arraigning Dad in some sort of family tribunal.

Mars-Jones Jr: Perhaps the clerk of the court will be good enough to read aloud the passage marked. There by my thumb. Speak up, man! You're mumbling.
'Her hand closed around an enormous, blood-gorged pole of muscle.

It pulsated in her hand like an animal and almost weeping with grateful ecstasy she pointed it into her own wet, turgid flesh.'

Prisoner in the dock, you there, judge of first instance – Is that something you would wish your cleaning lady to read? I hardly think so. Small wonder you are unable to meet my eye. Yet you left it in plain sight on your bookshelves, where it might cause any amount of distress to impressionable young people, tender-minded homosexuals among them, who might stumble upon it. I put it to you, judge in the dock, that you are no more than a *whited sepulchre*, yea a *whited sepulchre*, full of dead men's bones and all uncleanness . . .

For all I know, Dad had the same conflicted feelings about passages like that as I did about pages from Burroughs and Genet, which disgusted me but gave me a jolt of nihilistic arousal just the same. If we'd had that confrontation I was so well armed against, he might have admitted that this was his objection to the availability of pornography, not the fear that *Psychopathia Sexualis* might be bought by the lower orders from station bookstalls but the fear that he might buy something viler than *The Godfather* himself. Before this conversation could take place, of course, he would have had to start cultivating the habit of admitting doubts and vulnerabilities.

I had unwittingly bought an album to which Tina Turner and the Ikettes contributed backing vocals, but I wasn't yet ready to buy actual black music – my breakthrough came at long last with Marvin Gaye's 'Got to Give It Up' in 1977. Can it really be true that Dad was more open to black music than I was as a teenager? There's a certain amount of evidence to support the suggestion, and in our family we're crazy for evidence. We can't get enough of it, either to strengthen our hand or to inform ourselves about the high cards the opposition is likely to play.

Dad bought only two singles in 1968 and both of them were MOBO, as it's called now, Music Of Black Origin. In fact they book-ended the range of what the culture had to offer at the time. There was The Edwin Hawkins Singers' 'O Happy Day', gospel at its most submissive and serene. And there was Pigmeat Markham's raucous novelty record 'Here Come The Judge'. I thought 'O Happy Day' was soupy, and I was not the one in the family who habitually ordered soup. I thought 'Here Come The Judge' was infantile, and I was embarrassed that Dad got so much pleasure from it (*'This judge is hip and that ain't all / He'll give you time if you're big or small'*).

Pigmeat Markham was as much a comedian as a musician, almost a vaudeville act insisting on a bygone stereotype – it was only a few years since he had been appearing at the Apollo blacked-up, with his lips painted white. Of course Dad didn't pay attention to the racial angle. 'Here Come The Judge' was cashing in on the popularity of Markham's appearances on *Rowan and Martin's Laugh-In*. And naturally it was the catch-phrase itself that appealed to Dad.

For a while he used the song as his theme tune, entering a room ('Here Come the Judge, Here Come the Judge') to his own accompaniment of rhythmic speech. It seemed a bit amateur, somehow, even self-defeating. The Queen doesn't blow her own trumpet. She has heralds for that. Dad was a one-man band.

Gloriously, we had the last laugh. We listened to the B-side, billed as 'Here Come The Judge (Part 2)', which amounted to an extended smutty joke of exactly the sort that Dad hated. A defendant is up in front of the Judge on a charge of indecent exposure. Eventually it turns out that he has twenty-seven children. The case is dismissed by the Judge on the basis that the defendant hasn't had *time* to put his pants on. We knew how appalled Dad would be if he realized what he'd subsidized with his six-and-eightpence.

So we had the last laugh as far as 'Here Come The Judge' went. Unfortunately Dad had the laugh after that. The song's place in the history of popular music has been reassessed, and it's now sometimes described as the first rap record. Oh God. It's official. Dad was ahead of his time, while I was barely keeping up with mine.

When for example a record like Dave and Ansell Collins' 'Double Barrel' made an appearance on *Top of the Pops*, I was sincerely mystified, waiting for an actual song to appear, something properly equipped with verses and chorus. Lyrics too, please. It didn't occur to me that a groove might be enough in itself, more than enough – but now I've redoubled the fogey factor just when I was trying to make it go away. I should just punch the Gieseking button on the juke-box one more time, and give my rocking chair a stately nudge.

The counterculture embraced sleaziness pretty much whole-heartedly, but there were things in it that helped me just the same. Tim was more adventurous than me, a little more than can be accounted for simply by the twenty-month age difference. He had been given tickets to a preview of *Flesh* while queuing with a girlfriend to see *Klute*. *Flesh*! Girlfriend! *Klute*! He was seizing the day, seizing both the day and the night.

He also kept various underground magazines in the little chest of drawers between our beds in the attic of the Gray's Inn flat, through which I would guiltily rummage. In one of them there was a strip cartoon of two men in bed together. They weren't getting up to anything, except amusing each other by reading aloud from Dr David Reuben's *Everything You Always Wanted to Know About Sex*, published in 1969.

I knew about this book without having read it, making paranoiac use of my peripheral vision, flickering towards a headline and flinching away (still perhaps the perceptual mode of the closeted teenager, unless the Internet has made it obsolete) to absorb its dismal message from the attendant newspaper coverage. David Reuben was a doctor, and if he said that public sex was the supreme expression of attraction between men, and that quarrels between cohabiting men had a bitchiness beyond anything known in the normal world, who was I to doubt it?

I absolutely did not want to explore my sexuality, even before Dr Reuben told me that it was a territory of undifferentiated debasement.

The men in the cartoon, though, with their long hair and narrow chests, had a different reaction. When they had reached their favourite bit ('homosexual encounters are always about the penis, never the person'), the biggest joke in the whole hilarious book, they laid it aside and moved into a tender embrace. That stayed with me as an image, bigotry refuted with a smooch.

I wonder if the echo of Dante's Paolo and Francesca was intentional, with the morality reversed. *Quel giorno più non vi leggemmo avante. That day we read no more . . .* In Paolo and Francesca's case a book inflamed adulterous desire, but for Mike and Ralph (to give them names) a single kiss was enough to quench the calumny of print.

I hadn't actually read Dante, but was familiar with the passage by way of an eccentric source. Tim and I got a kick out of reading *The Plain Truth*, an eccentric religious magazine to which Dad subscribed. Possibly 'subscribed' is too active a verb, failing to convey his helpless struggles to escape the flypaper of a fantastically adhesive mailing list.

The Plain Truth once ran an article deploring sexual explicitness in literature, in which Canto V of the *Inferno* was cited as an example of good practice. No specifics of the adulterous act, something more along the lines of three tactful dots on the page or a cinematic fade, with no detail to pass on arousal by contagion. Hard to see, all the same, how this particular strategy, however admirable in its tact, could be rolled out across modern culture, displacing *The Godfather* and any number of other books from their places on the shelf.

There was particular pleasure, for disaffected sons leafing through their father's copies of *The Plain Truth*, in reading the columns written by its founder's son, Garner Ted Armstrong. What a toady to follow in the moralizing trudge of his father's footsteps! Except that as time went by there was trouble in televangelist heaven, with Garner Ted described by his father as being 'in the bonds of Satan' and relieved of his role in the church. There were allegations of adultery, gambling, even assaulting the stewardess of his personal plane.

Dad didn't have a radio station or a magazine to promote his views, but he didn't go short of lionizing. The only accolade a judge is unlikely to receive in court is an actual ovation. Dad hungered for that, and luckily there were opportunities to put himself in applause's way. He had been playing the guitar since his teens, and sometime in the 1930s had made a non-commercial recording, with a band, of a tune he had written himself ('Fellow Take the Floor'). He sang as well as played. The 78-rpm record was still in his possession, though his tenor voice, surprising light in his young days before his vocal cords developed the authority necessary to command a court, hardly made its way through the surface noise and scratches.

Twice during the 1970s he put on a show in Gray's Inn Hall after dinner, to an audience that included students as well as his fellow benchers. The programme was announced as 'Master Mars-Jones Makes Music', and Dad played a handful of pieces by Sor and Tárrega. He put in a certain amount of practice before the show. A certain amount, but perhaps not enough.

The drawback about having a career in a hierarchical profession (and actually living in its parochial stronghold), in terms of self-awareness, is that the hierarchical element, being constant, becomes invisible. It was never on the cards that he would be booed or slow-handclapped by the company of colleagues, but an acute ear for the timbre of applause might have detected something perfunctory and even resentful about it. Sheila to her sorrow, inconspicuous in the audience, saw and heard a student give a little shake of the head and murmur to a neighbour, 'power mad'.

The concert was successful enough for Dad to repeat it the following year, but on this occasion the response was more perfunctory, the rapture very moderate. Dad was presenting himself, after all, not as a guitarist among others but as a guitar-playing judge. This was essentially a novelty act, and novelty dare not risk repeating itself. He would have needed to raise the stakes somehow, to swap his Spanish guitar for a more crowd-pleasing instrument, assaulting the audience with shards of feedback or pouring lighter fuel, to cries of alarm, onto his beloved vintage Gibson, which though not electrified from birth had been fitted with a pick-up in its early adulthood.

On the bench, the unstuffiness of an amateur guitarist was a more dependable weapon. One of Dad's proudest moments presented itself during a case involving some Hendrix tapes that had been remastered for posthumous release. I think the original bassist and drummer (who would be Noel Redding and Mitch Mitchell) were suing for a share of royalties on the basis that they had been part of the recorded performance, co-creators who couldn't be cut out of the financial side of things just because a later decision had been taken to get other musicians to redo their parts. At one point a barrister started to explain to him the function of a particular piece of kit, and Dad (mindful of the ubiquitous myth of the judge as being all at sea in the modern world) was able to interrupt him with a plausibly tetchy 'I know perfectly well what a wah-wah pedal is!' It was no bluff – he had bought one for Matthew the previous Christmas.

It wasn't clear that Dad admired Hendrix's playing. He didn't have much time for gadgetry or electronics. Hendrix would certainly never depose Django Reinhardt, let alone Segovia, in his personal pantheon. He admired the way Django overcame the disadvantage (to put it mildly) of having two fingers paralysed as a result of a caravan fire when he was eighteen.

Dad's tip for the future of a truly popular music was always the return of that swinging, big-band sound. Nevertheless he had admiration and sympathy for singer-songwriters, creators as well as performers, even if he would pause by the television during *Top of the Pops* just long enough to mark Kris Kristofferson or John Denver down for using a 'capo', which allowed them to transpose music without refingering. According to Dad this was a cheat, and the sure sign of the dabbler. If I'd known more at the time about musical history I might have pointed out that the 'capotasto' was already in use early in the seventeenth century, with the word itself attested from 1640, so that this cheat's device can claim to be older than the guitar in its modern form – but perhaps on the whole it's a good thing that I didn't.

He presided over one significant case, *O'Sullivan & Another v. Management Agency & Music Ltd & Others* (1982), in which a downtrodden singer-songwriter took on his oppressive management company. It seemed to Dad that Gilbert O'Sullivan's innocence had not just been taken advantage of by MAM Ltd but positively mocked. At one point in early 1974, O'Sullivan was advised by his manager, Gordon Mills, that he must leave the country at once for tax reasons. He went to Portugal, a poor choice since revolution broke out there almost at once. He took refuge successively in Spain, Italy, Spain again and finally Holland. In October he was told it was safe to return to British soil. How much had these complicated manoeuvres saved him? Not a penny. They were pushing him around in the most obvious way, pushing him around the map.

It had been shrewd of O'Sullivan to project a gormless image at the start of his career – like an overgrown Bash Street Kid with his flat cap, pudding-basin haircut and long grey shorts. It had certainly got him noticed. But that was as far as his shrewdness went. He had signed a management contract without taking independent advice, and was being exploited in any number of ways. He was being paid a very modest allowance even after becoming a successful recording artist. For a long time he idolized Gordon Mills, occasionally even acting as babysitter for his daughter Clair, whose name he commemorated in one of his best-selling songs. An emotional dependence made him slow to act on his suspicions even when evidence of wrongdoing began to pile up around him.

The question for the judge was whether it was right to compensate this innocent for his self-inflicted financial wounds. He had signed a contract, and if he was foolish enough not to read it or ask for it to be assessed by a qualified third party then you could argue that he had forfeited the right to any intervention by the law. It could almost be a proverb: *the tightrope walker who cuts up his safety net in order to make a string vest should not be surprised to hit the ground with great force.*

O'Sullivan couldn't get out of his obligations as neatly as a much cannier musician, Arthur Lee of the 1960s' San Francisco group Love, who was able to flourish his birth certificate and instantly invalidate the contract he had signed as a minor.

All that seemed to invalidate Gilbert O'Sullivan's contract was its monstrous unfairness, which doesn't necessarily have legal force. An agreed set of operations must be carried out before a resolution can be reached. A judge is a sort of weaver bird, picking through the twigs of statute and precedent offered by the advocates for the parties involved, masticating them intellectually then gluing them together to build the nest in which he will lay the egg of his judgment.

The aspect of the law which seeks to 'mitigate the rigour' of common law is equity, and this was the paper in his Bar Finals that had won Dad his highest marks. As far as I understand it, which is hardly at all, common law and equity are like the complementary cerebral hemispheres of legal decision-making, with right-brain equity continually modifying the inhumanely precise discriminations of left-brain common law.

For his judgment in *O'Sullivan & Another v. Management Agency & Music Ltd & Others* Dad relied heavily on Lord Denning's codification, in *Lloyds Bank Ltd v. Bundy* (1974, reported 1975), of the various exceptions to the rule that signatories to a contract can't just walk away.

> There are cases in our books in which the courts will set aside a contract . . . when the parties have not met on equal terms – when the one is so strong in bargaining power and the other so weak – that as a matter of common fairness, it is not right that the strong should be allowed to push the weak to the wall.

This seems both promising and slightly empty. When does the individual ever meet an institution on equal terms? Whether it's a customer approaching a bank or a writer signing up with a publisher, bargaining power is so unevenly distributed that the word 'power' itself seems comical, even if this crazy-golf playing field goes by the name of 'the ordinary interplay of forces'.

Nevertheless Denning proposed that there was such a thing as an 'unconscionable' transaction. An individual so placed as to be in need of special care and protection might in the event be exploited by stronger agencies. Undue influence might be a consideration in deciding whether this was so. He was careful to stipulate that undue influence was possible without active wrongdoing. Self-interest was enough. In deciding whether a transaction was unconscionable it would be relevant to determine whether independent advice had been sought. Independent advice can't guarantee a balanced transaction, but the lack of it offers unfairness an opportunity.

It was a poignant moment to be recapitulating Denning's defence of the individual against institutional pressure. The day Mars-Jones J gave reasons for his judgment in *O'Sullivan & Another v. Management Agency & Music Ltd & Others*, 22 July 1982, was only a week or so before the near-legendary Denning's own last day in court. He had announced his retirement as Master of the Rolls, not exactly a voluntary departure from office but a political necessity after the Society of Black Lawyers took exception to questionable assertions in his book *What Next in the Law*. There was no question of his retirement going unmarked. He made a farewell speech to a court full to bursting with his colleagues (there were three hundred of them). A historic stepping-down, ripe in honours, with a hint of slow-motion defenestration.

Despite his reputation as the people's judge, Denning faced two ways. He was both liberal and illiberal. Perhaps the office has this Janus element inherent in it, there being no consistent way of resolving the conflict between individual rights and the imperatives of polity.

That's why I have my doubts about Geoffrey Robertson's full-throated paean to Dad ('a red-robed angel of mercy') in *The Justice Game*, however much I welcome it personally. As he sees it:

A, B and C were free, not as a result of their own courage (which was a precondition) or of their campaign (which gave them courage, but did not help the courtroom battle): they owed their release to a judge robustly indifferent to the State. Other judges, it is true, might not have recognized the oppressiveness of the indictment, or have called a halt to the case in the same way or at all. But for an era which is remembered for wrongful convictions and the liberties taken by the security services, the action of Mars-Jones is worth remembering, and worth celebrating. It says something for a system when the State, with all its power bent on conviction, cannot intimidate the courts or make prosecutors flinch from the duties of fairness.

I feel the need of a 'necessarily' before 'intimidate' in that last sentence, at the risk of taking some of the shine off it.

It's true that Denning could be very concerned with the protection of ordinary citizens, but he was also capable of arguing (in 1980) against those imprisoned for the Birmingham pub bombings being allowed to challenge their convictions. His reasoning was that if an appeal failed, a lot of money had been wasted, while if it succeeded,

> it would mean that the police were guilty of perjury; that they were guilty of violence and threats; that the confessions were involuntary and improperly admitted in evidence; and that the convictions were erroneous . . . That was such an appalling vista that every sensible person would say, 'It cannot be right that these actions should go any further.'

No mention of individual rights accompanied either outcome. There was just a calculation of the damage done to the public balance-sheet and the public confidence. It would be bad for the national mood if malpractice was exposed – but this was not Dad's view in matters of public probity.

By the same ignoble logic, it would have been wrong to prosecute the Obscene Publications Squad in 1976, since the proceedings would reveal they had been bought by the smut-merchants they were paid to keep down. It was as if rats had taken over the board of Rentokil and replaced the poison in traps across the country with multivitamins. This news might very well upset the company's shareholders, but how was that an excuse for keeping them in the dark?

When giving judgment in *O'Sullivan & Another v. Management Agency & Music Ltd & Others*, Mars-Jones J relied on Lord Denning for the chords (so to speak), but he had to make sure the tune of this particular case fitted them. In what sense was Raymond O'Sullivan, professionally known as Gilbert O'Sullivan, 'an individual so placed as to be in need of special care and protection'? (There exists no general duty of care, and no general principle of enforceable fairness, just a special dispensation in exceptional circumstances.) A standard type of this individual would be the 'expectant heir', someone who has assets he or she is unable to realize in time of need, but can transfer to someone else – greatly below their eventual value, as it may be – in exchange for ready money. O'Sullivan's talent as a writer qualified him as an expectant heir, entitled to be rescued from the consequences of his own decisions.

O'Sullivan was certainly unworldly, happy just to be making music, to be selling records, to be getting a reputation. He was given £10 a week spending money and lived in a cottage on the grounds of a substantial property owned by his manager. Somewhere in all this lurks the idea that Gilbert O'Sullivan was the child-man of his early image-making, not yet ready for long trousers, technically old enough to sign a contract but still a minor in psychological terms. He was being treated more like a ward of court than an autonomous adult.

The Bash Street Kid image actually seemed to suit him, certainly in terms of his bony face, better than the approximation to a hunky look that followed it. Fluffed-out hair doesn't work for everyone. He alternated unconvincingly between cosy jumpers and shirts open to the waist. No-one seemed to know if he was cuddly or sexy or not much of either, as he went through the available permutations of styling.

Having determined that the contracts should be put aside as void and unenforceable, Mars-Jones J directed that the master recordings be delivered to the plaintiff. Then he assessed the appropriate damages, and here he was in danger of going too far. He had already said that O'Sullivan had been 'fleeced' by Gordon Mills. Now he ruled that MAM should pay back all the profit made from the singer and his songs, with compound interest. A. J. Bateson QC, counsel for the plaintiffs, referred him to a ruling of Lord Denning's from 1975 (it's *Wallersteiner v. Moir*, if you're hungry for a reference) in which he stated that 'in equity, interest is never awarded by way of punishment. Equity awards it whenever money is misused by an executor or a trustee or anyone else in a fiduciary position . . .' Mars-Jones J accepted this, saying, 'I have found there was a fiduciary relationship here'.

He seemed to be equating a management company with a trustee, who would not be entitled to profit from the monies he handled. MAM, though, was in business to make money from the representation of its clients (who included Tom Jones and Engelbert Humperdinck). Mars-Jones J's directions did not recognize any legal element of profit. If the damages awarded weren't explicitly punitive, it wasn't easy to understand them in any other spirit.

N. A. Strauss, representing the First to Fifth Defendants, tried to protest: 'My Lord, I accept that your Lordship has jurisdiction to order interest on that basis, but I submit that it is inappropriate in the circumstances . . .'

He tried to spell out the flaw in the judge's reasoning, but Mars-Jones J was, as he said, 'not attracted' by his proposition. He wouldn't budge. After another couple of attempts, Mr Strauss could only say: 'My Lord, I have made my submission. I do not think I can take the point any further.'

I can find some sympathy in my heart for Mr Strauss. When there was something Dad didn't want to hear he could generate quite a force-field of negative interest. If he was 'not attracted' by a proposition there was a low hum in the air and the fitments began to rattle.

Mr Strauss's argument would have to wait for a hearing in a higher court. In 1984 there was an appeal in *O'Sullivan & Another v. Management Agency & Music Ltd & Others*, heard before Lord Justices Waller, Dunn and Fox. In their representations the defendants, or the relevant lawyers, found fault with absolutely everything that had been decided in Dad's court. That's one advantage an appeal against judgment enjoys over a family argument – nothing is lost by saying 'And another thing . . .' They objected to the notion that there was a fiduciary relationship between Gilbert O'Sullivan and his manager, to the voicing of personal criticism, to the transfer not just of copyrights but of master tapes, and above all to the fixing of compound interest as the appropriate mechanism for returning MAM's profits to the man who had generated them.

There was a certain amount of routine legal to and fro. Counsel for the plaintiffs proposed that the proper approach was that adopted in *Peter Pan Manufacturing Corporation v. Corsets Silhouette Ltd* [1964]. Counsel for the defendants felt rather strongly that the plaintiffs could not rely upon the support offered by *Peter Pan Manufacturing Corporation v. Corsets Silhouette Ltd* [1964].

The legal term for returning profits after the event is rather lovely. MAM was being required to 'disgorge' the money, a word that suggests a snake unhinging its jaws and yielding up some half-digested goat.

The disgorgement required of MAM was drastic. By making two changes to the system of repayment (factoring in past Corporation Tax and calculating simple rather than compound interest) the appellants sought to reduce the amount due by over four million pounds.

The original hearing had been long and intricate, the appeal brief but formidable in the intensity of its reasoning. The judge of first instance, sitting alone, had ruled that the contracts were void. The higher court was in effect an incandescent tube powered by three Lord Justices wired in parallel, legal luminaries whose individual wattage was already formidable. They disagreed with Mars-Jones J, defining the contracts as not void but voidable, being unenforceable so far as unperformed.

Sitting alone, like my father before me, I must huddle round the faint glow thrown by my little layman's Anglepoise and struggle to make sense of the shapes I see. I take this to mean that a void contract – void '*ab initio*' – would be one that could never have been performed. A voidable contract is one that can be set aside if its terms are not implemented, and this is the category to which the appeal judges decided Gilbert O'Sullivan's agreements with Gordon Mills and MAM properly belonged. They could be set aside because the obligations laid on the defendants had not in fact been discharged.

The emphasis here seems to shift from an unconscionable contract (and one in which Mars-Jones J detected not just

89

inequality of bargaining power but 'plain, unvarnished deceit') to one that was acceptably framed but defectively discharged. Even so, the effect was not to let Mills and MAM off the hook. The Lord Justices accepted that there was a fiduciary relationship, and that the defendants were in breach of it. They were therefore not entitled to profit by their wrongdoing. There was discussion about how amends might be made.

It turns out that you can't have rescission without the possibility of *restitutio in integrum*. Translating roughly: there's no point in saying a contract never happened unless you can restore the status quo as it was at the moment of signing. It's meaningless to turn the clock back if everything has been changed by the contract itself.

The use of Latin in legal argument and judgment has been drastically reduced since 1982. The effect is to make the proceedings less opaque, but they will always be opaque to some extent by virtue of being governed by past decisions, and hinging on distinctions foreign to daily life.

A legal system based on precedent is a monument to creative rot, a sort of cultural compost heap dating back, notionally, I suppose, to the Conquest. Not everything rots down into principle at the same rate, so that the decisions of a Denning, say, can resist the process in the same way that eggshells and avocado stones do, retaining their integrity and withholding their nutrients from the rich millennial mulch of insight and vested interest.

Just as the terminology of the early 1980s now seems very stiff, so the language of earlier cases referred to during the appeal proceedings has an additional fustiness that can sometimes be beguiling. Dixon, CJ, in *Alati v. Kruger* (1955) refers to the disaffirmance rather than rescission of a contract.

Purely as a word, I prefer 'disaffirmance' to 'rescission' (which sounds like bad news you might hear at the dentist's), and I've been disaffirming things like mad since I learned it, though made uneasy by not knowing if there's a shade of meaning involved. Does it make a difference that Dixon was Chief Justice of Australia? I know Australian law derives in some way from English, but how does Australian precedent impinge on English case law? My ignorance seems to increase with every moment of enlightenment. I've written with more confidence about Japanese cinema than I do about English law.

I do feel qualified to assess rhetoric, and the award for the most stirring utterance of the appeal must go to Michael Miller, QC, for the plaintiffs, who said:

> He who seeks equity must do equity. In the present case it is inequitable that the first plaintiff should seek to recover the whole profit made by the defendant companies as a result of the agreements, without being prepared to permit them reasonable remuneration for the very valuable services they have rendered in turning him from a relatively unknown song-writer to an internationally famous star.

(O'Sullivan had been working for the Post Office when he signed the contract.) Strongly put. What's sauce for the plaintiff must be sauce for the defendant.

Or as Lord Wright put it in *Spence v. Crawford* (1939), 'Though the defendant has been fraudulent, he must not be robbed, nor must the plaintiff be unjustly enriched, as he would be if he both got back what he had parted with and kept what he had received in return.' Yet this is more or less what the court of first instance had ruled, and even on appeal the defendants were held to be entitled only to 'a reasonable remuneration including a small profit element'. The underlying idea seems to be that someone who has been defrauded should sue for damages rather than relying on equity to make everything good. There's a grey area here, though, since in equity the term 'fraud' embraces not only actual fraud but certain other forms of conduct falling below the standards demanded by equity. Conduct of this sort is known as 'constructive' fraud. One of the examples of such a fraud would be a transaction procured by undue influence, or where one party is in breach of a fiduciary duty to another. Exactly what was held to have been the case here.

The judgment in the lower court was neither upheld *in toto*, nor comprehensively overturned. Instead it was upheld in part and the judge's order 'varied', with significant adjustments made to it. Mars-Jones J 'fell into error' when he accepted counsel's argument about the appropriateness of compound interest. (Excepted from this were the secret deductions made by MAM (Music Publishing) Ltd from monies taken in Germany and New Zealand. It was right that these sums be repaid with compound interest.)

One of the cases referred to in the appeal was *Erlanger v. New Sombrero Phosphate Co.* (1878). There isn't enough poetry in the law for me to risk leaving it out. Might that be a guano enterprise? The market value of birdshit has lessons for us all.

Dad would rather have had his order 'varied' than thrown out, I'm sure, but he can't have enjoyed the experience. If I've battled through the case and the appeal in as much detail as I can manage, and with as much clarity, it's partly to confront for my own benefit how different his world was from mine. In fantasy he would annex the world of books in his retirement. He also encouraged me to think of myself as a potential lawyer, but it isn't so. My wheels grind differently, and my ego is hungry for a different food.

The case of *O'Sullivan & Another v. Management Agency & Music Ltd & Others* was a significant one, though it hardly dominated the headlines. Dad would have listened respectfully to submissions made on behalf of a writer or an artist, but un-justice done to a musician, a performer moreover who wrote his own material, somehow struck him more forcibly and may have been part of what caused him to 'fall into error'.

Possibly there was an element of spurious underdog identification at work. Gilbert O'Sullivan had arrived in London by way of Waterford and Swindon, Dad by way of Llansannan and Aberystwyth. They had both come from nothing. After the death of our neighbour Os(wald) Terry, Dad would reminisce about his own early life using the phrase 'When I were a little lad . . .' which had been Os's trademark. Dad seemed not to realize that he was advertising the inauthenticity of his remembered struggles with the use of a borrowed tag, though I'm sure that Os picked it up somewhere too, just as the monologue of his we enjoyed so much as children, about Albert and the Lion, turned out to be Stanley Holloway's really.

Counsel for the defendants were working hard during the appeal to argue down the large sums whose disgorgement had been ordered by the court of first instance. They stated their objection to the master tapes being returned to O'Sullivan, but concentrated their efforts, understandably, on arguments that could save money right away.

It may be that the real importance of *O'Sullivan & Another v. Management Agency & Music Ltd & Others* was the precedent it set in the matter of master tapes. An anomaly of the case seems to be that Gilbert O'Sullivan ended up in possession of these valuable items, though if he had taken independent legal advice and signed a much more advantageous contract he would have enjoyed no such benefit. This is more or less a technicality in the case itself, because O'Sullivan had since signed other contracts that meant he then yielded up the master tapes to other record companies, but perhaps it expanded the possibilities for others. A singer/songwriter in an oppressive contract who only stood to win back his copyrights might think twice, but the prospect of getting ownership of master tapes would exponentially increase the attractiveness of a lawsuit.

There were musicians who took their cue. Sting sued over inequitable contracts (before the appeal in *O'Sullivan & Another v. Management Agency & Music Ltd & Others*, I think), with Mars-Jones J presiding. This was in the early days of the soundbite as an art form, and I imagine Dad must have wished he had worked harder on a truly quotable dictum when he remarked, after the defendants had finally capitulated to Sting and settled, 'This has been a very trying trial.' Elton John also sued Dick James Music, though before a different judge.

In all this I am feeling my way, humiliated by an inability to distinguish the core issue from the contingent circumstances, the steak from the parsley garnish. It has been a Socratic process, to learn how much I don't know, and I fully understand the feelings of the ancient Athenian citizenry, who might acknowledge that Socrates was a cultural treasure without equal, but would cross the road or remember a previous engagement rather than be drawn into dialogue with him.

From the dawn of pubescence if not before, my assigned role in the family was peacemaker, a not uncommon casting for a middle child, but Dad further characterized me as dreamy and unworldly, only too likely to be exploited by more savvy folk. Watching me as a child flitting from the piano keyboard to a book and the television, then back again, he would tell me that I had a butterfly brain. I wish I had had the wit to tell him I had something much more useful, a bee brain.

In many areas of life he simply ignored evidence that contradicted his fixed ideas, but this wasn't one of them. After the moment in 1980 when he learned that I had a book contract with Faber for the book eventually titled *Lantern Lecture*, he never seriously questioned my judgement. Did I start riding a motorbike (in 1988) when I was too old to be classed as a boy racer, too young for it to qualify as a midlife crisis with handle-bars? Dad was confident I'd ride safely. Did I venture into an unconventional family life (in 1991) by having a daughter with a friend? Dad was delighted. He would have preferred a grand-son but was prepared to wait for a further instalment of this pleasing twist in the family saga. He didn't imitate the ritual cry of his beloved Fred Flintstone – *Yabba-dabba-doo!* – but that may have been because he was too busy calling for champagne.

His earlier idea of me as dreamy simply fell to the ground, and he decided that I must have been planning the Faber coup more or less from the egg. Useless to say that good luck and social contacts – thank you, Rosemary Hill – had led me first of all to a magazine editor (Craig Raine of *Quarto*) and then, thanks to Craig's urgings, to a publisher, with the ragbag of fact-based fictions that was pretty much all I'd ever attempted. My dreamy side was still there, though I took care to defend it behind intellectual barricades, topped with all the razor wire I could rustle up.

The problem area was my sexuality, something not touched on in that first book, since Dad had always had such a horror of men who were attracted to men. He was more than a standard-issue homophobe, not far from a homophobe's homophobe. If there were Annual General Meetings of the Homophobia League then he would be an honoured guest if not keynote speaker, guaranteed any number of brief manly pats on the back.

Part of this was an unworldliness of his own. He was one of the very few judges of his day who hadn't gone to public school. He had studied at St John's, Cambridge, but only for a year after the end of his time at Aberystwyth. He didn't enjoy talking about sex of any sort, and wasn't comfortable when anyone else raised the subject.

It seems obvious that his metropolitan colleagues, once he had moved to London and started to practise as a barrister, were more relaxed, meaning more hypocritical, about such things, not unduly distressed when some of those funny people, who as everyone but Dad agreed could be highly entertaining, hairdressers and so on, were silly enough to get caught. Dad became every inch a Town Mouse, in his Church's handmade shoes and bespoke suits, but in this one respect he reverted to Country Mouse type.

I only know of one person who tried to alert him to the unreliability of his ideas on the subject of homosexuality, and that was Ronald Waterhouse, a junior colleague who sometimes worked for Dad as a 'devil' in his days at the Bar, working informally on aspects of a complicated case and being paid directly by Dad.

Working with devils was an arrangement that suited Dad very well. Perhaps it was a way of buying in the raw analytical power he felt he lacked, the X-ray vision of the natural lawyer. It was an intensive but also convivial system, not exactly democratic but not quite formally structured either. They all worked hard, in bursts, and Dad napped hard too. (Napping wasn't part of a devil's job description.) If he was in court and it was a matter of preparing the next day's material then he would have a nap after the afternoon session, before meeting the devil (or devils) for a drink and a briefing. They would meet again for dinner, when Dad would receive a progress report. Drinking at dinner would be moderate, by the standards prevailing. Dad would fix a deadline, perhaps for midnight, when the devil(s) would bring him comprehensively up to date. In the meantime Dad would have another nap.

I imagine all these lubricated parleys taking place in the Grosvenor Hotel, Chester, an institution I've never visited but one that seemed somehow to be Dad's spiritual home. Perhaps as the hub of the Wales and Chester circuit in his glory days as a barrister, neither Wales nor London, it was where he had the most seductive combination of ease and prestige.

Dad was a great exponent of the Churchillian Nap, a form of refreshment that has since been rebranded the Power Nap or the Disco Nap. He felt that you should play fair with the god of sleep by getting into your pyjamas and sliding between the sheets even if you only aimed for the replenishment of five brain-charging minutes offline. When the late-night pressure was too relentless for him to risk another nap he would keep going on cigarettes, putting his head under the cold tap every half-hour or so if the nicotine alertness began to fade.

He smoked every step of the way to the bench, and when he was told to give the habit up in the 1970s had to learn a different pattern of working. His brain needed to acquire the ability to walk again without the crutch of a cigarette, and Dad's solution was to move the intensity of his work life into a different sector of the day, not the late-late night but the early-early morning. He would set the clock for five or even four. When a long and complicated case was over he might still get up without fully waking and sleepwalk his way to his study, where Sheila would find him and coax him back to bed.

By suggesting to Dad that he was prejudiced, Ronald Waterhouse risked making an enemy who outranked him in a hierarchical profession, and also cutting off a useful stream of revenue. There's no more efficient way of killing goodwill than letting a friend know he's a bigot.

Of course he 'wrapped it up a bit', as advocates are always being urged to do . . . *Bill, you have a bit of a bee in your bonnet about these people. They are not as you suppose them to be.* Even so, this seems a case of File Under Moral Courage. I can't think of another category that would fit it.

Ronald Waterhouse didn't lose Dad's allegiance, and later he became a judge himself. He's perhaps best known for the painstaking inquiry he conducted, after his retirement, into the abuse of children in care in North Wales. There should be a special mention, though, for the question he asked during the proceedings against Ken Dodd for tax evasion in 1989. He asked, 'What does £100,000 in a suitcase feel like?' to which Dodd replied, unsatisfyingly to my mind, 'The notes are very light, M'Lord.'

Dad didn't forget that Ronald had tried to change his attitude, but he held on to the contested attitude as well as to the friendship with Ronald. He wasn't ready to be influenced, to entertain new thoughts. As far as he was concerned the subject was as exempt from renegotiation as a birth certificate.

Did he have any personal experience of homosexuals and their ways? He was once, as a young man, on the receiving end of a clumsy pass, though it was more apocalyptic than that in the telling. Unfortunately he gave few details, and didn't encourage questions. Any actual information value has disappeared under the build-up of competitively distorted versions Tim and I exchanged and found funny. Our final reworking went something like *Wallah at the Club bought me a few drinks between chukkas. Seemed a nice enough chap till he tried to slide his filthy paw into my dhoti – laid the blighter out with a chota peg.* (Sometimes 'polo mallet'.) Quite where the Anglo-Indian colouring comes in I have no idea. The incident took place, I think, in Geneva before the War, though Dad never otherwise referred to being in Geneva. The fact that our version ends with violence isn't part of the distortion. Dad said with a certain amount of righteousness that he had broken a bottle on the man's head, as if no other form of RSVP was possible.

Dad wasn't even sufficiently at ease with the existence of homosexuals to tell jokes about them. In fact he hated such jokes more than any other. Even an anti-gay joke gave perversion the oxygen of publicity, when by rights it should be smothered in the sulphur of oblivion.

I remember when Dad treated his brother, David, up from Denbighshire on a visit to the metropolis, to dinner at the Garrick Club. David embarrassed him by telling an off-colour joke on those hallowed premises. A joke about lesbians.

It was about as sweet as such a joke can be. *A man in a bar sees an attractive woman and asks the bartender to send a drink to her from him. 'I wouldn't bother if I was you,' says the bartender. 'She's a lesbian.' The man isn't deterred and insists on the drink being sent over. He waits a little while and then goes over to strike up conversation. 'So,' he says, 'which part of Lesbos are you from?'*

I know I'm a bit of a subtext hound, but there's something very satisfying about this constellation of joke, teller, audience and even setting. In theory David was much more of a Country Mouse than Dad, resistant to anything that was 'far back' (his code word, slightly mystifying to me, for 'posh'), but he chose to tell a joke making mild fun of provincialism and ignorance. And meanwhile Dad was appalled that the word 'lesbian' should have been spoken in the dining-room of the Garrick.

The Garrick Club was founded in 1831 (and named after the supreme actor of the previous century) as a place where 'actors and men of refinement and education might meet on equal terms', it being taken for granted that actors were unrefined and uneducated. That was certainly the general opinion, and the idea was to improve the position of this raffish line of work ('profession' was hardly the right word at the time). The founders hoped that by restricting eligibility to journalists, lawyers and actors, respectability might be leached from those who had more than enough by those who were badly in need.

The club achieved its goal, but the respectability of actors is as provisional as anyone else's. John Gielgud, for instance, a prominent member, was respectable (to the point of being recently knighted) when he entered a Chelsea public convenience one day in 1953, not so much when he left it in police custody. He had been advised (by Michael Redgrave, was it?) of the crucial importance of giving a false name if arrested. Accordingly he identified himself to the authorities as Arthur Gielgud. He seems to have thought 'John' was the bit that gave him away.

It seems thousands of years ago, the time when a vulnerable public figure could behave with such marvellous naivety. It's only fair to point out that Arthur John Gielgud was his full name, so he may have been trying in some quixotic way to avoid a lie while also masking his identity with an alias. He did dissemble about his profession, describing himself in court as a clerk.

Though worldliness was a very variable quality in those post-war years, when Dad was building his reputation in London, his own innocence and alarm seem hard to credit. Even in Aberystwyth, where he had been heavily involved in student stage productions, there must surely have been at least a few dodgy characters sheltering under the capacious skirts of Dame Theatre. There have been plenty of young men over the years who've joined a drama group when the only acting they were really keen to do was acting on their own prohibited desires.

Dad thought that such dark matters shouldn't be discussed – yet there was no lenience extended to those who were properly secretive. Dad harboured a particular animus towards Gilbert Harding, the 1950s television personality, famous for his rudeness, who broke down when interviewed (for the programme *Face to Face*) by John Freeman, who asked searching questions about death and his mother. The programme proved that television could be both intimate and intense, even harrowing. The impact was correspondingly greater in a culture more buttoned-up than today's.

Dad's logic was hard to follow. Gilbert Harding's sexuality only became public knowledge after his death, but Dad seemed to feel that there was an element of deception involved in his appearance on the programme. A monster had been allowed to lay claim to recognizable human emotions, things he couldn't possibly experience given the corruption of his desires. Such a person wasn't entitled to weep for his mother's death.

Ideally, crimes against nature should also be ignored by culture. Dad felt it to be appalling that Emlyn Williams, actor and playwright, should willingly address the issue in his autobiographies. One book, *George*, appeared before the decriminalization of homosexuality, the other (*Emlyn*) afterwards. A Welsh homosexual was a particular sort of traitor, a quisling between the sheets, a friend who chose to help the enemy. If there was a connection suggested here between the theatrical world and sexual double-dealing then it was all the less welcome for that.

As late as the 1970s Dad could listen with evident pleasure to a radio programme in which a pair of elderly spinsters, spending their retirement in the idyllic village of Stackton Tressel, reminisced about their long-ago operatic careers, without realizing that his beloved Hinge and Bracket were female impersonators. (Admittedly drag on the radio takes gender transgression into the domain of conceptual art.) When informed of the true situation he seemed baffled. What on earth was the point? It was hard to explain to him that however little point there was to the act in question, there was even less if they were really what they claimed to be.

David's lesbian joke had only made a ripple, but another comic routine caused Dad considerable offence. Since it happened in the 1970s, it gave his sons much joy. We weren't used to seeing him at a loss, and no pathos attached to the novelty at the time. Whether or not that decade was a difficult time to be a post-adolescent male, it must have been an excruciating time to be the father of such creatures. The occasion was Christmas lunch, displaced from the Gray's Inn flat for once. The reason was that Sheila was still recovering from the effects of a road accident, and wouldn't be up to the strain of catering, so the date is likely to have been 1973. The venue was the Waldorf Hotel in the Aldwych, and we went there as the guests of George Walford, a colleague of Dad's, family friend and in fact godfather of Matthew. On a cryptic-crossword level I enjoyed the fact that we were going to the Waldorf with the Walfords, but there was also a bit of history being invoked, since the Waldorf was where my parents had held their wedding reception. We would be near the very spot where Dad's father, Henry, had fallen on the sword of his abstinence in the name of family unity. There might be a plaque to commemorate this heroic ingestion of fizz, virtual hara-kiri of non-conformist temperance.

It started perfectly innocently. 'Do you know the story about the newly appointed judge who doesn't feel he's got the hang of the sentencing guidelines . . . ?' I wonder what had got into George Walford. Perhaps there was an element of the raconteur's Olympiad, a desire to tell a joke or funny story that would beat Dad at his own droll game. By this stage of the meal much food had been eaten, much drink drunk. Crackers had been tortured until they voided their trinkets. Paper hats had been distributed and put on with variously good and bad grace.

Dad expressed neutral interest in this recent appointee to the bench, praiseworthy in his concern to master the proper procedures.

George went on with his story. 'So he approaches a senior colleague and asks for the benefit of his experience. "What," he asks, "should I give a young man for allowing himself to be buggered?" "Oh," says the senior judge, "I'd say thirty bob and a box of Black Magic should do the trick."'

We sons were incredulous with delight but managed to suppress any manifestation of it. Sheila looked anxious and unhappy. Nobody round the table laughed. In fact a laughter-vacuum was created which could have annihilated a great deal of entertainment value – not just a single off-colour joke but Richard Pryor's entire 1973 Christmas show (assuming that by some anomaly of booking agency he was performing in the next room). Pryor was in his full foul-mouthed prime around then, but although Dad would have hated his comedy he wouldn't have felt betrayed by it, not personally attacked. He was so thunderstruck by George Walford's joke that he hardly seemed to react, though it was clear to us all that he had sustained a heavy blow.

George had danced on the grave of a number of his most precious assumptions. 1) A joke about a judge who was not just a pervert but a frivolous one, 2) told in mixed company, by which he would have meant not just that there were women present but that the younger generation was being exposed to insidious flippant evil, 3) at Christmas. He couldn't stage a protest because we were guests and thereby beholden, though I have to say such considerations hadn't necessarily held him back in the past.

It almost seemed to be too much for him to take in, this compound assault, being simultaneously stabbed (as it may have seemed) in the back, in the front and in the sides. Finally he managed to say, 'I'm afraid I don't see much humour in that sort of thing.' And after that nothing could put the bubbles back in the champagne. They had symbolically migrated to the bloodstreams of the Mars-Jones boys, black bubbles of mischief, and we had to pretend not to be made tipsy and exhilarated by them.

It was the same juvenile impulse that made us choose the Mille Pini off Queen Square (basic Italian) whenever a family meal in the Gray's Inn area was on offer – until there was an actual restaurant called A Thousand Penises we would make do with the Mille Pini. I don't know what had led Dad to choose George Walford to preside over Matthew's spiritual development, and perhaps that Christmas he regretted it. The godparents we were allotted were either neighbours and friends from Gray's Inn or colleagues of Dad's. So I was under the care of Cynthia Terry (Aunty See-See), who lived at number 5 Gray's Inn Square, and James Wellwood (Uncle Jimmy) from number 1. To complete the set I had a more august and remote presence, Sir Hildreth Glyn-Jones. I've never met a Hildreth since. It's a rare first name, and it means 'battle counsellor', usually given to females when given at all.

A godparent is supposed to watch over a child's interests, to underwrite renunciation of the Devil and his works, the vain pomp and glory of the world, not to mention desires both covetous and carnal. Informally there's some sort of residual watchdog function, though intervention would only ever be a last resort. During deadlocked arguments of the 1970s it would have been handy to empanel my trio as a higher tribunal, a family Court of Appeal (perhaps that was why we had been given three godparents each). In such a hearing I might not have done too badly. Cynthia was a layperson, not much of a match for Dad in argument, and Jimmy Wellwood, though a lawyer, was academic by temperament, easily distracted and easily overruled, but Sir Hildreth was a senior judge with rather a relish for barneys in court, who might have taken my side for the sheer hell of it.

Sir Hildreth didn't live in the Inn, but would seek me out every now and then when I was a schoolboy at Westminster. A message would be tucked behind the lattice of ribbons on the College noticeboard, making an appointment to take me out one afternoon. We would walk across Green Park to Fortnum & Mason for tea. I remember him telling me that Autolycus in *The Winter's Tale* described himself as a 'snapper-up of unconsidered trifles', and that the word for this indispensable faculty was 'serendipity'. Before he delivered me back to school he would dependably hand over a five-pound note.

All of this was highly satisfactory. This was godparental behaviour of a sort I could understand, with its own compass points: English Breakfast tea, Shakespearean conversation, anchovy-paste sandwiches, five-pound note. It was only long after the event, after Sir Hildreth had signed off on his sponsorial duties by giving me a copy of Peake's *Commentary on the Bible* – I had been confirmed, so in spiritual terms I was flying solo – that these visitations acquired an extra dimension.

Sir Hildreth was an acerbic judge notorious for the humiliations he visited on counsel appearing before him. Presiding over a court was his version of blood sport, and the blood spilled was unlikely to be his. It's virtually impossible for a judge to be defeated in a contest with a barrister (though F. E. Smith landed a few good blows), and any such victory will come at a cost. The bull never gets awarded a matador's ears. Technical redresses can be secured in a higher court, assuming that the judge is wrong in law as distinct from abusive in person, but this precious ointment can only be applied long after the bruises have faded.

So there was some calculation involved in awarding this oppressive personage a stake in my spiritual development. Giving Sir Hildreth this honour might confer a certain immunity on Dad. I was a sop to Cerberus, a studious little hobbit offered up to take the edge off the Orc King's appetite. Dad was trying to draw Sir Hildreth into the charmed circle of family with its qualms and taboos. When this senior judge stood by the font and undertook to watch over me, so that the old Adam might be buried and a new man rise in his place, I imagine Dad was looking for a related promise. That he himself wouldn't be stretched on a rack in open court any time soon.

Obviously I exaggerate. It's a family failing. Dad wasn't propitiating the Dark Lord of Mordor, nor even Torquemada (the actual Inquisitor, not the still-remembered crossword compiler). He was doing something I should have been able to understand even as a schoolboy, especially as a schoolboy. He was sucking up. The Honourable Sir Hildreth Glyn-Jones was twenty years older than Dad. He was never invited to drinks parties at the flat, or if invited didn't attend. I don't even know if he lived in London. He had a wife and three daughters but I never met them.

As for whether Sir Hildreth's bullying tendency was immobilized once he had been bound by the spider-thread of godparenthood, I don't know. Dad would take him occasionally to Twickenham to see the rugby, and may have thought that Sir Hildreth was eating out of his hand. But, according to what Dad said late in life, the habit of courtroom barracking was too strong for my godfather to break. Sir Hildreth admired Dad's advocacy but couldn't resist squashing him. And when he'd gone too far and had dragged Dad slowly over live coals, there was a ready-made way of making amends without needing to apologize. Almost a trick out of Dad's book. He could drop a note by my school and take me out to tea. He had realized that the relationship designed to tame him could be used for his own purposes. Tea for two at Fortnum's with a five-pound note thrown in came much cheaper than humble pie for one, eaten under the eyes of a junior colleague.

Sir Hildreth was near the end of his time on the bench by then, and it seems to be true that he wasn't popular within his profession. There's a tradition that at the end of the last day of a judge's working life, the advocate appearing for the Crown refers to this milestone and wishes him well in his retirement. On Sir Hildreth's last day the barrister who would ultimately speak those words, if in fact they were to be said, still hadn't decided what to do. It was only a custom, after all, not a requirement, and there would be no repercussions if it was omitted. He had a choice between seeming to truckle to power even while it was in the process of disappearing, or to expose a man to humiliation at the first moment when he could do so without fearing the consequences. Sir Hildreth's career as a judge of first instance was over, and he would never tear the wings off a barrister again.

Oh dear, I'm certainly ramping up the pathos, conjuring up a scenario perilously close to *The Browning Version*. My mistake. Sir Hildreth Glyn-Jones wasn't like the classics master Crocker-Harris in Rattigan's play, unaware of his unpopularity, mortified to learn he's known as 'the Himmler of the lower fifth'. Sir Hildreth made no attempt to soften his manner in court as his reign came to an end. It was almost a point of pride for him to play the tyrant and make things difficult. He must have considered the possibility that he would forfeit the gracious ritual of farewell on his last day, so that his career would go to its grave (so to speak) without a kind word to help the cortège bear up.

Finally counsel for the Crown stood up and spoke. He said, 'My Lord, I believe this is your last day as one of Her Majesty's Justices, and I would not wish to let the occasion go by without passing on the congratulations of this court . . .'

I have this from Esyr Lewis, Gray's Inn resident and family friend, the barrister who had to make his choice on the day. It wasn't that he felt an overwhelming urge to produce the proper gesture; he just found when the moment came that he couldn't not. And against expectation it wasn't a formality, but a moment of high stifled emotion. That *Browning Version* note again – not that it's a bad theme, the defencelessness of the well-defended. Sir Hildreth, having steeled himself against the likelihood of rejection, found himself still counted within the fold of civility. And when the Dark Lord of courtroom torture, Queen's Bench Division, went to hang up his full-bottomed wig for the last time, there were plausibly tears in his eyes.

There was never a real risk that Dad would be deprived of the customary send-off, when his turn came. He may not have been loved by those who appeared before him, but he was certainly respected, regarded as formidable rather than actively oppressive. No barrister ever steered a case inattentively while Dad was in charge of proceedings.

He had a heedlessness, even when not wearing the scarlet, which could sometimes seem heroic. Dad had his teeth looked after, for instance, by Sir Paul Beresford, an MP who set aside a portion of each week for his dental practice, or alternatively, as some of his constituents complained, a dentist who represented their interests in his spare time. By either account he was clearly not someone to be trifled with, but then nor was Dad, who might say, 'I don't think much of that bridge you gave me last time,' his delivery muffled by reason of the fact that Sir Paul was scraping and probing away inside his mouth at the time.

Brecht's Galileo admits that he didn't need to be tortured to be pressured into recantation – all it took was for him to be shown the instruments. That's how most people feel in dentists' waiting rooms, as they leaf miserably through *Vogue* and *Country Life* (or *Prima* and *Empire* if your dentist is less grand), on the brink of a general recantation. But it wouldn't have occurred to Dad to soften his criticism, or to delay the vote of no confidence until he and his tender gums were out of harm's way.

In his prime Dad's forthrightness was held in check by a certain self-censorship. (It made sense that if he approved of external censorship, of limits on what could be expressed and circulated, he should also be in favour of the internal Lord Chamberlain.) There were certain things he never discussed, even with drink taken. After he retired he made less of an effort to project a consistent persona. In conversation he let slip the news that the absolute wrongness of pre-marital sex that he preached to us in our adolescence was not something he had paid much attention to during his own. 'Let slip' gives the wrong impression, as if a guilty secret had escaped him. He seemed very matter-of-fact about it, and quite fond of his bad old ways.

I was hearing a new story and an unfamiliar sexual philosophy. In the days of trains without corridors, their compartments opening directly onto the platform, an enterprising man and woman taking refuge in an empty compartment could manage a 'quick poke' in perfect safety, as long as they remained aware on some subliminal level of the minutes remaining before the next station.

Perhaps this was how he spoke as an adult to adults, yet he had never enjoyed 'off-colour' conversations. He never swore, though that may have something to do with growing up with Welsh as a first language. It's a myth that there are no swear words in Welsh, but Dad would hardly have been exposed to any in a Congregationalist household in the 1920s and '30s. In fact, thanks to the consonantal impact of the language, almost any syllable can aspire to expletive force in Welsh. '*Pobl*

Bach!' for instance means no more than 'little people' (presumably along the lines of leprechauns), but can be given any amount of plosive attack.

Dad was a Welsh speaker and proud of it, though uneasily aware that there were rust spots on his mother tongue from not using it on anything like a daily basis. Nevertheless he had been that rare thing, a judge who could conduct court proceedings in Welsh, and he was instrumental in setting up summer schools for magistrates in Wales, to help them get acquainted with the new technical vocabulary in the minority language thrown up by new legislation.

Soon after his appointment as a judge he was made a member of the Gorsedd at the National Eisteddfod for his contribution to Welsh culture. Dad's sense of the honour being done him wasn't shaken by the discovery that the singer Mary Hopkin was one of his fellow cultural contributors. I remember the assembled Druids wearing wet-weather gear in the form of short white Wellington boots. Dad was very tickled by the headline in a local newspaper – 'LOCAL BOY MAKES BARD'.

He had spent a lot of time choosing his bardic name. This wasn't the down-to-earth sort of Welsh coinage associated with the need to differentiate between the many bearers of a single name, like Dai Central Eating for a man with only a single tooth remaining or Dai Quiet Wedding for someone who turned up to tie the knot wearing carpet slippers, to quote two of Dad's favourite examples. This was a serious and ceremonial business. He settled on Gwilym Aled, Gwilym being the formal Welsh equivalent of William, Aled being the name of the river near his birthplace of Llansannan, really more of a stream running across fields.

He told me I should have my own Bardic name in readiness. His suggestion was 'Adda Chwith', meaning Adam Lefthand, celebrating one of my more innocent deviations from the statistical norm. He didn't explain how I was going to make a contribution to Welsh culture without being part of it.

In the 1980s I was excited when I came across a gay activist in London who was doing something similar to Dad's translation project for the benefit of magistrates, helping to translate the technical terms of gay liberation into Welsh. I remember '*llon*' as the Welsh for 'gay'. I may not speak the language, but the ability to hiss that double *l* is part of my birthright, inalienable. If there are Welsh words that have added music to such terms as 'self-oppression' and 'heteronormativity', they haven't reached my ears.

The activist and I were getting on just fine (wasn't I an activist too?) till I mentioned my own Welsh connection. After that the engines of intimacy went into full reverse, since he regarded Dad as a sort of Uncle Tom for laying the treasure of his language at the feet of the foreign oppressor. As he saw it, a Welsh-speaking judge was a particular sort of traitor and fitted the same painful profile as Emlyn Williams did for Dad, an enemy who was born to be a friend. It was a moment of something like symmetry, the correcting of a balance. Normally I was Dad's shaming family secret but now he was mine.

In English Dad avoided four-letter words, though he could go as far as referring to someone as a 'four-letter feller'. In practice this was usually Bernard Levin, who had (as he felt) traduced him in an article written for *The Times* during the 1970s. A juror had tried to walk away from his responsibilities on the basis that he didn't understand the issues in the case. Dad responded by sending him to the cells for contempt of court. It's certainly true that if people could evade their civic duty so easily by claiming incompetence the system would soon collapse. It would have been better for the reluctant juror to stick to the traditional practice of turning up in a tracksuit and dark glasses, confident of being held back on the reserve bench as dodgy, presumptively druggy, then sent swiftly home.

Levin, as a columnist and contrarian, was bound to take a different line – to suggest, for instance, that this self-recusing juror was a hero of democracy, refusing merely to rubber-stamp the court procedures without true intellectual participation in the administration of justice. This was not a threat to the system but its vindication. The judge in the case who had slapped him down was, correspondingly, an agent of oppression and a sworn enemy of civil liberties.

What galled Dad was the relish with which the piece was written, as if Levin was tickled pink to be putting a judge into the public pillory, even the laughing-stocks. His article began: 'Mr Justice Mars-Jones was in a rare old paddy down the Old Bailey last week . . .' I remember reading it in a coffee shop in Cambridge, shocked by the eruption of the family name into my placid breakfast ritual. I was also undeniably thrilled by mockery at Dad's expense. We must have made quite a pair in Belinda's on Trinity Street, my ham roll and I, my tongue hanging out in stupefaction to match the pale meat lolling over the bread on my plate.

Dad felt he had been subjected to a personal attack camouflaged as commentary on something in the news. The worst of it was that he wasn't able to respond, either as one of Her Majesty's Judges nor as an individual. He had been targeted by the might of the fourth estate, and there was nothing he could do in protest or retaliation except rehearse the phrase to which Levin's name would always be chained with links of bitter contempt, 'four-letter feller'. The word suppressed in this formula rhymes with threepenny bit.

And perhaps there was another small thing he could do. He did have one small weapon at his disposal, the dark marble of social death. This he would fire from his catapult to strike back at the giant Levin, to bring the sneering Philistine-Pharisee down to earth. If ever Bernard Levin applied for membership of Dad's beloved Garrick Club, the black ball would fly swift from Dad's sling.

It was almost a pity that Levin was already so unpopular with the legal profession, largely as a result of his (very likely justified) criticism of Lord Justice Goddard in 1971, that Dad's additional veto would have had no effect. He could safely have risen above rancour and offered up a white ball in the spirit of charity and fair play. The result would still have been the one he wanted, with the Garrick Club turned for the occasion into a sort of Goth pinball arcade of careering black marbles.

Though it was understood that judges should not comment on any matter of public interest, sometimes Dad exaggerated the discretion that was required of him. It was an easy way out of family arguments in the 1970s for him to say that professional etiquette prevented him from expressing any sort of opinion on the issues of the day, as if there was no difference between the dining-table at number 3 Gray's Inn Square and a press conference bristling with microphones.

His first-born, Tim, having inherited a certain forensic zeal, once suggested that if it was so important to keep the political opinions of the judiciary out of circulation then Dad should read the newspapers in a protected environment such as the lavatory, since it was obvious what he thought from his expression while he read them ... after that the wrangle was on again, with Dad's attempt to claim the high judicial ground ruled out of court.

After Dad retired I felt the need to add a new element to a household that was at risk of becoming little more than the sum of its routines, unless and until Dad buckled down to that book of reminiscences, those songs, that radio play.

Rachmaninov symphonies weren't enough by themselves to make the flat hum with purpose.

I arranged to come round every Monday evening and help with the making of a meal. I had taken an interest in cooking in the sixth form at school, where Friday afternoons were set aside for non-academic activity under the banner of 'Guilds'. Cookery had easily sidelined the other two options, photography and social work (known as 'old ladies'). Westminster didn't do too badly by me if it taught me how to make a white sauce as well as an elegiac couplet.

Normally I made soup and Sheila would put together a main course, though sometimes we exchanged roles. From Dad's point of view soup was always the highlight of a meal. In fact soup was the meal. A meal without soup barely qualified as such. As teenagers we were well used to restaurant meals at which Dad would ask, 'Soup for everyone? Five soups?' as if he could imagine no other preference. Possibly he was just gingering us up to order promptly, rather than overruling our right to whitebait or prawn cocktail, but in that case he wouldn't have spoken for the lady as well, Sheila who had never chosen soup in all the time he had known her. Since roughly 1946.

The bargain over Monday dinner, as I explained it to Dad, was that I would make soup every week on condition that he laid the table. I was managing him. Perhaps I was trying to show Sheila that this so strongly counter-suggestible man could be controlled after all. Dad said, rather pitifully, that he didn't know where the cutlery lived. I pointed out that he had been living in the flat for upwards of thirty-five years, which should help to narrow the range of the search.

I warned Dad that if ever he left the table unlaid, I would pour the soup away. He would never see another of my making. Why does this now sound so insulting? In fact Monday evenings were generally enjoyable, and though Dad's laying was often approximate he never failed to make an attempt. One Monday I accidentally overdid the chilli oil, and Sheila was unable to choke down as much as a mouthful. Dad finished his bowl, and though his face was very red and his voice oddly hoarse said yes to another. It was as if soup was self-evidently such a good thing that the question 'More soup?' must always meet a Yes. The logic gates swung open irresistibly and there was no possibility of override.

He didn't like vegetables with a few exceptions such as beans (green ones and broad ones), but would relish any kind whatever as long as it was in a soup. He could never explain the depth of his attachment to a liquid first course. It didn't go back to childhood. He couldn't remember his first exposure but thought it must have been at a hotel. Soup carried no associations with the mother he had adored or the father he held up firmly as a model.

Until he died Dad spoke of his mother as the only perfect human being he had ever known. His voice went into a distinctive constricted register when he spoke of her. It throbbed with tears withheld. He had been twenty-one when she died and most sons, even the most devoted, have detected the odd flaw by then, but for Dad flaws were out of the question. His mourning, which had taken the form of being unable to sleep in the home she no longer occupied, so that neighbours had to take him in, exceeded the bounds of what was thought proper and became something of an embarrassment.

It seems terribly obvious that he loathed Gilbert Harding's emotional devastation when talking about his mother on *Face to Face* not because it was unfamiliar but because it wasn't. He wanted to share nothing with such a man, absolutely nothing, and to share the unhealed wound of his mother's death was close to unbearable.

On the other hand the Dad I came to know after his retirement had no great love for his own father, and not much affection. He gave no account of how and why a mother's boy, who had never fully processed her death (to the extent that death is something we process), should turn himself into a father who cracked down on any sign of unmanliness. He reproduced for our benefit the character, and the moral absolutism, of someone he claimed to admire but hadn't actually liked.

It was a theatrical performance, in a way, which made sense given that as a student he had done so much acting. It was in fact his father who wouldn't accept the idea of the theatre as a career for him. Dad's theatricality found an effective outlet in court. Playing his own father backstage, as a role in the family drama, was a capitulation perhaps subtly edged with revenge, but the rest of us didn't know that.

One of his favourite memories of his acting days was playing Hjalmar Ekdal in *The Wild Duck* as a student in Aberystwyth. He felt he excelled in the part, particularly at the tragic climax when Hjalmar finds his daughter Hedvig dead. During one evening's performance, even so, he became aware that he was not exercising his usual casual monopoly on the audience's attention. There seemed to be distraction, even tittering. He set himself to scale the tragic heights with ever more flair and boldness, climbing without ropes or oxygen.

What he didn't know was that the distraction was caused by the actress playing Hedvig. Dad had carried her in and reverently laid her down, but in such a way that her slip was showing. Hedvig was a Scandinavian lost soul, dead by her own hand, but she was also a young Welsh woman of the 1930s who didn't think such exposure was at all the thing. So the corpse's hand inched towards the offending edge of underwear, and set about tucking it out of sight. The play is much concerned with the *Livslognen* or life-illusion. The actress's *Livslognen* seems to have been that unrespectability in dress is a fate worse than death.

At this point Dad's *Livslognen* was that he could reconquer the audience with technique and ardour. At the end of the scene he threw himself into a rocking-chair, as he did at every performance, but with so much force on this occasion that the chair fell to pieces under him. The chair abandoned its *Livslognen* of being furniture.

Dad's only explicit complaint against his own father was that he never expressed approval, never offered praise. In his own role as father, Dad set himself to remedy this. Clearly he was less stern than his own father, though we weren't in a position to make the comparison.

He certainly offered warm words for good academic results, though it was undermined by his anxiety that praise would go to our heads and lead to an immediate slacking off. After good exam results he might say that of course every schoolboy worked hard in an exam term – it was the term after an exam that was the test of the true student and scholar, as opposed to the diligent mediocrity.

He told us that we could achieve anything we set our minds to, so how did I hear this as 'you'll never be good enough'? Blame the babelfish of adolescence, the cochlear implant that simultaneously translates everything into Desesperanto, the mother tongue of falling short.

Desesperanto from a book of Marilyn Hacker's poetry, too good a coinage to take over, in the manner of Ian Fleming, without an indication of its provenance. *Babelfish* courtesy of Douglas Adams, come to that, but in any case too well known to be passed off.

There was one episode of heroic parenting on Dad's part

during my schooldays, when he did everything possible to reverse my poor grade in one of my A-levels. The subject was Ancient History, and I had no aptitude for it, being hopeless at dates. I hadn't actively chosen it as a subject: the only way you could do Ancient Greek was as part of the whole classics package with Latin and Ancient History. I enjoyed the languages but could get no grip on the history that underlay them. Dad asked me well before the exam if I felt properly prepared. I bluffed unhappily, gabbling about Alexander's campaigns and my mastery of his battle plans, though my deficiencies in three-dimensional modelling drastically limited my understanding of the geographical aspect of strategy, Alexander's or anyone else's.

After the exam Dad asked me how it had gone. I had a sinking feeling, but it was no different from the sinking feeling I'd had the last time he asked. I talked about Alexander's campaigns and my masterful battle plans until he went away.

I got a D, which was more of a blow to my pride than an insult to my knowledge of the subject. Dad didn't reproach me, just asked me how I felt about the grade. I mimed incredulity, mortification, outrage, dismay, all (I feel sure) to a low standard of theatrical self-presentation. Dad was upset on my behalf but not reproachful. I felt I had got off lightly and was glad to hear no more about it, my dismal performance at A-level Ancient History.

It was a full fifteen years before I found that, actually, Dad hadn't left it at that. I was rootling through the drawers of his desk, with permission, looking for my birth certificate (the Passport Office was on strike and I needed paperwork for a temporary document) when I came across a correspondence between Dad and my school. Dad was pressing forcefully for my papers to be re-marked, since an injustice had obviously been done to my keen grasp of the subject. He hadn't kept copies of his side of the correspondence but drafts instead, since he wasn't always fluent on paper and benefited from second thoughts.

The letters from the school shifted in tone from warm and concerned to politely exasperated. Finally my housemaster reported that he had talked to all my teachers and that though a C might have been hoped for a D was not a grade that misrepresented my standard of work. Dad replied that if he was being asked to choose between the versions offered by the school and by his son, he would of course choose his son's. It was a magnificent crusade against injustice, spoiled only by the fact that no injustice had been done, since I had misled him at every point.

I was so astonished by this find that I'm not sure I found time to be moved. It had never occurred to me that Dad might be, as he claimed to be, a resource. I had seen him only as an authority to be placated and bought off.

It was the same with the Maundy money, the specially minted silver coins distributed by the sovereign that were sometimes given as prizes at the school. Theoretically the recipients of Maundy money are destitute, and the giving of the alms symbolically recapitulates Christ's washing of his disciples' feet at the Last Supper, but I don't imagine the headmaster of Westminster dressed himself up in foul rags and put himself in the Queen's path to importune her for Prize Day wherewithal. The school was founded by the first Elizabeth and no doubt royal links survive.

It happened that my little bursts of academic excellence failed to coincide with the times when Maundy money circulated in its eccentric fashion (the number of coins distributed each year, for instance, corresponds to the age of the sovereign). Did I hanker after this archaic accolade? I don't remember.

Whether Dad actively went shopping, or whether an item

in a jeweller's or antique-shop window caught his eye (there were a number of such shops in and around Chancery Lane), he found and acquired for me a complete set of Maundy money in a little case. The largest coin, the fourpence, was smaller than the sixpence that was then the smallest and most beloved piece of 'silver' money. I don't remember whose royal head endorsed my Maundy set – proof in itself that I didn't really connect with Dad's present. I must have it stowed away somewhere, but I don't know when I last set eyes on it.

I thought Dad had completely missed the point, by going to a shop to give money for something that couldn't be bought, though it was money itself. I didn't want to own Maundy money, only to win it. What it came down to was that Dad was cheating. I didn't see in his present what he wanted me to see, his proud face reflected in that row of tiny worn brownish graduated metal discs.

The correspondence about my poor grade at A-level in Ancient History, though, was a message that caught up with me in good time. It wasn't ancient history, it could count perhaps as early modern. A cache of letters is the classic posthumous find, particularly when it reveals an unknown aspect of the dead person. I was in a luckier position, with a wider range of options than mere grieving wonder. I wanted to tell Dad how much I appreciated his futile rearguard action against my well-deserved D grade, and I was prepared to take the time to do it well. I wanted to communicate in his style rather than mine. I felt I had a pretty good idea of the terrain of Dad's character by this time, better certainly than I had ever understood any of Alexander's battles. Emotionalism wasn't the way Dad did things, although he was on good terms with anger and its happy property of clearing the air, setting all dials to zero.

The ideal setting was the dinner table, with distinguished

colleagues and friends present, all glasses charged. What he liked about roles was exactly what other people dislike: the way they fix relations. He preferred formal occasions to intimate ones and a staged portrait to anything a snapshot might reveal. In such a setting all I needed to do was relate what had happened as an anecdote, playing up the comedy, and end up by toasting his valour.

There was an opportunity before too long. I think it worked. It seemed to go well. The trouble with doing something in someone else's style rather than your own is that you can't really expect the other person to notice. Dad wasn't likely to charge over afterwards to give me the full bear-hug with eye-leaks, saluting my consideration in playing 'For He's a Jolly Good Fellow' in his preferred key. He seemed gratified, he raised his glass with great willing, but this he often did, and perhaps I'm imagining the underlying message of 'See? Was that so hard? Let's have a lot more of that from now on . . .' A revisiting of *you have only so much time to make things up to me.*

Dad was very attuned, in the manner of his generation, to the oldest son, who was actively nicknamed 'son and heir'. By way of compensation I was dubbed 'pride and joy', which left only 'Christmas angel' for Matthew, which didn't seem very precise (despite his decorativeness) since he was born in mid-November.

I remember Dad once commenting with troubled admiration about Tim's physical beauties. Troubled because Tim, twenty at this point, wasn't particularly biddable, far from keen to walk in the paths laid out for him. 'Tim is very manly,' he said, 'very strong, with that heavy growth of beard – he should shave twice a day – and plenty of hair on his chest already.' At some point in this reverie he must have become aware that these were not ideal terms in which to discuss Tim in front of his younger brother, who at eighteen was plump and poorly groomed. He cast around for a countervailing compliment. 'And you . . .' he said at last, '. . . you have good posture.'

After his retirement, or at least after his Rachmaninov phase, Dad did less and less. There's a word that seems to describe the state towards which he gravitated: inanition. It's a word that might appear on a Victorian death certificate, and it has a technical meaning, to do with starvation. But it also conveys the slow emptying-out process of Dad's retirement, the physical and mental consequences of doing nothing. It wasn't that he turned his face to the wall. He turned his face to people when they spoke, he turned his face to the television, and still I had the sense that he was dying in small instalments, leaving us with no more than a digesting ghost to attend to.

When Sheila had upbraided him in retirement for laziness, he pulled together his intellect just long enough to defend his neglect of it: lazy people have something to do, and do nothing. Idle people have nothing to do, and are doing it. He was idle and not lazy. Case closed.

Even after Sheila's death he could play the part, from Holly's point of view, of the benign grandfather in a TV spot for heritage toffee – except that he might suddenly denounce her for eating the remnants of his brioche, though he had given gracious permission only minutes before.

Our three generations could watch *The Simpsons* together very harmoniously. I particularly remember the episode in which John Waters guest-starred as a 'collectibles' dealer new in Springfield, who admires Marge's style, assuming it's knowingly camp. He gains an ascendancy over Bart, to the point where Homer feels the need to toughen him up with exposure to blue-collar men and manly pursuits. Their first stop is the Springfield steel works, but it turns out all the employees there are gay. A workman pushing a vat of molten metal alerts his colleagues to the danger by trilling, 'Hot stuff coming through!'

Dry ice starts pumping out when the working day ends so that disco dancing, on suspended breeze blocks raked by searchlights, can begin without loss of time. In the next scene Moe the sleazy bartender lists the traditionally gay professions: 'Where you bin, Homer? The entire steel industry is gay – yeah, aerospace too, the railroads.' And you know what else? Broadway.

We laughed tri-generationally at the climactic scene, in which Waters's character saves the Simpson party from reindeer attack by skilful deployment of a remote-controlled Santa robot.

There was one last joke tucked away in the credits, an announcement that the episode was dedicated to the steel workers of America, with the slogan *Keep Reaching For That Rainbow!* It was a wonderfully unifying half-hour, even if I couldn't turn to Dad and make a comment about the subversive potential of popular entertainment, so rarely exploited, any more than I could have that particular discussion with Holly. Perhaps a sign of my decline rather than his, if I was so far gone in punditry that I now needed an audience for the most routine aperçu.

How much Dad took in of what was in front of him, or how little, became clear one Monday night. I was with Keith in the Highbury flat, leaving Matthew to look after Dad in Gray's Inn. We were watching a Channel 4 documentary on the 1976 Obscene Publications Squad trials, and the judge in the case was getting a certain amount of stick for deficiencies in his running of the case that led in the end to Wallace Virgo's conviction being overturned.

I took advantage of an advertising break to phone Matthew, worried that he and Dad might also be watching television. They were. Not Channel 4? Channel 4.

Did Dad realize that he was the unnamed judge being referred to? He didn't, no. He gave every sign of being fascinated by the programme, but fell short of making the personal connection.

I felt relief when perhaps distress should have been the dominant emotion. I certainly didn't want Dad to be aware that his past professional performance was being criticized, but it would have been better for him to be tuned to another channel rather than watching Channel 4 with empty attention, impervious, looking at his life from outside it.

My brothers and I didn't find it hard to believe that Dad might have blundered, particularly in a case combining two things about which he had such strong feelings, pornography and police corruption. It seemed obvious to us that he was instinctively an advocate, a judge only by hard work and scruple. It came naturally to him to shape an argument theatrically, not to hold the balance between opposing forces. We imagined him failing to stress the importance of reasonable doubt, when it came to the guilt of a police commander betraying the public trust.

In this particular case, the case of *R. v. Virgo*, we were wrong, at least according to Matthew's godfather Monro Davies, not the least of Dad's devils. Monro can remember even after the lapse of half a century how many days a particular case lasted. The successful appeal against Virgo's conviction challenged the admissibility of a diary entry. Dad had accepted it as evidence, and now he was being overruled. Nowadays the admissibility of such material is uncontroversial, and in any case there was no damage done by admitting the diary entry in *R. v. Virgo*, since it was the only direct evidence of guilt. Without it there was no case. Mars-Jones J had exercised the only option that could have put Virgo behind bars.

Even before Dad's mental presence dwindled to this point, I had come to rely on help, both what was supplied by the council (or the agency subcontracted by it) and by private providers. It might happen that a carer sent by the council on a morning shift was so clearly efficient and likeable that I would hire him or her to work at other times. The agency's name that sticks with me is Care Alternatives, with its faint double meaning (alternatives to care, as opposed to options for caring), though there was a change of contracts halfway through the year. First-time callers, particularly at weekends, had to be told the location of Gray's Inn Square in great detail or they were likely to overshoot in strange directions.

One of the morning reliables was Nimat, a Sudanese woman of great beauty. She was tall and poised. The starkness of her haircut emphasized the roundness of her head. She was perhaps in her forties, with a son of about ten, whose father she had left behind with some relief in Sudan. Since then she had found another relationship, in London, but the man in question had been run over and killed. There was a sadness about her, a sadness that didn't take away from her vitality but was part of it. This vibrant sorrowing may have preceded the events that gave it depth.

When I heard the lift mechanism start its whirring at about eight o'clock, I would go in to Dad and say, 'It's our lovely Nimat.' Usually he said, 'Who?' When she came into his room she lowered her head to be near his as she explained who she was and why she had come. Her voice was both husky and cooing. Then he would say, 'Don't you have wonderful teeth!', which would make her smile even more of a world-historical event.

He would follow Nimat down the corridor to the bathroom without her needing to help him with his Zimmer frame. She simply drew him along in the wake of her magnificence.

After his shower he would have a neutral cleanness. Historically the smells he had borne were Vitalis (hair oil), Old Spice (aftershave) and Badedas (Swedish horse-chestnut-based bath essence). A triple chime of naffness, a three-bullet-point suicide note in the language of male grooming. I don't remember any advertisements for Vitalis, but perhaps they simply said that the product would make your hair look like oiled metal, and as a bonus that its smell would remind your children of the oil they applied to their Triang-Hornby oo gauge electric toy trains. Old Spice implied a sort of daft sportiness with its footage of surfing and the crypto-fascist pulsations of *Carmina Burana*. It was Badedas (though the advertising copy stylishly omitted the capital) that was most obviously a strong solution of wish-fulfilment, as much an extract of the male menopause as of the Swedish horse-chestnut.

The campaigns for the product were classy, tending to appear in Sunday colour supplements. The tagline was 'Things happen after a badedas bath'. What things? Well, a man in black tie might step out of a sports car to the un-surprise of a blonde wrapped only in a towel, surveying from a bathroom window the suavity of her visitor.

This was in the days before women learned to respond to crass sexual implications in advertising, if they ever really have. It seemed obvious that the target market wasn't female, and it was the male reader who was being offered a vision of steamy Scandinavian nakedness, whether he owned a sports car or not. Women seeing the advert and identifying with the woman in the towel would be likely to respond with social panic rather than arousal, thinking *Oh GOD! I thought he said seven-thirty!*

At one point in the Aids years (the phrase has some short-hand value, though they're hardly over) I slipped into a bath behind a friend and held him tight. He was recovering from shingles, and found that pressure on his skin could relieve the agonizing twinges he was experiencing, which are a sign of improvement, of nerve cells regenerating, but feel like anything but. Hugh hadn't yet had his diagnosis of Aids, and was willing to embrace his shingles as tightly as I was embracing him, as long as he wasn't in the firing line for anything worse. The bath was a mass of foam produced by bubble bath, and at some stage I recognized the bubble bath as Badedas.

The intimate distress and comfort of the experience was so intense that it stripped all the Dadly associations from the smell of Badedas, overwriting them with tenderness and sorrow. Now both Dad and Hugh are dead, with Hugh dead long before Dad, but it is Hugh who is summoned back in welcomed pain by the smell of those Swedish horse-chestnuts. All the naffness has melted away, and my heart and my nostrils open up.

I didn't like to delay Dad's carers with chat when they had other places to go, but I learned a certain amount about Nimat. She lived on Royal College Street in Camden. She had been brought up as a Christian. She had worked in Africa as an air hostess (I think she used that phrase, rather than 'cabin crew'), though I imagine her height was a disadvantage in those cramped spaces. Her great pleasure on stopovers was to put on her hottest hotpants and make her way to the bar of the hotel where she was staying. There she would order a cocktail and make it last, pacing herself and letting the ice-cubes melt at their leisure. Everyone would know she wasn't a renegade Muslim displaying herself and drinking poison but simply a Christian enjoying legitimate privileges, relaxing in her own way, though her presence in the bar is unlikely to have been sedative.

Another morning helper was Damon, a slight, softly spoken man in his early twenties. He would shuffle off his boots the moment he entered the flat, as if he had spent time in Japan. In the corridor to the bathroom he had no wafting powers to compare with Nimat's, but he spoke gently to Dad and persuaded him to co-operate pretty well. Most days he seemed not to have another job to go to, and I would happily squeeze oranges for him and brew coffee of quality.

One morning over the coffee and orange juice Damon asked

me if I had noticed his speech impediment. It was a strange thing to ask, because yes, I had in fact noticed that he had a speech impediment, but only on the very day he had asked the question. Before then there had been no detectable lack of fluency.

He explained that on previous days he had been choosing his words carefully to avoid problem consonants, vigilantly manning the points (in effect) so as to send his sentences along stretches of track where there was nothing blocking the line. From today, though, he was putting into practice the principles of a radical speech-therapy method.

It seemed odd that the immediate effect of speech therapy was to impair the fluency of speech, but it didn't seem helpful to point this out. I hoped it would work for him.

Over the next week or two the radical approach to speech therapy acquired a name – this was The McGuire Programme. Part of the technique seemed to be a matter of mastering the art of 'costal breathing' and part of it was clearly psychological. The system sounded so American that I was surprised to learn that the David McGuire who devised it was a Briton, a semi-professional tennis player who had drawn on his knowledge of sport for both aspects of the programme, the physical and psychological.

Damon was set targets for some exercises, such as 'VS with walk-away'. VS is Voluntary Stuttering, and Voluntary Stuttering with walk-away meant that he should approach a stranger and initiate a conversation, but exaggerate his stuttering to the point where the other person, yes, walked away. He was supposed to achieve this, say, five times between one group meeting and the next. There was also the electronic equivalent, VS with hang-up I suppose, in which he would act out a similar level of blocked speech on the phone until the stranger on the other end of the line hung up. I remember Damon saying that to save money he would call free helplines. He didn't need to have a question prepared for the relevant product or service because he wouldn't be getting beyond the first syllable anyway.

This was fascinating and alarming. It made psychological sense for stutterers to take control in this way. If there is a link between shame and stuttering, what could be more empowering than seeking out the humiliation you have always feared? I don't mean that shame is the origin of the behaviour but that it becomes an inextricable part of it. Having provoked rejection under controlled conditions, you can come to realize that it's not so unbearable, and take some of the pressure off a self-reinforcing pattern.

On the other hand there were elements in the programme reminiscent of minority politics, of twelve-step groups, and, most obviously, of cults. To stop passing as fluent, to start insisting on your imperfect articulation, seemed to be some sort of speech-therapy equivalent of coming out of the closet. Yet the notion of the 'recovering stutterer', endorsed by McGuire, seemed to describe stuttering as an addiction. It was hard to see that a stutterer who 'relapses', when unable to consolidate the progress made with the group, was in the same existential boat as the alcoholic unable to stay sober without the safety net of the meetings and the emergency parachute of the sponsor. Did the stutterer have to accept the fact of helplessness as a precondition for recovery?

I even thought there was something rather ominous about the phrase 'the road to freedom' – it seemed to say there was only one. Still, I enjoyed having conversations on a subject so far outside my experience. Damon maintained direct eye contact while he spoke, which was particularly disconcerting when he was telling me about the unbroken eye contact which was a requirement of McGuire Programme meetings. It was only when I was tactless enough to ask if the sessions were expensive that he moved his gaze away.

One day he took a further step in his shy boldness, asking me if I could recommend a gay bar for him to visit, since he was 'bi-curious'. Inevitably I had preened a bit about the way I could balance divergent impulses, filial, sexual, paternal, as if I was Blondin coolly cooking an omelette on a rope above the Niagara Falls, when my little balancing trick was only over the Serpentine. I pointed out that I wasn't much of a bar-goer, and that he should consult a listings magazine, but he was very keen on a personal recommendation. What he wanted was a bar that was 100 per cent gay, so that everyone in the whole place except him had a fixed sexual identity. Only then could he satisfy his bi-curiosity in safety, conceivably even setting his feet on another road to freedom.

Almost from his first visit I had encouraged Damon not to be defined by the duties which brought him to the flat. I wanted to reward his excellence as a carer, but the result was that his excellence was eaten away by the rewards I devised for it.

There was the day when after Dad's shower was finished Damon popped his head into the kitchen and asked, 'Any chance of some fresh squeezed orange juice?' There was every chance, as long as I got busy and squeezed some oranges. I might not have been made uneasy by the request for juice, but I certainly was by his stipulation of the process.

And there was the day when he popped into the kitchen to ask a personal question before finishing his tasks. After about a minute I became aware of the creaking noise as Dad shifted his weight on the Zimmer frame, and realized that Damon had left him in the corridor leading to the bathroom. Having no momentum of his own, Dad was waiting patiently for the resumption of cues. By this point the personal attention I had given to Damon had more or less destroyed his professional performance.

Luckily the agency that employed Damon lost its contract with Camden Council shortly afterwards, so I didn't need to deal with the problem I had created.

One helper from the Care Alternatives roster who stayed on to look after Dad in the evenings even after the agency lost the council's contract was Bamie. Bamie, from Sierra Leone, wasn't tall but was certainly strongly built. Not only did he think the British had done Sierra Leone a power of good, he claimed that this was the general opinion of the inhabitants. Imperial guilt is such a reliable reflex, even in those born after the days of Empire, that I would have suspected a joke if Bamie hadn't been so solemn and insistent. In some impossible way we were the good guys, and anything that had gone wrong since we left was a matter of local culpability casting no shadow on our collective honour. Whether he meant to do it or not, Bamie was chipping away at a fundamental part of modern British identity.

One thing about Bamie which took a little getting used to was that he called Dad 'Dad'. At first it seemed possible that he had misunderstood and thought that this was his client's name in the world, until he explained that in Sierra Leone it is the polite way of referring to an older male person.

Though in his North Wales childhood an awareness of racial diversity went no further than the admission that South Waleans might be human, Dad soon became used to Bamie. But the first time this muscular black man, not only black but somehow monumentally black, his skin tone very dark, his eyes flashing, used the form of address 'Dad' while tucking him into bed, Dad's own eyes went very wide and he sent them wonderingly over towards me, seeming to signal *Something I've forgotten?* I was able to reassure him that his bloodline hadn't taken a strange turn by saying, 'Dad, you remember Bamie, he comes to look after you . . .' Holly, though, never really got used to being referred to in his darkly growling voice as 'Aunty Olly', aunty being the respectful form of address in Sierra Leone for female persons of whatever age.

Bamie was proud of his wife and toddler son, but it was only in his dealings with Dad that I could see his tenderness. He was a Christian, much involved in the activities of his church, yet to my eyes his strongest underlying characteristic was anger. In conversation he was very big on Matthew 10:34 ('I came not to send peace, but a sword'), less mindful of Matthew 5:39 (turning the other cheek). It might be from a different gospel or a different religion.

When his church went on pilgrimage to Walsingham, it was Bamie who drove the bus. But on the way back into London after they had paid their homage to the Virgin, Bamie came very close to an incident of road rage when another driver tried to cut in ahead of him. What stayed with him from the day was not serenity.

I enjoyed discussing religion with Bamie in the sitting-room of the Gray's Inn flat, while Dad turned his face from one of us to the other in low-level surprise, though I had a definite feeling of playing with fire. Riding in the bus with Bamie might well be exhilarating, trying to nose out into traffic ahead of him would certainly not be.

I invited him to consider that he liked the bits of Christ which were like himself, but had no time for the bits of Christ which were unlike Bamie. Debate wasn't his natural element, but he maintained his position forcefully, with quotation, repetition and the occasional rhetorical question.

Did I mention to Bamie during our chats that my private life was not as standard as was implied by the occasional presence on the premises of that miniature aunty, my daughter? I did not. This was feeble, though I could tell myself that I had no business preaching a gospel of sexual non-conformity if the result might be to upset the crucial aspect of the arrangement, namely the smooth bond between Dad and his carer. This was a truth but not a sufficient one. If Bamie was minded to take Matthew 23:27 ('Woe unto you, scribes and Pharisees') as the text for a homily, I would need all my debating skills. I could hardly deny I was a scribe when it was how I made my living. If he decided I was a Pharisee into the bargain, hypocrite and whited sepulchre, things would not go well for the household.

It made a great difference to me to know that Dad was in Bamie's care, in his strong, scrupulous hands. Bamie worked a long shift, from three in the afternoon to ten at night, which was when I would return after spending time *en famille*. One evening he told me, 'A lady came to see Dad and shouted at me.' I didn't need to be told that this was Edith Wellwood, though in fact Edith ended up (to everyone's surprise including perhaps her own) approving of Bamie. Her initial mistrust wasn't based on race but on long experience of other people's unremitting incompetence. Confronted with such conscientious skill she surrendered. Her only concession to contrariness was to insist on calling him Bamber, as if his Sierra Leonean parents, great fans of *University Challenge*, had decided to name him after the long-ago quizmaster.

When the school summer holidays came around I was able to take a break, borrowing a converted barn in Normandy from a friend so as to spend two weeks there with Holly and her mother. Set free of Dad-related routines I immediately devised replacements. I would get up early for a shower, then cycle many kilometres to the bakery that made the best brioches, wearing a clinging vibrant orange singlet which I was fairly convinced I could get away with, though I knew better than to look at my reflection in shop windows *en route* in case the verdict went the other way. My timing was sufficiently predictable that the plunger in the cafetière would just be beginning its descent when I returned with the baked goods.

We made a day trip to Mont Saint-Michel during which I carried Holly on my shoulders across the causeway for what seemed several hours, knowing that there was absolutely nothing in Mont Saint-Michel to engage a six-year-old's attention when we got there. The expedition was a failure even before the setbacks of crowded pricy restaurants and smelly dustbins, the generally oppressive atmosphere of a historic spot gone rancid from sheer picturesqueness. Tourists and supplies were being imported in order for one to consume the other before the tourists traipsed off to fill the buses again and the dustbins were emptied at last.

On the way home Holly fell asleep in the back of the car and the drive back to the barn outside Gourbesville, through fog over unknown roads, was oddly magical. In her brain memories of the day were being coded to record the stoical enjoyment that makes family expeditions special, when people have fun on principle, whether they want to or not. We adults listened to Mark Lamarr on some esoteric radio station, playing even more esoteric rockabilly. I hadn't even known I didn't hate rockabilly. With that rapturous winding-down of mood in a silence alive with twangs, the trip had to be classified all over again, as a success. The fogbound afterglow backlit the whole day.

Between them my brothers had been looking after Dad for that fortnight, and then I was back in harness. He seemed balanced in his static decline, though of course decline is never static.

He began to have difficulty swallowing, coughing and spluttering almost with every mouthful of tea or coffee. This was diagnosed as 'dysphagia', which my ghostly Greek A-level allowed me to identify as meaning no more than 'difficulty swallowing'. Not exactly a revelation. The solution was to add a thickening agent to the liquid in the cup. In theory this was what Dad had always wanted, with every drink promoted to the status of soup, but the coughing and choking didn't really go away.

I was mortified when I found that Dad had a sore on his heel. This wasn't a surprising development, considering how little encouragement his blood was getting to circulate with any vigour. Dad was proud of the manly shape of his legs but had never done anything either to earn or to maintain it. Even as a young man he didn't enjoy walking as an activity. In his prime he would get into his cherished Jaguar on a Saturday morning, then drive two hundred yards to John Brumfit, the tobacconist's in Holborn Bars, to buy cigarettes.

When he had taken up 'jogging' in the 1980s, buying matching New Balance running shoes for himself and Sheila, he moved so slowly that I had to discipline myself not to overtake him at a comfortable walking pace. In retirement he had offered masterly passive resistance to any attempt at keeping him mobile.

Nevertheless I took the sore on his heel, this site of necrosis, personally. I was mortified at the failure of care. This time ancient Greek provided a more vivid etymology. *Nekros* means a corpse, and necrosis is a patch of local death.

One day as I was changing the dressing on his sore, Dad patted me on the back and murmured, 'Dear Adam.' This was so unlike his usual style that I bridled at it, saying something thoroughly ungracious like 'What brought this on?'

His preferred manner was formal, a matter of raising a glass to Sheila when she entered the room and saying, 'You elegant fowl', the endearment safely sourced from a nonsense poem.

After her car accident he went through a phase of calling her 'the salt of the earth', which I thought thoroughly patronizing. When he started abbreviating the phrase to 's.o.e.' I would bare my teeth silently, as if I had taken a mouthful of salt myself.

He didn't have a late-life nickname for me, which was no loss if Nogood Boyo was the template. While I was looking after him he would sometimes say that I was a 'good guy', or 'one of the good guys', in a tone of mild surprise, as if my reputation had suggested otherwise.

I provide this context to explain my surly response to an endearment, and Dad's surprising reaction to it. Instead of retreating from the territory of intimacy and tenderness where he had spent so little time, even (to all appearance) in his dealings with Sheila, Dad advanced further into it, replying, 'I was just admiring the lovely curve of your shoulder.' It has to be said that reflexive charm was part of his armoury, but this didn't seem an armoured moment.

If I hadn't appointed myself caregiver, I would have discounted this aspect of Dad's character altogether, whether by rights it should be called latent or suppressed. I would have thought such a dreamy response not just uncharacteristic but actively alien to him.

It seemed possible that the 'Dad' I had experienced in my teens and his maturity, a man both driven and driving, had been a long charade, both professional and familial, undertaken between the dreaminess of his own childhood and the undefended state to which he was returning. This was a mask I knew better than the face beneath, which perhaps I wasn't trusted to see.

Dad in his prime didn't want to have needs, preferring to think of himself as the fount of prosperity at which all were nourished. The least endearing aspect of this character trait was the desire to show someone that a present offered to him was in point of fact worthless, whatever trouble had been taken over it. When I was sixteen I bought him a decanter from Heal's for his birthday, and stood there mortified while he explained that unfortunately the cork stopper would absorb off odours, rendering it for all practical purposes unusable. How would I know? I was a perfect innocent in wine, having at that stage not drunk even a thimbleful.

In fact my brothers and I had been promised a hundred pounds on our twenty-first birthdays if we abstained till then (and the same sum if we kept away from cigarettes). None of us led virtuous lives for long enough to claim his bounty, though if the threshold had been eighteen I would have cleaned up.

In 1970s' conversations I noticed that Dad presented himself as the primordial bottom layer, the massive foundations of the pyramid from which the family tapered to a point, but there was a tremendous feeling of strain there too, not to be acknowledged, as if his mental image was likely to invert at any moment, and then he would feel the whole unstable edifice bearing down on him, driving him into the sand.

In terms of the day-to-day, in fact weekly, running of the house Dad's function was ceremonial, and the name of the ceremony was carving the joint.

At any family meal featuring roast meat, his carving expertise trumped the mere cooking. He claimed rights, royal and retrospective, over the food the moment it entered the dining-room. The holy trinity of implements would be set before his place at the head of the table, fork, knife and steel for sharpening it. He would run the knife against the steel with innocent Sweeney-Todd professionalism, a whetting sound which had the effect on diners of the bell Pavlov rang to set his dogs a-drool.

The little fanfare of knife-sharpening gestures seemed to

have almost the opposite effect on the man who produced them. It relaxed any urgency. This was one of his preferred moments for launching into an anecdote – 'Have I told you about the time when . . . ?' or 'the funny story about . . . ?' He was confident enough of his raconteur's gift to announce a story as funny before setting out to make it so.

He would pause with the honed knife raised above the Mason's ironstone serving-dish (in the Regency pattern) of turkey, beef or lamb, or even arrested in the eternal moment of carving a slice, while he laid out the background or built up comic tension. Sheila would look anguished and eventually make a muffled plea ('Bill, please! People are starving – meat now, story later . . .') on behalf of group appetite, and then the carving would resume until the next time narrative pulled rank over mere plate-filling.

While I waited for food, particularly if the story was a familiar one, I would gaze at a strange feature of Mason's Regency design on the plates, a chimera or portmanteau creature, combining elements of slug and grasshopper in an unattractive new ensemble. Something with a long yellow neck that would scuttle rather than slither or creep, a little Loch Ness Monster skulking at the edges of the Dutch still life. My mixed feelings about family meals were laid down as a queasy extra layer of colouration on that curious transfer.

It was natural enough that Dad had the skill to disassemble a roast animal, since his father had been a farmer as well as a postmaster. Henry Jones had killed his own livestock and made his own bacon, and in a more direct way than the current Prince of Wales makes biscuits, to be sure. If he delegated those tasks it was because he had more important business to attend to, not because he didn't know how. Presumably he passed on his carving secrets to his first-born son, but Dad offered no instruction in his turn, either to the first arrival or the after-comers. There was a side of him that wanted us to follow in his footsteps, but the desire to make sure we would never eclipse the big man was also strong.

Dad's mother had also had dealings with meat. Dad spoke admiringly of her brawn, not in the metaphorical sense of physical strength but literally the jellied-meat dish she made from a pig's head.

In my imagination of the rustic past there are wives who refuse their husbands certain sexual acts or positions, and wives who refuse to make specified items of charcuterie. Brawn would have to be high on the list – the American phrase is 'head cheese', translating the French *fromage de tête* without the recoil you'd expect from a culture that renders offal as 'variety meats', as if animal glands and disregarded cuts were putting on some sort of nightmare revue, a butcher's burlesque show.

It's cleaning the head that makes for much of the unpleasantness. Do pigs have the good manners to blow their noses before they're slaughtered? No they don't. That job falls to the housewife who feels unable to refuse the marital obligation of brawn.

My grandmother did her duty, but there's no evidence she enjoyed it. Perhaps women weren't expected to, and it was only another thing men wanted.

Involvement in the processing of meat is a distinctive variety of carnal knowledge. Close contact with meat drags us down into the meat we are. A woman whose father is a pork butcher, who attracts a man's attention by slinging a bull's pizzle at him, will not be appealing to his higher nature. Isn't that the great lesson of *Jude the Obscure*? Yet Dad's mother was still the angel in the house as far as he was concerned, however many pigs' heads she rendered down.

In marital by-play Dad would sometimes suggest that Sheila make him up a lovely crock of brawn, in the same jovial spirit as he would suggest, every time her birthday loomed, that a brush-and-crumb tray would make the ideal present, fulfilment of any woman's dreams. She was too defensive about what she perceived as her weaknesses as a housewife to ignore him or banter back. If ever he paid a visit to the village of his birth, staying with his brother, he would rhapsodize about being woken at seven-thirty by the joyful song of Dilys's hoover, and Sheila smiled grimly.

Carving was an activity that he carried on with for some time after he had retired from other occupations, but at Christmas 1998 Matthew was deputed to wield the knife. If he made an imperfect job of it he certainly managed better than I could have done, while Dad looked on in neutral wonder.

If Christmas 1998 was a rather perfunctory festival, with Dad so evidently depleted, then Christmas 1997 had been almost too festive, with a mood of exhilaration that edged into hysteria. Sheila had received her terminal lung cancer diagnosis at the beginning of December and was bizarrely full of energy, busily signing off on her life, tying up loose ends. After lunch she led the three women who were more or less her daughters-in-law (there had been no marriages) into her bedroom to choose things they might like from wardrobe or jewellery-box. She set a brisk pace towards the grave, and the rest of us were made breathless by trying to keep up – except of course for Dad, who hadn't been told there was anything wrong.

Sheila seemed almost disappointed that Matthew's partner, Angela, didn't jump for joy at the offer of a sage-green leather coat from the 1960s, though everyone agreed that it would look well on her. Matthew had brought along a digital camera to film the get-together, not so much on his own account as to provide some sort of record for his baby daughter, Ella, who wouldn't otherwise have memories of her grandmother.

Sheila's only worry was about where she would go after death, not a theological matter but a question of storage. Her final destination wasn't in doubt – she wanted her ashes interred in Llansannan, Dad's birthplace, next to his ashes when they arrived there. But where was she to go until then? It seemed silly to be planted in terrain where she had no independent sense of rootedness, twiddling her immaterial thumbs while she waited for company.

To me these seemed abstruse considerations. If you imagined your ashes as sentient, it was hard to think of a place where they were likely to be happy, but if you didn't, how could it matter where they were stowed? Even so I realized that I was missing the point. Sheila was temperamentally a worrier, and not all worries can be taken away, least of all from those who have put in the hours, but perhaps this one could. 'I could look after you here, if you like.'

'Here? Where exactly?'

'Upstairs. In the top of a cupboard. Would that be all right, do you think?'

It turned out that this little piece of symbolic hospitality was enough to bring her peace of mind. After she had died, early in the new year, I had no feeling that she had moved to the top of an upstairs cupboard, but in other ways my feelings took an unexpected turn. After the elevated mood that accompanied her last weeks, I had expected a comedown and a grief proportional to my love and liking, but nothing similar happened. Instead there was a stable sense that she had died in character, with nothing left undone or unexpressed, and that I had made a satisfactory job of helping to make that possible. She seemed absent without being missing, and mourning was beside the point. It didn't match anything I felt.

Dad had been going steadily downhill while in my care, but I managed not to notice. I suppose friends who hadn't seen him for a while were in a better position to notice. The obvious comparison, with its kitsch symmetry between early and late life, first and last steps, would be with parents being too close to observe developmental spurts in their children which are very clear to outsiders – but there are other examples of the outsider having a privileged view. Friends who meet you after a gap will notice that you've lost a few pounds, and say you look marvellous, or that you've gained a few stone, and say you look well.

I was slow to acknowledge that Dad was fading. He seemed to have been fading for a long time, and there seemed no necessary end to that fading. There's an element of that old philosophical conundrum, Zeno's Paradox. Dad had to cover half the distance to death, and then half of that, and half again. Logically he would never get there, and perhaps that's what people feel about their parents in particular.

If I was partly in denial, I may have also been hiding from the possibility of exhaustion. By convincing myself I was in for the long term, I could guard against the running out of filial energy, never a very dependable fuel. How long would it be before I was resenting Dad for taking up my time, my hand trembling with suppressed violence as I stirred the thickening agent into his tea?

Being an attentive son could co-exist with some low-level posing. While my mother was dying I had once needed to take an oxygen tank to University College Hospital for refilling. Such things are heavy, unwieldy, whether empty or full. I couldn't imagine taking one onto a bus, but it would be awkward lifting one into a taxi. In the end it seemed simpler to walk to the hospital, only about a mile away. It was a rational decision, but I couldn't help being aware of the figure I cut, reminiscent of the beefy man in a Guinness advert from my childhood, shouldering a girder. Now while ministering to

142

Dad's needs I got a certain small kick out of parking my fat motorbike outside John Bell & Croyden on Wigmore Street and striding in wearing full leather for a bumper box of incontinence pads. Posing can be a defensible strategy, a way of skating on the surface when you suspect that it won't be possible to return from lower down.

Dad was admitted to hospital early in the new year, and died of pneumonia on the 10th of January. It happened while he was being turned by the nurses, with no family member present, though Tim was visiting and I was on my way. A discreet exit, and a common pattern, as if the person dying was tiptoeing away from the body with the minimum of fuss, though of course the assisted movement of being turned in bed may be enough to give the software of shutdown its prompt.

There's a famous study that shows that death rates among the terminally ill go up after family festivals (Christmas, Hanukkah, Easter, Passover), as if people could somehow hang on for a celebratory event and then stop the struggle, choosing in some limited way their moment to die. I say 'famous study', but I can't find it anywhere on the Internet, which is a pretty strong indication that it doesn't exist. It's not exactly proving a negative to any elevated standard, but it's a good rule of thumb: if you can find something on the Net it may or may not be true, but if you can't find it then it isn't. So perhaps I made it up or have garbled some quite different piece of research.

Even so, the first time someone died in my presence I had a sense of intention. This was the artist Mario Dubsky, who was the first person with Aids I was assigned to 'buddy' as a volunteer for the Terrence Higgins Trust. The year was 1985, early days for the Trust's buddying initiative, so that a handful of us did our best to meet the basic needs of sick people spread out across London. In his teens Mario had been diagnosed as manic depressive, and couldn't be described as an easy person, but then he would have disliked the very idea of easiness, in people or anything else. In theory he was very self-absorbed, but he also had a marked ability to stand outside himself. I remember once, when he was bringing up with great difficulty small quantities of yellow liquid into a bowl, that he looked up at me and said, 'This must be very hard for you.'

When he was ill enough to be hospitalized in the Middlesex, the institution that had given him both his diagnoses, thirty years apart, first manic depression and then Aids, I would visit him several times a day. He wasn't conscious, but I hoped to find him alert sooner or later so that he could make a will. Mario hated his mother, or rather 'hatred' was his name for the love he felt (he phoned her on a regular basis to keep her informed of the progress of his loathing). If he died without a will she would inherit as next of kin, in theory the last thing he wanted.

I had fudged the opportunity of suggesting the making of a will earlier on. Now it was a priority. I understood perfectly well that his dying intestate, leaving his property to someone he claimed to hate, was the outcome that most closely corresponded to his feelings for her, refusal without disconnection. I had to take his stated wishes at face value, just the same. If he was lucid on one of my visits I would contact a solicitor through the Trust and see what came of that.

Mario died, without returning to consciousness, the first time I spent more than a few minutes by his bedside. The nurses weren't expecting this, and nurses at the Middlesex were knowledgeable and canny. Certainly he seemed to be recovering from this latest infection. It happened late on a Saturday evening. Flibbertigibbet that I was, I planned to go on to a bar for some night life after an hour or two by Mario's bedside.

Of course Mario didn't 'know I was there', but to absorb the event in the immediate aftermath I needed to think that he did. He had many friends, but I was the only person who was at all close to him not to have known him before he was ill. Death was part of the part I played in his life. In my presence his body seemed to shut up shop with great efficiency, as if dying was no more than a knack, something like double-declutching (in the days of gearboxes without synchromesh) or even throwing a frisbee with the proper flick of the wrist that sends it sailing.

His death seemed expressive of him, and so did Sheila's, in very different circumstances. It seemed exactly right in terms of her character that she should die at home, not professionally attended, but while waiting for the transfer to a hospice that she claimed to want. It was a trait of her generation amplified by temperament and history to shrink from being any trouble, choosing to tidy herself away among strangers rather than make demands on her sons. What actually happened was what suited her best, dying at home, whether or not she had the boldness to say she wanted it.

I struggle to put Dad in this category of expressive deaths. If he had been able to script his last moments in his prime, then he would have faded away with a stern smile on his face, benignly absolving, while the three of us told him how sorry we were never to have lived up to the example he set. That impresario-patriarch side of his character had died before he did, and perhaps there were less extrovert traits that had not found much expression in the man we knew.

I made the funeral arrangements with A. France & Son of Lamb's Conduit Street, just as I had done when Sheila died. The premises were pleasingly ramshackle, with awkward spaces and varnished partitions. There was none of the plushness of modern death. It was like an old-fashioned provincial doctor's surgery, except that the patients weren't bored or anxious. There were framed press cuttings on the wall, and one of them caught my eye while I was waiting to be attended to. As it turned out the firm, or its ancestor W. France of Pall Mall, by appointment to His Majesty, had been the undertakers ('upholders' was the word used at the time) who made the arrangements for Nelson in 1805.

This piece of information wouldn't have made the slightest difference to Sheila, but it would have tickled Dad very much. Nothing could have been more appropriate for a Navy man like himself than the association with the splendid Horatio, who made the journey back from Trafalgar in a barrel of rum. Sailors on that voyage of triumphant melancholy are supposed to have paid their respects by taking nips from the barrel. This must qualify as the ultimate Nelsonian beverage, grog doubly fortified, spirit infused with a spirit well over proof, from which they took tots of the great man's essence, helping themselves on the sly to sippers, gulpers, sandy bottoms of immortality.

Some time had passed after the funeral before it occurred to me that we hadn't provided our funeral directors with a set of clothes for Dad to wear in his coffin, and that therefore he must have been kitted out by them in some rudimentary way from what had gone with him to the hospital, pyjamas or a tracksuit. Utter violation of his dress code in his prime, the bespoke double-breasted suits with their hint of Cosa Nostra.

How could this have happened? Sheila's arrangements the year before had been taken care of more scrupulously, but then the circumstances had been different. She had died in the flat, with her clothes to hand, and it had been an obvious priority to make sure she was turned out as she might have wanted. It seems extraordinary that France & Son could have made no enquiry about our wishes, but extraordinary too that I didn't think of it.

How did I imagine that Dad was going to be fitly costumed for the event? That Messrs France would sneak into the Gray's Inn flat and make their own selection of mobster suit and club tie (the Garrick, please God)? How else except through my agency was Dad to be properly treated, at any stage after I had volunteered to take care of him? The fact is, he was my prisoner, as he is on this page, with no redress against caricature or cheap insight.

It's perfectly possible that a discussion about clothes took place, one that passed through one of my brothers (or both), or even one that I was part of but don't remember. In that case my fretting over the possibility of his going to the flames improperly kitted out is the same sort of mental tic as not being able to sleep for worry that the alarm hasn't been set or the gas turned off.

Was there a part of me that wanted Dad to be unsuitably dressed in the coffin? Feelings about parents are such primal things that it's safer to assume you harbour any and every disreputable emotion rather than give yourself a clean bill of health. The Oedipal agenda doesn't lay itself out neatly, in the style of a PowerPoint presentation. My first book, *Lantern Lecture*, for instance, is almost entirely made up of insults to father-figures, something I managed not to notice for years.

The first-written piece was a fantasia in which the Queen contracted rabies from an infected corgi (the origin of the illness being a bat blown off course). Obviously the Queen is a mother-figure, except that her position of supreme authority makes her an honorary man, and Dad was not just a judge but one of Her Majesty's Judges. The title story was a commemorative character sketch of one of Dad's friends, Philip Yorke, the last squire of Erddig near Wrexham, and someone with about as much authority as the Milky Bar Kid. The withheld warmth of the story makes clear that I was choosing him as preferable to the father I actually had, a sort of antidote to the patriarchal poison. The fact that it was of course Dad who introduced me to Philip adds to the ungraciousness. In the final piece of the book, 'Bathpool Park', I returned to the patricidal fray but this time managed to do without the Queen getting in the way. The story analysed the operations of Dad's court in the case of *R. v. Donald Neilson* and tried to show that it, and he, had missed the point. At the time of writing I thought of each piece as an exercise in a given genre, whether satire, elegy or analytical journalism, and so it is, but the impulse of antagonism is consistent across the group.

There were a few procedural hiccups before *Lantern Lecture* was published, but it wasn't Dad who made difficulties. Faber submitted the typescript to his old instructing solicitor Peter Carter-Ruck for a professional opinion about its vulnerability to legal action.

The advice he gave was clear. Author and publisher would equally be open to charges of seditious libel. A stay in the Tower of London was not out of the question. Established authors on the Faber list were likely to express their distaste by changing publishers.

(Note to younger readers: treatment of the royal family was very kid-gloved in those days, a time that pre-dates even the decorous lampooning, as it seems now, of *Spitting Image*.)

Carter-Ruck was an old friend of Dad's, it's true, but I don't think his opinion was a put-up job. Nobody ever said Dad backed down from a fight unless he was clearly going to lose it, and if he wanted the book squelched all he had to do was withhold his permission from the part of the book that couldn't be published against his wishes, 'Bathpool Park'. I had taken the precaution of showing Dad 'Hoosh-mi', the satirical fantasy about the Queen, only after he had rubber-stamped 'Bathpool Park', which was good tactics or sneaky dealing according to taste. When he read the more obviously problematic text, he praised it uneasily, adding, 'But we're in trouble!' First person plural, not second person singular. His attitude was troubled support rather than alarm, though of course he might have had second thoughts about having given his blessing to another part of the book. An instinct of solidarity doesn't necessarily have staying power.

To me it seems more likely that Carter-Ruck was acting unilaterally, convinced that Dad would be embarrassed by the book and doing what he could to help. Or perhaps he sincerely believed the book was a bombshell and a call for republicans to take up arms.

This wasn't the general reaction. Faber took the sensible step of taking a second opinion, this time from John Mortimer, a lawyer of a different stripe. Having defended the editors of *Oz* on obscenity charges, he was unlikely to panic over my little squib about the Queen. Mortimer's opinion was that it was in thoroughly bad taste, as was more or less required by the genre of satire, but far from actionable.

Dad can hardly have avoided coinciding with John Mortimer at the Garrick Club, but had mixed feelings about him. On the one hand Mortimer was the best-known example of the lawyer-turned-writer, even if he had started early, while Dad's creativity was waiting for the ripeness of retirement. Dad would certainly have approved of my borrowing the title of Mortimer's play *A Voyage Round My Father* to serve as subtitle here, carrying the suggestion of a personality so large that only chartered shipping could get a proper view, even if his real admiration was for an earlier play, *The Dock Brief*. Dad responded with sentimental fullness, and no identification whatever, to Mortimer's central character of a washed-up barrister given a last chance of glory. On the other hand, John Mortimer consistently aligned himself with opposition to censorship, and disputed the corrupting effects of pornography. Hadn't he said, in court, that if pornography really had the power to corrupt then the Old Bailey would be chugging to the sound of massed vibrators by now, considering how much smut their Lordships had seen in their time? Well, apparently not, since I can find no evidence for such a statement, though it was one of my favourite quotations for many years. There's no search engine as powerful as wishful thinking.

When *Lantern Lecture* came out, Faber were hoping that Hatchards of Piccadilly, booksellers by appointment to Her Majesty, would refuse to stock it, so as to provide a starting-point for some whipped-up indignation in the press. Unfortunately they denied us that publicity coup, ordering twelve copies rather than their usual six, a favourable verdict but overall a disappointment.

In the pages of the book I had given Dad an invaluable hostage for use in future disagreements. From then on, if ever we were getting testy with each other he would announce, 'I'm not going to take that from a son who described me in print as "wizened"!' and we would each hare off in search of a copy of the book. When the text of 'Bathpool Park' was consulted I would make my case that its reference to the judge's expression, as caught by the press photographers, being one of 'wizened disapproval' when he emerges onto a bright street after a day in a dark courtroom was a very different thing from saying he was actually wizened in the general run of things and under standard lighting conditions. Dad would grumble and be soothed.

In writing about the dead it's not possible to give them the last word, except in the most artificial, self-admiring way. There can't be a power struggle – the writer, the survivor, has all the power. You can try not to use it, or to use it responsibly, but the real gulf isn't between the various ways of using the power you have, it's between having the power and not. If, for instance, I want to mention a couple of occasions on which I humiliated Dad in his powerlessness, reproaching him for lapses he couldn't help, being brusque and even sarcastic, I humiliate him all over again. Yet, given that I have written about my mother, there is no neutral position. Not to write about him, having written about her, implies a statement in itself, either that he's not worthy of my attention or that I can't find a way to do it.

Writing about Sheila was different. I wrote about her in her lifetime, with her consent and power of veto. I was surprised that she didn't exercise that power, since I had included many potentially embarrassing details. Sheila was happy to attend the Virago party launching *Sons and Mothers*, the book for which the piece had been commissioned, and seemed to have a sense almost of ownership about what I had written. *It's funny*, she said, *I want to turn the page over and see what happens next, although I know what happens next and on the whole I didn't enjoy it when it actually happened.* 'Are there any more reviews of our book?' she would say, and stick them in a clippings file. Since my contribution was much the longest in the book it was likely to be singled out for special praise or condemnation. I particularly enjoyed reading one review aloud to her, which suggested that she had never taught me how to shut up.

When Sheila was in hospital after diagnosis, she asked me to explain to the consultant that she didn't want to prolong her life with minimally promising treatment. I found I was repeating things I had already written about her attitude to life, and broke off to say, 'I don't think you realize! This is a famous woman. She's had her life story published . . .' He was extremely disconcerted. It was nice to turn the tables on authority for a moment, and for Sheila to feel that she was more than one patient among many. The paperback of *Sons and Mothers* had just come out, as it happened, so I was able to nip down to Foyles to pick up a copy, which we both signed and presented to the consultant.

Would Dad feel a sense of ownership about what I've written here? Unlikely. (Too parsimonious with the short sentences to fit the strict Denning template.) He would have enjoyed his obituaries more, with their properly formal lists of honours and famous cases. In fact one of my friends had a slip of the tongue when referring to them, and said, 'Didn't your Dad get great reviews?' He became flustered and corrected himself, but it seemed the right choice of word, just the same. Perhaps obituaries should have star ratings (everything else does these days), in which case Dad would have got four-and-a-half across the board. How would that appear on a poster – a jaw-dropping roller-coaster of a life? A live-out-loud? Unambiguous success at any rate, pats on the back from every quarter.

I learned a few surprising things about his career from those columns, such as Dad's having passed the longest single sentence ever imposed in this country. Nezar Hindawi had tried to blow up an Israeli aeroplane by planting a bomb in his pregnant girlfriend's luggage. Dad gave him forty-five years in 1986. I remember him in conversation at the time, expressing grave dismay that a human being could do such a thing, but I never quite knew if he was being sincere at such moments. Sometimes it seemed that he needed to rehearse his outrage in a slightly stylized way, to prove (whether to himself or others) that he was still capable of registering civic horror rather than professional inurement.

The abolition of capital punishment was a measure that had Dad's approval, but it didn't make the problem of evil any more tractable. Seeing Myra Hindley on trial hadn't made him reverse his judgment on the issue, and nor did the Hindawi case, but he seemed to be reaching for some extra measure of punishment by passing that sentence.

Dad certainly wouldn't appreciate being made out to be a hypocrite in matters of sexual morality. *Eminent Victorians* was published in the year he was three, but he never really cottoned on to the disappearance of piety from biography, the eclipse of deference in general. He didn't go along with this trend but had instead suppressed his own resistance and presented his father as wholly admirable. There seemed to be a law of succession in operation, as he saw it, governing the emotional dealings between successive generations of fathers and sons, so that only those who didn't challenge their fathers were entitled to inherit respect from their children in turn. Even in the 1950s there must have been other models for the transmission of family feeling, but that seems to have been the one Dad was stuck with. I honestly don't understand the benefits of this system. Why would I want a father who was identical with his principles, the same person inside and out, leaving nothing to be found under his bed more startling than a copy of Pamela Hansford Johnson's *On Iniquity*?

Respect seems such a meagre currency, so unsatisfying if you've ever been paid in brighter coin. In the pre-history of the family it seems likely that Dad wanted transactions of love rather than duty. His moral fixity made him hard to please, of course, and we became wary of him, consciously inadequate. I'm speaking for myself here, though reaching for the shelter of a first person plural. In his turn he registered distance and defiantly claimed it, saying to Sheila that she had spoiled us, would do anything to be popular with us, while his was the stern love that refuses to fawn. Finding his soft feelings rejected he rejected them too.

I see myself as taking after my mother, but then he had the same idea about himself, and if Dad was a judge with a fixed objection to the death penalty then in the world of book reviewing I'm presumably regarded as a proponent of capital punishment. Not just a hanger but a flogger too. Possibly even an actual hangman, measuring a book for the drop. Pulling the lever with professional slickness and a pride, *à la* Pierrepoint, in my work rate.

There are some odd secondary symmetries in our professional lives. By writing 'Bathpool Park' and suggesting that Dad's court failed to understand what happened to the kidnapped teenager Lesley Whittle, I opened up his workplace to the methods of mine, and treated the case as a verbal construct that could yield results if subjected to practical criticism of a wayward sort. In his turn, a few years later, Dad was called upon to adjudicate on how far critical comment could go before it attracted potential penalties in law.

The TV critic of the *Sunday People*, Nina Myskow, had written a catty review of a programme in which Charlotte Cornwell played a rock star. She remarked that Cornwell's bottom was too big to belong to such a person. The title of the programme was *No Excuses*, which might have whispered caution to the indignant performer. The personal nature of the comment struck her as outrageous, and she sued. The case came up before Dad, who ruled that although the comment was highly disagreeable it fell within the limits of free speech.

Returning to the question of suits in the sense of clothing rather than cases in court: let's assume that the alarm has been properly set, the gas turned off and that A. France & Sons did the decent thing as regards Dad's wardrobe. There was only one definite respect in which the firm let us down as clients. We had stipulated that Dad's ashes be put in a casket like Sheila's, since they were to be interred together. It's the word 'like' that let us down, I imagine, with its spread of possible meanings. Dad's casket was indeed like Sheila's, in the sense that it was an elongated wooden box of modest size. What it wasn't was identical. Why would an undertaker's think that rough resemblance was all that was required? It seems doubtful that the firm was making an elegant demonstration of the fact – it was indeed a fact – that our parents, though a couple, were very far from being a pair. By the time we had discovered the error it was too late to ask.

The ceremony of double interment in Llansannan, Denbighshire, was given an awkward undertone by our self-consciousness about the mismatching caskets that were to be carried out of the chapel, at the end of the service, and conveyed ceremoniously to the tidy hole prepared for them. The graveyard at Llansannan always seemed a peaceful place, the baa-ing of sheep from the hill more restful even than bells or birdsong.

We invited Bamie to attend the ceremony. It would have seemed wrong to leave him out, after the large contribution he had made to Dad's last year. There was a slight element of embarrassment about his attending, just the same, and we didn't press him to make an extended visit. The ethnic diversity of Denbighshire has presumably come along a certain amount since Dad's childhood, but it seemed painfully obvious that the only non-white face in the community, the only possible candidate to keep him company, was the inn sign of the smoky pub where the family group was billeted, the Saracen's Head.

After the ashes of our parents, though asymmetrically canistered, had been safely stowed away in a single billet, Tim took on the task of commissioning a gravestone for them. The task seemed appropriate not because he was the eldest but because he had a strong interest in layout, design, typography, which extended naturally enough to the medium of stone. The inscription finally agreed on was the one adorning Dad's coat of arms. It's in Welsh and means *Justice The Best Shield*.

Having your own coat of arms is undeniably grand, though in Dad's case this was grandeur acquired along the way. It's the custom for Treasurers of Gray's Inn to be honoured after their term of office with a portrait and a coat of arms. The Treasurer is the figurehead of the Inn, and benchers occupy the position in order of seniority, so that it is possible for distinguished benchers to see their eminence approaching, mortality permitting, year by year. Sometimes of course mortality not only permits the appointment but shortens the wait.

Dad's turn came in 1982. There's little scope for glory in a Treasurer's tenure – if a new building or the renovation of an old one is accomplished during your time, then your initials will be incised on it, but Gray's Inn is a compact parish and major works are needed only at considerable intervals. Perhaps Dad was trying to sneak his way into this marginal immortality with his decision to install lead planters on the steps leading up to the Benchers' Entrance to Hall in South Square without consulting the governing body. He had a good relationship with the Inn's gardener, Malone, thanks to the years he had spent in the position of Master of the Walks (the Walks being the true name of the fine gardens, originally laid out by Francis Bacon), and they had dreamed up this pretty scheme together. His fellow benchers were not pleased to be left out of the decision-making process, and ordered the removal of the planters. Not quite Watergate, but the kind of thing that stirs strong feelings in a small community.

I remember Dad dropping into conversation that he'd had a useful meeting with the Garter King of Arms. He certainly seemed to get a kick out of the fact that the Inn would stump up for the expense of researching a suitable blazon. Presumably some of the Inn's Treasurers are snugly pre-escutcheoned by the time they ascend to the office, but Dad's modest origins ruled that out.

His village background, neither privileged nor deprived, had left him with a few thrifty foibles. He loved getting things through the post, and would enter any competition the *Reader's Digest* thought fit to offer him. Once a compendious book arrived at the Gray's Inn flat, a complete guide to gardening with all the basics for the beginner but plenty of tips to satisfy the expert. Sheila proposed sending it back with a stinging letter. How dare they demand money for an unwanted, unsolicited compendium of anything? Dad was looking rather sheepish, a milder version of the expression he wore with a hangover, when his whole body was like a dog that knows it has done wrong and wants to be forgiven without meeting his master's eyes.

'Bill . . . you didn't!' But it was true – Dad had knowingly ordered a complete garden guide when he didn't have a garden, unless you count the Walks in all their magnificence, since he was Master of the Walks at the time, the Walks where blooms were whisked into the flowerbeds the moment they were approaching their best and whisked away in disgrace the moment a petal was out of true.

'Why, Bill? Why would you do such a thing?'

Dad rallied his self-respect. 'I'm not a fool, darling. Give me some credit. I wasn't born yesterday. I know perfectly well they don't put you into the Grand Prize Draw if you don't order *something*.'

Dad's motto about Justice being the Best Shield was in Welsh. I was able to remember it for a few months after the interment of his ashes, then it left me for good. It didn't have the memorability of some phrases in the language, like for instance the standard Welsh way of referring to a microwave. *Microdon* would be correct usage, though it's no more than a back-formation from the English word, *micro* meaning *micro* and *don* meaning *wave*. But everyone in the North says *popty ping.* The oven that goes ping. Then there's the Welsh for a jellyfish, which my cousins assure me is called *pysgod wibli wobli.* There is of course a long tradition of mocking the ignorant outsider, or 'soaking the Saxon', and the Welsh word *saesneg* has some of the disparaging charge of the Scottish *sassenach.*

There were other ways in which I could have refreshed my memory about Dad's Welsh motto, but they involved a little embarrassment, since I would have to admit to family members that I'd forgotten it. So why not contact the Royal College of Arms instead? Stick out my thumb and hope to be given a ride in the mother ship of heraldry.

There turned out to be a website and an e-mail address. What had I expected – specifications of the maximum wing-span of the owl to be despatched with the parchment of enquiry (A4 or smaller, please)? Something of the sort.

Does the Royal College of Arms have a Facebook page, even? Actually I'd rather not know.

There were some wearily polite answers on the website intended to nip Frequently Asked Questions in the bud. It was particularly requested that large amounts of genealogical data should not be forwarded at the initial stage. On the other hand there was little point in submitting an enquiry that consisted of no more than your name and a request to be told your coat of arms. Enquiries that displayed a complete failure to have read the website might not receive a reply. There was no point in asking about clan membership, clan badges and the like, since the clan system was entirely Scottish and the College of Arms had no responsibility for Scotland. English families could not be associated to a clan, still less form a clan themselves, unless they were ultimately of Scottish descent. The belief, apparently quite widespread but new, that everyone has a clan, and can wear some specific tartan or display a clan badge, was quite erroneous.

The idea of forming my own clan had never occurred to me, until the stern warning intended to quash the desire inflamed it.

I submitted my enquiry to 'the officer in waiting', not knowing a particular officer of arms and feeling that this was not a case for the Garter King of Arms, a heraldic emergency, even if there was a possibility of his remembering his meetings with Dad. I imagined him on call, twenty-four hours a day, sleeping in crested pyjamas next to a hole cut in the College floorboards to accommodate a pole like the ones in fire stations, only made of solid gold.

This nervous mockery of mine seems to suggest that I'm secretly impressed, whether by antiquity, poshness or arcane precision of language.

The next day an unfamiliar name showed up in the sender slot of my e-mail display. It's 'Bluemantle Pursuivant', but the software processes it as if it was an ordinary name, no different from 'First Hull Trains' or 'Nigerian Not-a-Scam', though it seems to have stronger affinities with (say) Montezuma or Rumpelstiltskin. It's only because of the comical grandeur of the title that I notice how it is displayed, as if on a pale-blue plaque with rounded edges. So are all the other senders' names, on miniature versions of locomotive name plates, but it's only now that I see the style of display as heraldic in its own right, an oblong shape in the tint of *bleu celeste*. There's a plus sign next to the name. Do I want to add Bluemantle Pursuivant to my contacts list? Well of course I do. I press the button.

Bluemantle Pursuivant confirmed that a grant of Arms was made to 'Sir William Mars-Jones of Gray's Inn' by Letters Patent dated 25 March 1986.

The blazon, or description in heraldic terminology, is as follows: Sable a Stag trippant Argent attired and unguled Or on

a Chief Azure three Roman Swords erect point upwards
Argent their hilts Gold. The Crest is On a Wreath Or, Azure
and Sable A Dragon's Head couped Gules langued Or and a
Griffin's Head couped Or langued Gules both addorsed and
gorged with a gemel dancetty per pale Or and Gules. Mantled
Sable and Azure doubled Or and Argent.

How lovely! The Inn had conspired with the College of
Arms to commission a symbolist poem on Dad's behalf, its
vocabulary Old French but its perfumed hieratic sensibility
closer to Mallarmé.

> Sable a Stag trippant
> Argent attired and unguled Or
> On a Chief Azure
>
> Three Roman Swords erect
> point upwards
> Argent
> their hilts Gold
>
> The Crest is On a Wreath Or, Azure and Sable
>
> A Dragon's Head
> couped Gules   langued Or
>
> and a Griffin's Head
> couped Or   langued Gules
>
> both addorsed and gorged
> with a gemel dancetty
> per pale Or and Gules

Mantled Sable and Azure
doubled Or and Argent.
{Chorus: '*With a gemel dancetty per pale Or and Gules-O,*
with a gemel dancetty per pale Or and Gules . . .'}

Dad's motto turns out to be GORAU TARIAN CYF-
IAWNDER, which had been Flintshire's watchword until the
county's abolition in 1974, when it passed to the successor body
the Borough of Islwyn (formed by the amalgamation of the
Abercarn Urban District, part of the Bedwellty Urban District,
the Mynyddislwyn Urban District and the Risca Urban District).
This unorthodox bit of twinning, with a motto being shared by
a borough and a judge, carried on until 1996, when Islwyn too
was abolished. At the time of his death, Dad seems to have had
an exclusive claim on his chosen slogan.

Along with the technical description of Dad's blazon my
new friend Bluemantle passed on the information that his
Arms would descend to all of Sir William's children and be
passed on by his sons to their own descendants. It was open
to me (and my brothers) to place on record a brief pedigree
setting out details of the descent, thus establishing our own
right to the Arms. If this was done certified paintings of the
Arms could then be issued. He attached an example for my
information – but at this point I got a faint whiff of the
Reader's Digest all over again and decided not to go any further.
All the same, it was nice to know that if I developed heraldic
cravings of my own they could be satisfied with a pedigree
and a cheque.

Dad's concern with his status seems to have become almost
legendary. In an informal interview in the *Financial Times* (18
January 2013) doubling as a restaurant review, the barrister
Sydney Kentridge, aged ninety and going strong, mentions
him as a sort of cautionary tale, an example of 'judge-itis' or

elephantiasis of the self-esteem. Kentridge (who ordered herring with beetroot and mustard, followed by sole goujons with duck-egg mayonnaise) recounts that it fell to Benet Hytner to pay Dad tribute on behalf of the Bar when he retired, saying, 'There is one distinction that your Lordship and I share. We both have sons who are more distinguished than we are.' Hytner was referring to his son Nick (already well established as a theatre director) and, presumably, to me. Kentridge goes on, 'He infuriated the judge and delighted the bar.'

It seems perverse to contest reports of Dad's pompousness when I had so much experience of it at first hand. But it happens that Dad passed on this incident, good-humouredly, as a compliment to me, and Ben Hytner made no appearance on his list of four-letter fellers, clearly rascal rather than weasel.

I'm not making claims for Dad's modesty. I was in the room, after all, when he had a negotiation on the phone with American Express about how many of his honorifics – MBE, LLB – could be crammed onto his Gold Card. It was explained to him that there was a physical limit to the space available. Perhaps he imagined an exception being made in his case, and a special extended format devised for the credit card, making it as long as a chequebook, along the lines of the outsized platform ticket that used to be available at Llanfairpwllgwyngyllgogerychwyrndrobwyllllantysiliogogogoch railway station.

After tough negotiation he agreed to drastic surgery on his first name and become *Sir Wm*. Very few people would ever see the form of words on that Gold Card but that wasn't the point. His first name he had been given. Those qualifications had been earned.

He didn't exactly come from nothing, but he came from a much less promising social background than most of those he came to call his brothers. The other case of over-developed self-esteem that I knew about in Gray's Inn, Edward Gardner, was also a self-made man. Strictly speaking he can't have suffered from judge-itis since he didn't get as far as the bench, moving into politics instead. Dad had at least gone to university, to Aberystwyth and even Cambridge. Ted's family ran a small jeweller's in Preston, and he worked as a journalist after leaving school. After having an outstandingly 'good war' in the Navy, starting as an ordinary seaman and ending up as a Commander, he managed to read for the Bar directly. His political attitudes were more coherent than Dad's, in that he not only opposed homosexual law reform but actively campaigned as an MP for the restoration of the death penalty, getting as far as a free parliamentary vote on the topic in 1983.

Underlying the self-importance must have been a sense of disbelief at how far he had come. He mastered Received Pronunciation, the vocal intonations of those in power, perhaps later in life than Dad did, so that it was only in his last illness that his children ever heard his underlying Preston voice. In a sense he died a stranger to them, emigrating to his home region of speech.

He once framed a half-smoked cigar he had been offered by Winston Churchill, with a plaque testifying to its provenance. There was also a time when he encountered difficulties (I have this from his daughter Sally) when re-entering the country after a holiday. It was pointed out to him that his passport had been defaced. He denied it. He was shown where handwritten letters had crudely been inserted. At last he protested at the unfairness of it all. 'I have recently been knighted. By the Queen, in whose name as perhaps you know passports are issued. I am now *Sir* Edward Gardner. I haven't *defaced* my passport, I have *corrected* it.'

Clearly neither of these men had acquired the knack of

playing his achievements down, but then they didn't go to the sort of school where such skills are taught, the informal sessions of self-deprecation practice beside the fives court.

It wasn't his own crest that Dad displayed in the domestic spaces of the Gray's Inn flat but the escutcheons of the four ships on which he had served during the War, *Euryalus* being the ship, or the crew, for which he felt the most fondness. I don't know the position of the College of Arms on heraldry for ships.

One day soon after Dad's life-reviews had been published, I fielded a phone call from a woman who expressed condolences, saying she had known my father long ago, and seemed anxious to know if my mother was still living. One of the obituaries had seemed to indicate that she had died first, but she wanted to be sure. I confirmed the fact, and then she told me that Dad had proposed to her in Malta during the War.

It seemed almost excessively scrupulous, to make sure there was no widow to consider before revealing an association which could hardly hurt her, going back as it did to a distant period, before he and Sheila had even met.

According to this Esmé-from-Malta, Dad had said she should marry him because he was going to be Prime Minister. He would drive her around in his Bentley. She knew he hadn't become Prime Minister, but had he got as far as the Bentley of his dreams? I had to admit he had only got as far as a Jaguar Mk II, though that had seemed pretty much the best car in the world when we were children and urged him (in those days before a speed limit) to accelerate on the approach to humpback bridges.

It seemed that Dad's courtship technique included a fair bit of jovial braggadocio. It was hard to believe he was in earnest rather than playing a part. I asked Esmé why she didn't accept his proposal. Because she was Catholic, she said, and he wouldn't commit himself to having any children of the marriage raised in the faith.

If he wasn't willing to compromise on something that was so important to her, I wondered whether Dad had only been honing his wooing technique with this Esmé. 'Do you think he was serious about you?' I asked.

'Oh yes,' she said. 'I know he was. He carved my name on his ukelele.' There was no answer to that. We shared a moment of respectful silence, until I spoiled it by saying there was no answer to that.

Esmé had married another naval officer in the end, who had the advantage of being Catholic. She was now a widow, or she wouldn't dream of making this phone call, but there was no possible harm now. She had moved to Britain with her husband, so this phone call was coming from Guildford rather than Valletta.

She said she had seen Dad once in London by accident. It was on the top deck of a 38 bus going along Theobald's Road, just by Gray's Inn. Dad and buses seems an unlikely pairing, but if forced to that extremity he would certainly choose the top deck, stronghold of smokers. 'I was with my husband,' Esmé said, 'and Lloyd sat near me. He didn't speak. He was wearing a bowler hat and I could see he was trembling.'

And you, Esmé? How did you feel? 'How did I feel? I felt jolly glad I was wearing my new Marshall and Snelgrove hat.'

I had registered a faint shock at hearing her refer to Dad as 'Lloyd', his name in the family when he was growing up, discarded in favour of 'Bill' for his post-war life at the Bar. In a strictly limited sense her attachment to my father was deeper than my mother's, by dint of going further into the past, reaching back to a simpler, more dreamy form of life, with luxury cars and offices of state lined up like ducks in a shooting gallery, his for the picking off.

At the end of our phone conversation Esmé mentioned that she sometimes came up to town. Would I care to join her one day for tea at the Ritz? I would, with pleasure.

Tea never came about. Perhaps I should have called 1471 and made a note of Esmé's number (risking the discovery that she had withheld it), though I'm not sure I would have wanted to bother her.

It must have been a habit of Dad's in those days to personalize the instruments he played. The guitar he took with him on active service ended up inscribed with the names of any number of shipmates. At the end of the War he took it to a shop on Denmark Street, hoping to get a good price, since many of the friends whose names it bore had attained high rank in the service. He was disappointed to be told that he had virtually destroyed its market value.

The ukelele seems a rather flighty instrument on which to inscribe the name of a beloved when there is a more high-toned one available. The guitar is the serenader's weapon of choice, after all – but perhaps Dad's guitar was already rather crowded out, like a teenager's plaster cast, with the names of his messmates. Even if there was room physically I can see that there might be a social qualm. Dad might be reluctant to make a nice well-brought-up girl consort, even on the body-work of a guitar, with rough male company, a contingent from below decks. Better to be the admiral aboard a ukelele than share the bridge of a guitar.

The best that Denmark Street could do for Dad was to accept the reverently vandalized guitar in part-exchange for another instrument. Dad dug deep into the pockets of his demob suit and forked out sixty pounds (excluding the exchange value of the inscribed guitar) for the Gibson L4, beautiful to look at as well as to play, lacquered and already a vintage item (made in 1928), subsequently an heirloom inherited by Matthew, the guitarist among the brothers, while Tim took away the Monington & Weston, also lacquered but less precious, and I made off with the contraband Clavinova.

I stayed on in the Gray's Inn flat, negotiating with the Inn with a view to being given a tenancy. Dad had paid very little for the flat, both because he moved in under an earlier, more smiling Rent Act and because he was one of the Inn's eminences. I was under the impression that I was a member of Gray's Inn because Dad had paid £50 to make me one, just before the minimum requirement for being a student member was raised from a rather basic level (though I think you had to have a Latin O-level). I was entitled to eat lunch in Hall, that grand canteen where the *Comedy of Errors* was first performed, though I can't say I exercised the privilege much.

I would pay a lot more than Dad had, the Inn wouldn't have to renovate the flat and would benefit from an uninterrupted income stream. Those were the advantages I could argue. What was in it for me? Sentimental continuity and an ample flat in central London with views of the Walks and the Square. Could I afford it? No.

In fantasy I was already drafting advertisements to run in the *New York Review of Books*, offering academics on their summer vacations the use of an ample flat in central London with views of the Walks and the Square, a stone's throw from a Hall steeped in associations with the Bard, equally convenient for the British Museum, British Library and West End theatre. I would keep afloat by renting out my flat in Highbury, then make a mint with this illegal scheme from July to September, retreating to my own little nest in the eaves (peeing into a bucket, presumably) but descending cheerfully to make breakfast – other meals by arrangement – hoping all the while that the CCTV cameras in the Square, or the Inn staff supposed to be monitoring them, would turn a blind eye to the unauthorized traffic.

Keith meanwhile was producing low-key variations on a theme of common sense, saying that the Gray's Inn flat was fine but a little unreal. There was nothing wrong with my premises in Highbury.

At first the Inn seemed to have no objection to my staying on, at a greatly increased rent and with no more than a short-hold assured tenancy (that abominable innovation of the Thatcher years), and then it did. I wasn't a possible tenant. But I'm a member of the Inn, I said. You're a *student* member, they said. Yes, I said, I'm a student *member*. Apparently my little entitlement was meaningless in real terms. I felt like a novice financial trader shouting for shares on the floor of the Stock Exchange, waving what turns out to be a Timothy Whites voucher with an expiry date in 1964.

For some reason I felt it necessary to insist on being expelled, though physical eviction (bailiffs, weeping children) wasn't called for in the end. I understood that in a legal showdown an institution almost entirely composed of lawyers was unlikely to lose – but like many people who have written journalism, I had an exaggerated notion of the power I could wield. Surely if I hinted that I was writing a piece for *The Times* about the Inn's inhospitability to someone who had actually been born there, though its own hypocritical motto was *Domus*, the Latin for a home, the benchers would fall over themselves to make peace on my terms?

Let's assume that they were terrified, but nerved themselves to calling my bluff. They may have felt that, as a true son of the Inn at heart, I wouldn't go nuclear with the warhead of a bittersweet and implicitly scolding family reminiscence.

I seem to be portraying myself as someone who dealt with

his parents' deaths comparatively coolly, but had a bit of a tantrum when called upon to leave the pleasant premises they had never owned. That's not how I see it, obviously, but it was easier to hold the fact of their deaths steady when I was moving through the familiar spaces they had occupied.

Still, I had almost eighteen months to adjust, a six-month period of grace granted by the Inn and then a year of illegal occupation. There would have been some sort of hearing, but I was making out that Gray's Inn had always been my main home, with the Highbury flat serving essentially as a work space or office, and it became clear that telephone records would not substantiate this notion. Like Ian Fleming before me, I realized that it was better to cave in than be disgraced.

As a true son of the Inn, but one who had inherited some of the bloodymindedness of the law itself, I wanted to do what I could in the way of collateral damage, and duly wrote for *The Times* a nostalgic article incorporating sardonic sideswipes at the Inn's hypocrisy. I thought it would be cowardly to publish such a thing after the event, much more satisfactory if it appeared while I was still in residence. Peeking out of the curtains on to the Square that Saturday morning, I expected to see benchers flat on their backs, pole-axed by my righteous rhetoric, stiff arms raised to hold the paper open in front of their sightless eyes – if not actually vaporized by the blast, leaving only white shadows on the pavement.

One of the luxuries of the flat was the amount of storage space available on the attic floor where I had been based. The sloping walls of the side-attics had provided ideal repositories over the years for black plastic bin-bags containing unsorted papers, clumps of bank statements cheek by jowl with letters from Iris Murdoch and Jeanette Winterson. All of these now had to be sorted through prior to disposal.

My brothers and I managed to divide up our parents' effects

without tension or disagreement. There were various farewells to our childhood home (though Tim as the eldest might possibly have memories of a previous flat across the Square, at number 12). I remember an evening when we watched a video of Tim Burton's *Mars Attacks!*, which my brothers hadn't seen, in shared rapture, the vinegary nastiness of the satire intensified in some indefinable way by our planetary affinity. When we were children Dad had told us as a matter of fact that we were from Mars, and presumably enjoyed the moment during a visit to the Planetarium when I called out, 'That's ours!' as the guide singled out Mars with his torch, whose cutout projected a glowing arrow shape onto the velvety dome above our heads.

A slight divergence in fraternal temperament showed up on the last night of all, when one brother intentionally smashed a glass in the fireplace, to signify defiant Russian largeness of soul, and another brother fetched a broom to sweep it up. The fireplace had been a functioning one until the Clean Air Act, and had subsequently been fitted with an upmarket simulation. In the common spaces outside the flats were substantial coal bunkers with locks and immensely heavy wooden lids. Though the flats were only built in 1954, the indispensability of coal was unquestioned, built into the fixtures. When there was no more coal for our bunker to hold, except in the form of stubbornly persisting dust, it came into its own as miscellaneous external storage space. Dad installed wine racks inside it, into which I would often be called upon to transfer bottles after the delivery man from Oddbins in High Holborn had called. While Sheila had favoured everyday whites and an unfussy cava called Segura Viudas (though 'Sigourney Weaver' rolled off the tongue more reliably, particularly after a couple of glasses), Dad liked the prestige of a grape variety or a region and would ask guests if they fancied a glass of Sancerre. In

Indian restaurants he would ask if they had 'such a thing as a Muscat de Beaumes de Venise', articulating with exaggerated clarity as if taking the hard work out of lip-reading for the benefit of someone deaf.

Some wine was kept upstairs, on the attic level where I lived. Under the concrete roof the temperature was far from constant. In summer it could become so hot that sleeping on the flat roof became an attractive option, while in winter it sometimes happened, thanks to the skylight's ventilator being rusted open, that snow fell on my bed. These conditions don't suit wine over any length of time, and none of the bottles that Dad had kept up there turned out to be fit for drinking, and barely for cooking purposes. There was a melancholy gap between label and contents, not to be bridged by the palate, hardly even by the imagination.

Since the spiral staircase to the attic level had been installed at Dad's expense before the family moved in (he told us when we were children that it had come from a submarine), it made sense that we would have a right, perhaps even a duty, to take it with us when we left. A brief look told us that this plan was impracticable, a pity since it had such a strong visual appeal, almost in terms of conceptual art, to leave the alienated domestic space pulsing with absence.

Moving out of Gray's Inn didn't mean I wasn't allowed to set foot on the premises. There had been no ASBO element in the Inn's legal victory. I stayed in contact with residents I'd known from childhood, most of whom tactfully treated my article for *The Times* as an aberration that need not be mentioned. It seemed natural now to think of the plutocratic enclave as their present home rather than my past one. Seeing fresh paintwork on the nameboard of number 3 at street level was slightly shocking at first, but as I continued to visit no. 5 (bringing fresh sprats from Peckham Market for Lady Henry

Wilson's Sunday lunch) and no. 1 (delivering to Edith Wellwood pans of the egg custard that constituted almost her only food) I soon got used to it. I found I could use the Inn as a short cut to other destinations without feeling I was venturing onto ground that was either sentimentally charged or forbidden.

Digging my heels in and refusing to leave a flat to which I had no legal right seemed to do the trick in psychological terms. When I was finally turfed out I was able to leave the past behind and walk away clean. Eviction has some modest merit as an agent of emotional resolution. It doesn't come cheap, though, and I'm sure there are thriftier ways of breaking the spell of the past. I'd urge others in my position to shop around.

Sometimes there were direct reminders of my dead people, tiny resurrections. One day I took a watch-chain to have a new swivel fitted, which seems a fantastically fogeyish errand, though my excuse for preferring a pocket watch is that I'm allergic to metal and would get a wrist rash if I wore a watch there. (Now that mobile phones have replaced watches this excuse seems very thin, but habits have a habit of becoming entrenched.) I took the chain to Sanford's the jeweller, located in 3 Holborn Bars, that little remnant of London before the Great Fire. The row of shops has been made over any number of times but is historically grounded by the fact that you step down into them, down to the old street level. The past has subsided and resists the hydraulic imagination that would pump it up to the level where we live.

Sanford's is a family firm, though recent (established only in the 1920s) compared to the Tudor building that contains it. Its near neighbour was the tobacconist's where Dad would pick up his cigarettes, John Brumfit's, though subsequently rebranded Shervingtons, since the new owners couldn't afford the fee demanded to keep the name and the illusion of continuity in business. An old building attracts businesses keen to benefit from the ennoblement of association, but there comes a point when the clustering of parvenu enterprises exhausts the stock of transferable grandeur, and then the transaction goes into reverse. Then it's the building itself that seems fake, discredited. Even without an actual wand emporium the edifice takes on a Harry Potter tinge, and the skew-whiff angles and planes of 3 Holborn Bars come to look as if they had been worked up, sketch after sketch, by a production designer with set builders by the hundred on his payroll, ready to lay the required square footage of prefabricated cobbles at a moment's notice.

Already there seemed something hopeless about the sign on Shervingtons' door. *Thank You for Smoking* – a slogan that was meant to sound jauntily defiant seemed to carry an undertone of forlorn pleading.

Jewellers' shops in films starring Catherine Deneuve or Audrey Hepburn are palatial premises, but a jeweller's can also be snug, cosy, like a jewel box – or shoe box – in its own right. That's the style of Sanford Bros (the 'Bros' in much smaller lettering on the shopfront, as if added later at the insistence of an affronted sibling). It's an unfussy establishment the size of a country-house pantry, holding itself a little apart from the concentration of competing trade in Hatton Garden. This is a jeweller's shop where the word 'bling' has never been spoken.

When the man serving in Sanford's asked for my name he seemed to hesitate for a moment before writing it down on the docket. In such a small room our interaction necessarily seemed social, and the hesitation an invitation to something more than small talk. I asked if the name rang a bell. He thought for a moment, then he asked, 'Was your father a stout man?' I said that he would have rejected the word, but that the waistbands of his trousers sometimes led stressful lives. Why did he ask, though?

'This is going back a bit,' he said.

It was when he was a teenager, manning the shop on Saturdays. Between us we worked out that it must have been in the early mid-1960s. This chap had come in to buy a pair of earrings or something, and he had three boys with him.

I had no memory of the event, but the occasion wasn't hard to reconstruct. Dad had forgotten Sheila's birthday, or their wedding anniversary, until the day itself (or the day before) and was doing what men in those days were expected to do, slipping into the nearest shop to spend his way out of trouble.

The man assigned the boys places to stand – one, two, three – in Indian file, and they took up their marks, not as if this was a drill they were used to, but as if their Dad was in a good mood and it was fun to go along with him. Then the man raised his finger and wagged it, saying with pretended sternness, 'Don't steal.'

That's all, the most fragile piece of drollery imaginable, based on the presumed unlikeliness of our misbehaving and the small scale of the shop, but it had stayed with the Saturday boy for a third of a century. It helps that the name is distinctive in the first place, and Dad's professional success had the side effect of refreshing casual memory with regular mentions in the newspapers, but still Dad had an ability (not continuously detectable by his family) to charge small events with charm and presence. I could just about think myself back into the line-up, looking at Matthew's curly hair from behind, sensing behind me the incipient resentful curl in Tim's upper lip, but of course I'm just making it up.

There have been a couple of other occasions when I've been told an anecdote about Dad since his death, without being in a position to confirm its authenticity, as I could in the case of the Sanford Bros Saturday boy. A quantity surveyor who had learned the basics of Building Contract Law from Dad's lectures at Brixton School of Building in the late 1940s told me that he was popular with his students, unpopular with other members of staff, who complained about the gales of laughter emerging from his classroom. One of the funny stories that caused the trouble concerned the court-martial of an officer who had been intercepted more or less naked, chasing a woman in a similar state through the public spaces of Shepheard's Hotel. The disciplinary authorities had trouble deciding exactly what the charge should be, and settled on his being improperly dressed. Dad, defending, combed through the King's Regulations and found that there was an exemption in place for sporting activities – you counted as properly dressed if you were appropriately dressed for the sport you were pursuing. Not a defence that would pass muster for a moment nowadays, but supposedly that was the argument Dad pursued and his client reaped the benefit.

Except that Dad never mentioned it, and I never heard the anecdote from family friends, many of whom were lawyers. It's not so salacious an anecdote as to be impossible, revealing nothing more disreputable than roguishness, so perhaps his prudish side led him to be discreet by the time he had children, children whom he wanted brought up in the belief that a wedding night was an encounter between two trembling virgins. Or perhaps the story has been misattributed. It sometimes happens that an anecdote becomes detached from its original subject, and either melts away or migrates towards a new owner, someone deemed to be larger than life.

In the case of another story I can immediately declare its falsity, though its source is an ex-registrar of Westminster County Court who knew Dad at the relevant period. If Dad had appeared as an extra in the film of *Thunderball*, thanks to the intervention of a grateful Kevin McClory, if it had even been mentioned as a possibility, over one drink or twenty, we would have heard all about it.

There were times in his lifetime when Dad's exporting of his vitality seemed actively preposterous. I remember returning to the Gray's Inn flat one evening in my teens when a small parental drinks party was breaking up. I used the stairs, slowing down as I heard the social hubbub above me on the third floor, so that I hung back instead of showing myself and joining the group of half-a-dozen guests gathered on the landing, putting on their coats.

Dad was presiding over the dissolution of the party. He pressed the button to summon the lift and then pinched his nose with his fingers to give his voice a grating Tannoy quality. Oh my God, I thought, he's not going to do that old routine, surely! The lift-operator routine, so embarrassing, predictable and out of date. 'Third floor, going down . . .' he intoned. 'Ladies' lingerie, hats and gloves . . .' Was he going to find some new twist to freshen up the whole cringe-making performance? No he wasn't. He didn't need to. Still holding his nose, he bent his knees so as to give a poor impression of someone sinking out of sight . . . and everyone copied his stance, laughing helplessly. Sophisticated grown-ups seemed to be entirely under his spell, though admittedly with alcoholic help.

I might have been watching footage of some strange cult. Dad was some sort of hypnotist, and his audience was well and truly under. It was like the children's game of 'Simon says', except that Dad was Simon, and so he didn't need to say 'Simon says' to get his way. He just said things, and people surrendered all resistance.

How do I measure up to Dad? I'm a taller make of man than he was, so wearing his trousers would be out of the question even if I had them taken in. Any shirt of his would leave my wrists to dangle, but I keep his singlets of sea island cotton ('Sunspel for Austin Reed') in circulation, and for quite a time wore his Japanese Burberry knock-off fawn raincoat, which was almost long enough in the arms.

The splendid Preacher of Gray's Inn, Roger Holloway, was about the same height and build as Dad (though trimmer) so it was to him I offered first refusal on his clothes. I've really only seen agitated clergymen jumping up and down wearing nothing but their underclothes in Ben Travers farces, but Roger was powered by wild joy rather than panic as a succession of velvet smoking jackets came to light. It turned out also that some ceremonial items of judicial wear were indistinguishable from what clerics are supposed to wear on similar occasions. Perhaps some buttons needed to be altered, but from that day forward Roger didn't need to visit Westminster, in the run-up to gala events, to pester minor canons of a suitable size for their finery.

Dad's cheap-looking wardrobe wasn't itself a coveted piece of furniture, and even desirable items like the dining-table went off to auction – in Yorkshire, since we had been advised that larger pieces sold better there.

The little utility chest of drawers, though, from the bedroom I shared with Tim (where the comic that showed me the instructively tender men lurked) now sits immediately next to the desk where I write, as if it had followed me patiently around with its message of reassurance, wagging its tail, waiting for this moment of acknowledgement. Its bottom drawer no longer contains anything that might challenge the patriarchy.

In fact the chest, as well as its cargo of not quite Gatsby-grade underwear, is now the home of miscellaneous patriarchal souvenirs, such as a pair of white kid gloves trimmed with gold braid. These are relics of the old assize system – it was traditional in various towns to present a judge with such gloves when there were no criminal cases needing to be heard, symbolizing and celebrating the innocence of the populace. Dad received three pairs in his early years as a judge, before the assize system was replaced. I wore my pair in public just the once, at a party with an eighteenth-century theme on Coldharbour Lane, teamed with a loose white shirt, aiming for a dilute Byronic effect. It felt exhilaratingly unwise to be dressed so fancily on a street where you could get into enough trouble wearing clothes of the current epoch.

There's also a gleaming cigar box lined in green felt, with a dedication inside: 'To *Mr William L. Mars-Jones, Q.C.* In appreciation of the preservation of my stainless character. *Swansea Assizes July, 1958.*' Stainless steel, of course, though the effect is slightly undermined by the message merely being typed on a piece of paper and stuck inside the lid of the box. This was from a client who was charged with stealing scrap metal and then trying to sell it back to the people from whom he had stolen it, accused of both law-breaking and idiocy. Considering the way he had been delivered from disgrace, the client might have stumped up for silver, if not platinum, and suppressed the little joke – except that, as Dad tended not to mention, he didn't work for free.

There's also a grey jewellery box (covered with a material vaguely mimicking either velvet or suede) containing another of Dad's treasures, swathed in cotton wool although the object in question isn't actually delicate. It looks like a bookmark, about two inches wide, four and a half long, and it's made of silver. There's a dove engraved on it, flying downward with a scroll and ribbon in its beak. This is Sheikh Yamani's Christmas card from 1984. The message in flowery script runs, 'Ahmad Zaki Yamani / Wishes you a Merry Christmas and a Happy

New Year', then an engraved imitation of the sheikh's signature in English script, and finally '25 December 1984'. The emphasis on the date of Christmas seems excessive and awkward, as if the sender thought it might vary from year to year. On the other side is engraved a calendar for 1985.

This is clearly an object *de luxe*, though I'm not clear about how it's supposed to provoke admiring comment. Actually used as a bookmark? It's a bit bulky for that. On a mantelpiece with the other cards? An elaborate but more conventional Christmas card would do the job better. As a desk-top accessory and talking-point? You might say, 'Shall we make it April the second? According to Sheikh Yamani it's a Tuesday . . .' Leaving it open for your companion to say, 'I think you mean the day before . . .', not believing you until the card has been handed across, with a show of reluctance (he's a close personal friend), and its full three-and-a-bit ounces weighed in the palm of the hand. Perhaps not even then.

Three-and-a-bit ounces! To put it in context, if this was luncheon meat, it would make a substantial portion for one.

As for why Dad was on the receiving end of a silver Christmas card from the Saudi oil minister, I have no idea. If he had been involved in international trade negotiations, I'm sure he would have said. He showed off this mega-trinket at the time, but was mysterious about why he had been sent it. He may have been as much in the dark as anyone else.

It's possible that Sheikh Yamani simply carpet-bombed the pages of *Who's Who* with his seasonal greetings. I wonder how many of the recipients responded in kind. It can't quite have been the usual oh-God-they've-sent-us-one-we-have-to-send-them-one mid-December flurry. If there wasn't a return address as such, there was always the Saudi embassy. I imagine various failed attempts at striking the right note, with drafts beginning 'Dear Sheikh' and 'Dear Ahmad' following each other into the waste-paper basket. Conversation, perhaps, about whether it wouldn't really be more sensitive, more reciprocal, to send an Eid greeting (either Eid al-Fitr or Eid al-Adha) at the appropriate time instead, perhaps with a photograph of the family, even some of the children's artwork, crayon sketch or potato-print. A bit pushy, maybe?

Silver Christmas card, kid gloves, cigar box. Not a bad haul from the trolley-dash of clearing the parental flat.

There are other less exotic relics in my keeping, mainly books. The non-legal books in the Gray's Inn flat were either leather-bound and gold-tooled trophies (*A Child's Garden of Verses*, *Thy Servant a Dog*) that we sons were given as children, or novels belonging to Sheila, either in Book Society editions or The World's Classics imprint, with its pleasing solid though dinky format. I remember being shocked at the age of twelve or so by Kipling's brutal realism in *Thy Servant a Dog*. 'I found a Badness. I rolled in it. I liked it.' – was there no limit to the filthiness of print? It seemed astonishing that such obscenity was felt suitable for leather covers, and put in the hands of children.

The book titles that most tantalized me in Sheila's library took the form of phrases, like Audrey Erskine Lindop's *The Singer Not the Song* (made into a famously campy film, with Dirk Bogarde very much leather-bound in the trouser department and verging on the gold-tooled) or Enid Bagnold's *The Loved and Envied*, both of which I read in due course. The World's Classics books, though they sat very satisfyingly in the hand, were heavier going, *Lark Rise to Candleford*, *Esther Waters*, *New Grub Street*. I don't think I finished any of them.

Dad wasn't a novel reader (if you except *The Godfather*), saying that he did too much reading in his work to enjoy it as a leisure activity, which is a perfectly reasonable attitude although it's a distinction that wouldn't actually occur to a book-lover.

His taste in reading matter off-duty ran to financial guides and investment magazines, some of them standard news-stand fare and some of them verging on the cabbalistic. I took just one of them from his bookshelves when we cleared the Gray's Inn flat. It's called *The Campione Report*, written by Dr W. G. Hill, JD, and published by Scope Books in 1989. I've only just now looked at it. As far as I can see, it might just as well be called *Protocols of the Elders of Mammon*.

The Campione Report announces sternly that it 'may **not** be reproduced or copied in any way' and is 'for use of original buyer only'. Dad's is 'confidential registered copy' no. 748. There's a disclaimer on an inside page: 'Whilst reliable sources have been sought out in compiling this book, neither the author, publisher nor distributor can accept any liability for the accuracy of its contents nor for the consequence of any reliance placed upon it.'

The main text is rather more seductive. 'Tax havens are like beautiful women . . .' purrs a passage headed 'Is Campione your cup of tea?'. 'Each one has different charms. Unfortunately, as with the ladies, they often offer a negative characteristic or two as some sort of price in return for enjoying their favours. The charms of Campione are many, the price is low, and the negative aspects are few . . .'

It certainly sounds lovely.

The artificial-sand beach with real palm trees, maintained beautifully at public expense, looks like a set from a Hawaiian travelogue. The churches and schools are absolutely gorgeous, and kept up like no others in Europe. Garbage is picked up free. Unfortunately, the locals still have to pay something for water, gas, electric and telephone. But these services are subsidised . . .

There's no VAT, and foreigners pay no income tax. Visitors can renew their tourist status indefinitely, by walking across the street every three months, into another country, and will never be asked to register with the authorities.

Subsidized Shangri-la! VAT-free Brigadoon innocent of garbage! Where is this haven? Well, Campione turns out to be a rocky little enclave of Italy entirely inside Switzerland, a square mile huddled round a municipal casino – whose takings are what subsidizes local services. Population (in 1989) 3,000. Historically a place where monks trained local boys to become master masons and stone-cutters, and not exactly a haven, just a place where no-one can be bothered to collect tax, certainly not from foreigners. Campione offers all the benefits of Switzerland, including efficient communications and neutrality in wartime, and none of the disadvantages, such as military service (two months of active duty every summer, for life).

The philosophy advanced by Dr Hill is Permanent Tourism, though I wonder if Dad was tempted by any of his other publications. Permanent Tourism sounds like anything but fun. Wasn't the Flying Dutchman a permanent tourist?

He didn't consult me about money matters, and to be sure I would have had no economic knowledge to contribute, but there are other paths to prudence. I would have warned him against any financial scheme seemingly inspired by *Passport to Pimlico*.

The book's intended effect of privileged information, oligarchic insiderdom, is immediately undone by the choice of material used for the cover. As Dad's fingertips stroked this 'leather-bound' book of dreams, for which he had paid £50 – more than a pound a page! – didn't he notice they were in fact meeting a texture reminiscent of the notebooks that were always offered as prizes by the *Reader's Digest*, those abject booklets bound in 'luxurious' Kidron or Skivertex?

This is a dream that crumbles at first touch. It dies under the fingers.

In real life Dad's financial dealings were unsteady. After Black Monday in 1987 he asked if I could lend him some money. He had come unstuck with futures – now futures had come home to roost and were sharpening their claws on the present. He seemed only slightly embarrassed about it. No more than if he had run out of stamps, and needed to catch the post.

In fact it was a good time for him to ask for money, probably the only time in my life I could have helped, since I had a regular income from the *Independent* without yet having saddled myself with a mortgage. Even so it felt more like a test of loyalty (would I pass him by on the other side?) than a case of real need on his part. How could my few thousand stave off bankruptcy? – which was what he seemed to be saying. But I stumped up and he got his affairs in order, paying me back inside a year.

We had a family joke about Dad and his reverse financial acumen, wondering what would happen if he ever invested in Krugerrands. Would his fellow benchers be making panicky calls to their brokers from the Senior Combination Room, falling over each other in their rush to get out of what had for so long been a watchword for safe investment, now that it was clearly marked for destruction?

When I say 'family' joke, I mean only the surly confederacy of sons. We didn't include Sheila in jokes about Dad's reliable unreliability in money matters. She had to manage its consequences in earnest. Her judgement was better than his, just as her purely intellectual powers were greater, but without the confidence required to impose these advantages on others they go for nothing.

Only on the humble level of the chromosome did she have

the power to overrule the man she had married, in the one small department of life where he could accurately be described as recessive. Her crisp brown-eye instruction overruled his tentative blue-eyed suggestion, so that there were no blue-eyed boys in the family, just the blue-eyed man.

She also threw her short sight into the mix. Dad was long-sighted and in later life wore half-moon spectacles of the sort that seem so perfectly designed for incorporation into judicial body language, particularly the sceptical upward glance at counsel over the rims, that no-one would be shocked to learn that they were worn by judges whose vision needed no correcting.

Another easy target for our jokes was Dad's collection of busted bonds – highly decorative certificates conferring rights in abandoned ventures, such as mines and railways, that might in theory be revived and yield a return. (I would love to pretend that one of them was for the New Sombrero Phosphate Co.) In the meantime, framed up, they were attractive examples of nineteenth- and early-twentieth-century engraving. Financial dealings often have an erotic tinge, as witness those sultry, pouting tax havens, and so we decided that 'busted bonds' was as close as Dad would allow himself to get to busty blondes.

After his retirement Dad decided to sell the portfolio of busted bonds he had built up over a decade or more. The bonds tended to be large in format, unmanageable as objects, so he asked my help in taking them to market. He phoned for a taxi and we travelled in high spirits to the address in Regent Street of the dealers who had sold them to him. I think he was expecting grand premises rather than a small office on an upper floor near Hamleys, which turned out to be our destination.

I don't quite know why Dad was expecting a hero's welcome and a large cheque, except for this being the script his temperament always wrote for him. In the end he settled for about a third of what he had paid in the first place. He was crestfallen, naturally, perhaps more about having lost face in front of me than because of the setback itself. Even so he had resilience, and bounced blithely back in a matter of minutes.

If there was pathos in the dreams of wealth of a man who by most standards had done well for himself, it was part of a wider pattern of dissatisfaction in the family. Dad and his brother David didn't exactly feel cheated by each other, but separately they felt that life had cheated them in terms of the distribution of its rewards. The tension between them never came to a rolling boil, hardly even a simmer, but that didn't mean it was inactive. One cooking method described in Jane Grigson's book on fish is to heat a whole salmon in a simple stock (the technical term is court-bouillon) until you see the first bubble, then turn off the flame. There is by then more than enough heat in the fish-kettle to penetrate every fibre, until the flesh is ready to fall off the bones. It was in this fashion that the brothers slowly poached in the court-bouillon of sibling rivalry.

Dad, the older brother, struck out on his own. He went to university, served in the Navy during the War, moved to London and ended up with a title. David wasn't academic and was expected to stay out of uniform, farming being a reserved occupation. There was no need for him to reinvent himself, and the lilt that Dad had scrubbed from his voice was alive in David's.

When their father died, the brothers inherited as many liabilities as assets. My grandfather hadn't troubled the Inland Revenue with paperwork for many years, and the family firm (farming and distributing farm feeds) was in disarray.

David's instinct was to follow the farmer's code (let the Revenue smoke us out if they can) while Dad's decision was to come clean and arrange some sort of repayment plan. This was both morally sound and practical. Dad could claim to have saved the business, but not long afterwards he endangered it all over again. Dad had no real knowledge of farming-related business, but he brought down an expert from London with him to give the enterprise a sort of audit. Perhaps it was a way of exerting some older-brotherly authority.

The firm was earning an annual profit of 5 per cent. The expert observed that it should be making 10. In fact 2 per cent was a respectable figure in that sector and that decade, the 1950s. Dad, though, was impressed by the expert's verdict, and decided he should sell his share of what he was persuaded was a struggling business. His money would do better elsewhere.

David had the choice of buying his brother out, which would dangerously stretch his resources, or to lose control of the company. There was another person with a stake in the business, Eddy Batty, originally a refugee from Liverpool, and between them David and Eddy kept the business afloat.

Not only did the family firm keep its head above water, with one less family member on board, but it prospered remarkably. Soon David was a wealthy man. From then on there was a mild underlying resentment between the brothers, expressing itself in little jibes about status and money. If Dad mentioned going to a royal garden party, David might say, 'Bill, your car's looking a bit shabby. Should I buy you a new one?'

His mismanaged exit from the family business formed no part of Dad's story about himself, and he would certainly have had a version of his own. Presumably David felt that the older brother had been disloyal, risking family prosperity by selling his own stake. Dad had his own reservations about David's success, suspecting that sharp practice had played a part in it.

In particular he seethed when in the 1970s David bought some farms from their aunts Bessie and Minnie for much less than they were worth. According to Dad, Bessie and Minnie had told him, 'David said it would save us trouble if we let his people do the valuation. Always so thoughtful!' He almost choked on his 'whisky sour'. The case of *O'Sullivan and Another v. Management Agency and Music Ltd and Others* was in the future, but his objections were as obvious as if they had been spelled out as a headnote from a reported legal judgment: *Undue Influence – Fiduciary relationship – Sharp Practice within the family clearly constituting Constructive Fraud – Aunts were 'sitting ducks'*.

Bessie and Minnie, by the time I knew them, lived in Colwyn Bay in no great style. They were cultivated, with their piano stool containing the inevitable 'Rustle of Spring' and an arrangement of Delius's 'Cuckoo', but not dazzlingly sophisticated. They had never married and in late life didn't seem anything but strait-laced, but had perhaps been a little friskier in their youth. They had owned the first Hispano-Suiza in North Wales, and took the car to Paris when they travelled there in the 1920s. They were worldly enough to know that as women of means they might be targeted on this expedition by venal and unscrupulous men, and came up with a novel method of keeping out of harm's way. They spoke only Welsh during their visit, reasoning that it was safe to ignore the risk of there being a Welsh-speaking gigolo on the prowl in Paris.

No doubt David was a shrewd businessman and at times even a sharp one, but Dad's mistrust of his brother's probity had a slightly mad side to it. He seemed to think that any cash transaction was suspicious in itself, including the gifts David made to his nephews at Christmas and other occasions – as if a farmer's failure to use a chequebook for every piece of business was proof positive of dishonesty. Uncle David's wallet fell open very easily, and he was always trying to ply us with cigarettes (John Player Specials, not just in packets of twenty but drums of fifty) and Castella cigars. Not being a smoker was regarded as a poor basis for refusal. Dad always considered

David's open-handedness suspicious, though it was a trait the brothers shared. We who benefited from that incontinent wallet didn't see it as defective in any way.

Whatever Dad did with the money from selling his share of the family business, it was unlikely to have prospered. He wasn't good with money, and if this is a heritable characteristic, then he certainly passed it on to me. Money is a cat that will never curl up in my lap, however devotedly I make kissy sounds to attract it.

I have no other technique. In my case, lack of financial sense is straightforward, almost one-dimensional. Dad's was more complex, since he had delusions of flair. He thought that wealth was a dog that would come running if he blew the right whistle, and even if he couldn't hear the summoning blast himself he was confident it would get an answer sooner or later, and then he'd be hard put to keep the muddy paws of riches off his suit. Judges are not poorly paid, but it's a free country and anyone is allowed to flirt with debt.

Dad reminisced mistily about the far-off days when judges were paid huge sums as a matter of public policy. The idea was to defend justice by making its administrators so wealthy that no-one could afford to bribe them.

Dad would never have thought of himself as a gambler, and everyone agrees 'speculator' has a rather nicer sound. In fact he did gamble in a homely way, putting moderate sums on horses and feeding one-armed bandits in the hope of making them sick. It was only with the horses that he had any sort of form, racking up some decent wins and no significant losses. When we sons were below drinking age he would treat us, on an Anglesey Sunday, to a trip to the Plas Club, where there was a slot machine. He would stake us to a few sixpences, but though a jackpot would have transformed our finances rather more than his the gambling fever didn't take with us. Dad was the one who always wanted one more pull, and his ears would strain as we were driving off to catch the crash of the jackpot that was rightfully his. A club was also the only place he could legally get a drink on a Sunday in a dry county, but I don't think that was the strongest attraction.

There was never an actual break-up with the Llansannan side of the family. David had provided some of the money to buy the Anglesey house in 1960, for instance. Naturally he was entitled to stay there himself, though as time went by Dad began to suspect him of offering use of the house (far from luxurious, but right on the beach) as a sweetener in some of the business relationships that seemed to him so deeply suspect.

It didn't help that David was a mason. Their father had been strongly opposed to freemasonry, and Dad saw his joining a lodge as an opportunistic move and a betrayal of family principle. David for his part thought that Dad didn't know how business was done in the country. He wasn't necessarily wrong about that, to judge by the expert-auditor-from-London fiasco. Perhaps David felt that a self-righteous insistence on going it alone had done their father harm. If the old boy had chosen to be *on the square* himself, then he could have come through his financial difficulties more smoothly. Freemasonry wasn't a nest of devils but a harmless social network, no more sinister than the Garrick Club.

Even now I don't feel comfortable aligning membership of the Garrick with freemasonry, even though it's perfectly obvious that Dad felt at least as much for the poached-salmon-and-avocado stripes of the club tie as any mason feels for the apron and compasses, or the mystic pressure that blossoms inside a routine handshake.

There were little rituals remaining between the brothers and their families. A turkey or goose raised on one of David's farms would be put on the train from Denbigh as a Red Star parcel, to arrive at Euston in time for Christmas or Easter. Then one year the parcel turned out to be a bit whiffy, and after that the custom lapsed, having lost its justification (immaculate bird) and its ability to regulate family tension.

The first-born seems to have all the advantages, but it doesn't need to be so. There was a Jenny Mars some generations back in the family tree, and David had been given 'Mars' as his middle name. In his case it was natural and organic rather than something surgically implanted by deed poll, even if it wasn't technically part of his surname. There was no reason why David shouldn't add it in hyphenated form to the name of the family firm. It certainly lent a bit of class and memorability to the side of a lorry.

Still, when in the 1980s David's daughter Jenny was getting married, the printed invitations included the hyphen for the whole Llansannan branch of the family. Dad wouldn't have minded that, except that the invitation sent to the London branch omitted ours. This gave the impression of a calculated snub, since family names are so deeply rooted in the brain, not subject to the ordinary erosions. But why would David want to snub him, at the same time as asking him to make a speech at the reception? Sheila advised him to hold his horses and say nothing. With an effort, he did.

His speech at the reception, held at the Hotel Seventy Degrees, Colwyn Bay, went down well. Of course public speaking is what barristers and judges do for a living, and it's no more surprising that they should perform satisfactorily in social space than it is for the schoolchild's dad who happens to be a professional cricketer to make a creditable showing at the Fathers' Day match. Dad's approach to the art of the after-dinner speech was an odd combination of the slapdash and the scrupulous. He would often not know what he was going to say when the meal began, and would make notes on the menu as it progressed, but after the event he would make a record of what jokes he had told on what occasion, so as to avoid repeating himself if he was asked back after a great success.

I studied his method of preparation for Jenny's wedding. Five minutes riffling through the entries on Love and Marriage in his dictionary of quotations became a robust quarter-hour of jovial showmanship. Any hyphen-based tension between the brothers melted away in the glow of his performance.

It wasn't long before David's second daughter, Eleri, got married in her turn. Again Dad was asked to speak, and again the invitation suppressed our rightful hyphen and paraded the impostor. This time there would be no holding of horses, and Dad would not be reined in. I remember Sheila hovering in the background while he made the phone call to his brother, willing him to a moderate statement of grievance. He didn't do badly, saying he would be happy to speak at Eleri's wedding reception, but only if a new invitation was issued with his name correctly spelled. David tried some conciliation of an inflammatory sort by saying, 'It's a very small thing to get so worked up about, Bill,' and Dad said, 'Then you will oblige me in this small matter.'

A hyphen is indeed a small thing, but if David had really thought so his usage would have been less consistent. He was certainly making a point of some sort. Hyphens weren't rationed. There was no originary hyphen, primal platinum ingot of nominal linkage, kept in a vault somewhere (like the ur-kilogram), protected by the sort of double-key protocol devised for keeping nuclear weapons in safe hands.

The hyphen is the Janus mark, precisely that sign which both joins and separates. Undergraduates of my generation learned to produce emptily suggestive sentences like that by reflex, as we moved into French weather in terms of literary theory and criticism. Such formulas are more fertile in the realm of psychology, where this way of thinking started and where perhaps it should have stayed. *Families are divided by the things they have in common*. That one might actually be true.

The tug-of-war over the hyphen symbolized an enduring tension. Dad wanted cash and David craved honours. Early on in my first year at Cambridge I met someone at a party who recognized my name and asked if I had any odd relatives in North Wales. I couldn't categorically deny it, though I had never thought of David and family as odd. It turned out that this fellow student had been holidaying with his family in Colwyn Bay and taking a stroll through the town when they were approached by a jovial man who offered to show them round. This was David during his term as mayor of Colwyn Bay, volunteering his services as tour guide. He offered to change into his robes and regalia, complete with chain of office, if they were wanting to take photographs. He kept them in the back of the car, the municipal equivalent of a superhero costume, so they were ready to hand when duty called.

Dad had all the advantages in terms of ceremonial, with galas of pageantry like the State Opening of Parliament handed him on a plate. David had to improvise, and to take his photo opportunities where he could find them.

Neither brother had a healthy style of life, though David reached his physical limits first. He had heart troubles in his early seventies. While he was convalescing after an operation, his wife, Dilys, or the children if they had charge of him, would leave him in the car while they ran errands, with strict instructions not to move. When they returned to the car, he had usually disappeared, but all they had to do was find the nearest pub and then pluck the glass from one hand, ease the cigarillo from between the fingers of the other.

He died in 1992. Naturally we attended the funeral, and I think we were all concerned about how Dad would take the death of his only close relative, not just brother but younger brother. We travelled by train. Dad's mobility was already poor. I remember we had to change trains at Chester, and that Dad made use of the lift when we transferred between platforms.

At the reception after the funeral, he gravitated towards the room where small children were watching videos. There he became entirely absorbed by the adventures of Pingu, a penguin animated by stop-motion whose tribe all spoke a delightful Scandinavian-inflected gibberish. Dad became convinced this was Welsh, and that he understood every word. Often he made such statements half-seriously, then defended them in a spirit of fun, but play-acting seemed unlikely on such an occasion, and his move away from adult company was slightly worrying in itself.

We ate in the restaurant car on the train back to London. As he took the first sip of his drink, Dad said, 'This is the first time I've enjoyed myself all day.' As if the whole idea of a family funeral was to put a spring in your step. There were times when his positivity seemed another name for disconnection.

The standard Welsh attitude to death is the subject of a joke I have heard told by Rob Brydon, though I expect versions of it go back to the era of the *Mabinogion*.

Rhys Pugh is dying. Dying. His little old head lies sunken in the pillow, as if it had been dropped there from a height. Won't eat, won't drink, barely remembers to breathe. Day after day his wife, Bronwen, holds his scrawny hand, brushes his scanty hair. Day by day he sinks. Then one day he says, in his little cracked voice, 'Bron-wen?'

'Yes, Rhys?'

'I feel a bit better today. I could eat a bit of sal-mon.'

Well, Bronwen is made up. Delighted. She scampers to the kitchen and gets busy with the pots and pans that have seen so little use of late. Minutes later she brings a bowl, faintly steaming, to Rhys Pugh's bedside. She raises him from the pillow of his sickness, cradles him tenderly in the crook of her arm. She lowers a spoonful into his mouth. He mumbles it for a few seconds, raking it back and forward with the stiff blade of his saurian tongue. Then a look of bewilderment and distress settles on his superannuated peasant features. 'Bron-wen?' he asks with a tremble in his voice.

'Yes, Rhys?'

'Bron-wen, I asked for sal-mon. This is not sal-mon. This is tu-na.'

'Well, the thing is, my love,' says Bronwen, 'I was saving the sal-mon for the funeral.'

That's one account of the national character, by which the Welsh are perfectly at home with death. It's life that makes them uncomfortable.

Dad wasn't like that. His way of being Welsh was very different. If there's a spectrum of Celtic moods then he tended towards its volatile end. Though he saw himself as rock-solid in the consistency of his principles, you could never quite tell how he would react to anything. The mixture of gravitas and unpredictability made him a remarkable courtroom animal, but it was less of a winning formula in the domestic settings of kitchen or sitting-room.

This was something I had to try to anticipate when I realized, in the late 1970s, that I would have to inform Dad that I belonged to the category he hated and feared. Yes, the moment of coming out, cardinal rite of passage in gay life, though of course the term 'rite of passage' can cover anything from bar mitzvah to *auto-da-fe*.

I had already told Sheila (before I called her anything but

Mum), not making a very good job of it. Rose-tinted spectacles is the rule when looking back at the past, though pink cataracts might be the more accurate expression, since spectacles can be taken off. Researchers have found ways of correlating people's wishful impressions with hard data, checking the age at which children learned to walk or talk (as recorded by healthcare authorities) against parental boasts of precociousness, or establishing the true amount given to charity over a given period as opposed to the inflated claims. So if I'm convinced that I played my coming-out scene to my mother in a key of sickly self-pity, then the reality was surely worse. Did I compare my sexual orientation with her road accident of a few years before, as something that had to be dealt with in all its damage rather than wished away? I'm afraid that I did. As the years went by she must have been surprised to realize that my life contained both fun and meaning, intimacy and a moderate level of self-respect, but then so was I.

It was strangely hard, talking to Sheila, to take the robustly defiant party line in the face of a reaction that contained no criticism. An instant response of sorrowing sympathy gave me emotional cues that I wasn't able to overrule.

Between us, though, we laid to rest the rather tepid fantasy of my heterosexual future, in which I would be an academic living in a big house outside Cambridge with a grand piano and a family. In this wishful prospect the piano seemed more solid than the shadowy children and a wife who was hardly even a shadow. The whole fantasy depended on the proposition that an academic was a sort of vibrant neuter, and professor the apotheosis of eunuch. The family idea derived from my fondness for children, which was real but didn't necessarily indicate a baby-making fire in my loins. I was on easier terms with people significantly older or younger than me. Until I had learned how to have a sex life, so as to be able to approach men with the possibility of desire and women without the possibility of misunderstanding, it was people more or less my own age who presented the problems.

Finally Mum asked the question mothers nerve themselves to ask: Would this life make me happy? I said that it would, but I couldn't avoid a vocal wobble and an implication of martyrdom.

The role of martyr was one that I adopted early and relinquished late. I can blame the family dynamic for that, if I put in enough work. Tim was only twenty months old when I was born, and as I grew steadily more eager to grasp he didn't automatically become more eager to loosen his grip on what he held. Sharing anything was an artificial and imposed piece of behaviour. It wasn't likely to survive the withdrawal of parental oversight. Sensibly Tim would snatch the disputed object back. In these circumstances, lacking the physical resources to grab and keep what I wanted, I learned to pretend not to want it, to play the role of the sort of self-sacrificing person who gives things up willingly, in the interests of a larger harmony. It was true that I still didn't get what I wanted but I had the great joy of knowing that Mama (her earliest name) was pleased with me for being such a good boy.

None of this creaking character armour would be in play, luckily, when I confronted Dad with what he least wanted to hear.

It was a big scene in the making, and that was just what I didn't want made. Dad's thespian side was strongly developed, mine nipped in the bud for that very reason. To some extent over the years I had observed Dad's behaviour and learned to modify its excesses. It was sometimes possible to resist the theatricalization that was Dad's normal response to crisis, to de-dramatize conflict. For instance, if he ordered the three of us out of the house during Christmas lunch after some blow-up at table, a certain amount of de-escalation could be managed as long as we stayed put.

The inventive act was not to push back your chair and throw down your napkin but to peel a tangerine or to reach for the nutcracker, to wait a while and then ask Dad why he was so fond of Kentish cobnuts when they were so fiddly, so hard to get out of their shells.

Breaking off the conversation marooned us in our roles. Refusing the script as he wrote it would guarantee at the least a new configuration of conflict, and might lead to novelties all round.

What I needed to do, on the brink of my rite of passage, was to shape the event so as to bring something small and truthful out of Dad, taking him away from reflexes and set attitudes. I needed to change the character of his performance by restricting its size, as if I was Peter Brook called upon to direct Orson Welles or Donald Wolfit (if anyone remembers that name) in some warhorse of the repertory.

The obvious priority was getting rid of any possibility of an audience. If it was just the two of us there would be more prospect of my being able to damp down his reactions. There was a less selfish aspect, too. Dad wouldn't have to consider putting on a show of consistency with his previously expressed attitudes, for the benefit of anyone else.

I would need Dad to myself for several days, which by this stage in the evolution of family life wasn't a natural state of affairs. The tail end of the Christmas holiday in Anglesey offered the obvious opportunity. It wasn't difficult to persuade my brothers to be reunited with their girlfriends rather than remain fused to the family group. My mother agreed to head back to London early. I don't remember what pretext we gave for this piece of behaviour, which could legitimately have struck Dad as odd if he had been in a mood to suspect any sort of ambush. Accomplished lying isn't much of a family characteristic, though it's hard to be quite sure, since it's the other sort that gets found out.

I strongly suggested to Mum (she wasn't 'Sheila' then) that she didn't answer the phone on New Year's Eve. This was a sensible precaution, since I was trying to release Dad's rage and sorrow in a controlled explosion, far away from other people. I wanted to minimize the possibility of collateral damage.

Dad's reflex and survival instinct was not to absorb unwelcome information and emotional disturbance but to re-export it immediately in a new direction. He would start a fight externally in preference to experiencing his own conflicts. How glib that sounds! And psychobabble had barely been invented in those days. But I knew that left to himself, he would pick up the phone, ventilate some anger in Mum's direction (you let them walk all over you, and this is what happens!) and then feel much better, leaving her struggling to recover the shreds of her poise.

There was already an interpretation of family history in place, available to Dad in times of crisis, according to which he had stuck to principle and refused to 'buy his sons' love', while she had capitulated at every stage and never made a stand against permissiveness. This wasn't always the way he saw things, but it was the version of events that emerged under stress.

Even at the time I understood that this cover story was a result of pained disappointment not just in his sons but in himself. Not only were we turning out very different from the go-getting brood he had so confidently anticipated, but he had somehow managed to reproduce the atmosphere of his own young manhood, with a father-figure reluctantly obeyed but not much liked. He had wanted to be our friend, and to break the pattern, but had no idea how to realize this new approach to family. Much easier to blame Mum for her tenderness than acknowledge that his own, proudly disguised, had been ignored.

Mum in her moods of frustration sometimes said she felt like 'kicking hell out of a dwarf', not in reality revealing an impulse towards discriminatory abuse but conveying that she felt like the final recipient of a long line of tensions passed on in distorted form, and wished she could discharge them in her turn to someone with even less status. When she wasn't able to be Dad's comforter and strong support she was likely to be cast in the more oppressive role of scapegoat-in-waiting.

This pattern was available, hallowed by use, and it wasn't likely that Dad, under great emotional pressure, would fail to blame her in the case of a warping for which mothers are traditionally held responsible. When sons turn out not to be the marrying kind, fathers can play *cherchez la femme* with a vengeance.

So I recommended to Mum that she phone relatively early in the evening to exchange New Year messages, and not answer the phone after, say, ten o'clock. This was a married couple who spoke on the phone every day when separated, though they had no special ritual for the end of the year. They hadn't needed one – I imagine this was the first New Year's Eve they had spent apart since 1947. There's a risk of overplaying the psychodrama here, and portraying myself as the son who seeks to divide his parents so as to have his mother all to himself (as in accounts of 'The Psychology of The Homosexual', orthodox though very *passé*), but I admit that I didn't hesitate to impede a ritual communication that was likely to turn nasty under the special circumstances prevailing.

New Year's Eve is a good time for a family confrontation

since there's never anything worth watching on television, and if you're very lucky alcoholic bonhomie will carry the day.

The deadline was midnight. I wanted 1977 to be the last year I saw a hypocrite's face in the mirror, and there were only minutes left of it. I ushered in the new era of frankness by turning off the television and topping up Dad's wine glass. The era of the 'whisky sour' was over – he had been told when diagnosed with his stomach ulcer that he must give up spirits. Then at last it was time for 'Dad . . . There's something I need to tell you.'

That's the formula for this ceremonial event, though perhaps I should give myself the benefit of the doubt and say that I introduced some slight variation – 'There's something you need to know', or something of the sort. There's not a lot of room available for improvisation. The coming-out speech is a relatively unvarying form because the event has only two parts, a clearing of the throat to demand attention (hear ye! hear ye!) and then a simple phrase that can't be taken back (I'm gay). After that, as it seems to the person making the declaration, the fixed points disappear. All clocks return to zero hour and the speakers have new voices issued to them, voices that stray so far from any previous conversation that they might as well be talking in tongues. They might say anything at all.

The details of that evening are a blur, not just because it was a long time ago but because it was a blur at the time. I was in shock. Dad was in shock, of course, but I was in shock too, from having administered one and also from the fact of having kept my nerve. Samson had pulled down the temple and the masonry had bounced off him as if it was no more than blocks of expanded polystyrene. Patriarchal authority, as it turned out, was balsawood under the mahogany veneer. It wouldn't crush me just yet.

That first night Dad was stricken but not rejecting. When we finally went to bed he said everything would be all right. There was no hug but then he wasn't a hugger. There was no sense of a hug withheld. His wish of 'Happy New Year', returning mine, was subdued but seemed sincere, bearing no trace of satirical aggression, no suggestion that I'd already blighted the twelvemonth to come.

Dad didn't much go in for New Year's resolutions, left to himself. If pressed on such occasions, he would say his resolution was to drink more champagne. Franker exchanges with his sons were not something he wished for as such.

I was buffeted by strong currents of vertigo and anticlimax. Tim had described the confrontation in the making as me 'holding a sex pistol to Dad's head' (punk rock had detonated only recently) but I had pulled the trigger and so far there were no casualties. I had made an existential leap, but maybe it was a leap into the void *à la* Gloucester in *King Lear*, and over a cliff-edge that existed only in my head. When at last I could pull air back into my flattened lungs, I was all too obviously the same person as I had been before. Less was changed than fear had promised.

Everything would be all right. During the night Dad had second thoughts about this. Under the first impact of the news his concern had been to reassure me, but overnight he had looked at things from other points of view and revised his conclusions.

He brought me tea, an indication in itself that he had slept badly, or at least woken early. He had his pipe between his teeth, an ex-smoker's stratagem to ward off oral craving. According to Mum he ground his teeth in his sleep, and if he was going to be grinding them during the day it made sense to erode a replaceable object rather than the fretting mechanism itself. In the same way it's sensible to introduce a pencil between the jaws of an epileptic in spasm. It may be that at this point Dad was torn between the dangers of speaking his mind and the pain of biting his tongue. Overnight he had come up with a number of arguments to prove me wrong. He would argue every step of the way, he would (as lawyers say) 'put it to me' that I was mistaken about what I thought I was and wanted.

In normal life Dad didn't do self-catering. He would indicate his needs by saying, 'I wouldn't mind a cup of tea, if you're making one,' which sometimes made me seethe with its omission of the word 'please' – why had I been encouraged to take manners so seriously as a child when it turned out they were optional? Now he was playing an unaccustomed role by bringing me tea, though he sent a signal, by leaving the bag in the mug, that there were limits to mollycoddling.

As a general thing, the mollycoddling went the other way. Some household tasks would be evenly divided, true. He would attend to the kitchen range and I would clean out the grate and lay a new fire in the sitting-room. But if food was going to pass Dad's lips it would be me preparing it. At some stage I hoped that Dad would see the irony of warning me against unmasculine behaviour while expecting me to cook and serve his meals. He liked to be waited on, even in small matters like the clicking of tiny saccharine pellets from a dispenser into his tea.

He could muster a reasonable family meal out of tins in an emergency. The menu would start with Baxter's Royal Game soup, a splendid brown concoction, and move on to a Fray Bentos steak and kidney pie, actually baked in the shallow circular tin with its appealing, steeply sloped sides, a regular solid easy to describe: a truncated cone, with the missing apex pointing downward. Concentric grooves pressed in the lid left marks on the pale wet surface of the pastry-to-be. Dad's only creative touch was to anoint the surface with milk, before putting it in the oven, to enhance the crust. Frozen peas to round off the main course, tinned fruit to follow.

When Mum was put out of action by an accident in 1973, Dad bought a Penguin book by Desmond Briggs called *Entertaining Single-Handed* and briefly raised his game in the kitchen. One simple but spectacular pud was Briggs's Hot Jamaican Fruit Salad, made with tinned fruit (pears a particular success) and fresh banana further sweetened with brown sugar, then splashed with rum. How did people's teeth not explode at the impact of so much sugar? Perhaps they did, and dentists rubbed their hands in glee. Briggs suggested putting the dish in a hot oven when you served the main course, so that the potent Caribbean fumes gradually seduced your guests' senses.

Since that time, Dad had reverted to type. He had relapsed into the proper helplessness. Desmond Briggs gathered dust on the shelf, and his knowledge of kitchen geography reverted to a masculine blank.

In any case kitchen tasks performed during our sexuality summit would drain energy required for the preparation of his case. This was a judge after all, and the case was only closed when he said so. Our few days together turned into a courtroom drama rather than a soap opera, a long cross-examination broken by domestic routines. An actual day in court would be interrupted by lunch, possibly by a conference in chambers. This more free-wheeling inquisition was interrupted by me making Dad coffee or an omelette, maybe pork chops with gravy and carrots.

To an extent he treated me as a hostile witness whose testimony he was determined to discredit, which didn't necessarily make him aggressive since undisguised aggression is a very limited courtroom tactic. His manner was sometimes almost seductive, and he knew the effectiveness of seeming to agree with the opposing arguments from time to time. But there was also a sense that I was his client, someone to be got off the hook however strong the evidence against him, however stubbornly he incriminated himself. He had campaigned hard over an unsatisfactory grade at Ancient History A-level – he would do a lot more to get my failing papers in heterosexuality sent back for re-marking.

I hadn't made the mistake of trying to soften the blow. It would have been fatal to say for instance 'I think I might be gay', a formula which with its hint of doubt would turn anyone into a lawyer quibbling about exactly what was meant. Dad was in no hurry to accept my verdict on myself, even without equivocation on my part.

One of the first things he said on that New Year's Day was that my situation was anything but unusual, and I should be initiated into the joys of natural love by an older woman, or by older women plural. This was the first indication he had given that the sexual code he preached, with its embargo on exploration of any sort, admitted any flexibility. He assured me, though, that the older-woman procedure had done the trick for Prince Charles, though several courses of treatment had been needed to make sure the cure was fully rooted.

Dad had met Prince Charles and liked him, dutiful Welsh small talk and all. Both parents had attended his investiture in 1969, travelling on the special train laid on for the event, and buying the scarlet bentwood chairs, designed by Lord Snowdon, on which they had been seated while the Prince received his insignia, coronet, mantle, sword, gold ring and gold rod. In fact they had bought an extra chair, to match the number of their sons, prudently forestalling any future squabble over heirlooms.

It seemed extraordinary to me that Dad should at short notice turn the heir to the throne into a latent but finally triumphing heterosexual. According to Dad Prince Charles had lain back and thought of Wales, and I should follow his example. Of course it wasn't news that Dad had a tendency to tailor reality to the demands of fantasy. Keeping fantasy in check may have been one of the things that a life in the law did for him, by requiring him to finesse the facts rather than setting them aside. If I had suggested any ambiguity about Prince Charles's sexuality before New Year's Day 1978, Dad would have been outraged.

That was his first gambit, the Princely Parallel. There were others over the next few days, the Auntly Ambush, the Bisexual Fork, the Bisset Surprise.

Auntly Ambush. Dad asked me to find his address book and look up his Aunty Mary's phone number. I was surprised by this sociable impulse. Were we planning family visits? It hardly seemed the time for that, the air being so strongly charged with tension.

Aunty Mary, widowed since the 1950s, lived in Denbigh. It was true that we sometimes saw her over the Christmas holidays. She made mince pies, and had a little superstition about them. Each mince pie eaten between Christmas Eve and New Year's Day guaranteed a lucky month, so it was necessary to get through a dozen to be fully protected, and each mince pie must be paid for with a kiss. Those kisses of hers, bristling and oddly intent, put me off facial hair for a while.

I asked Dad why he wanted to speak to Aunty Mary. 'I don't,' he said. 'You'll be doing the talking. Don't you think you should tell her what you've told me? She's family, isn't she? She has a right to know.' He started to dial the number, confident that I wouldn't let him finish the process and make the connection.

I went over to him and pressed down on the prongs of the

phone, cutting off the call, and stayed there to prevent him from making another attempt. Dad's Orson Welles side couldn't be kept in check indefinitely. He got quite a lot of mileage out of using the telephone as a prop in our family theatricals.

According to his script, if I had a duty to tell him about my sexuality (this was how I had described my situation), then likewise I must inform the rest of the family, directly. He had chosen Aunty Mary as the most rhetorically effective figure for this line of argument, someone so far removed by age and long-standing widowhood from the urges of the body that I would have to explain basic acts from scratch, pouring unwelcome information into the scandalized funnel of her Welsh-county-town-dwelling, Congregationalist-sermon-saturated ear. I explained that there was no need to explain myself to Aunty Mary because she wasn't part of my life, while Dad was. This was true in its way, but perhaps he was noticing something else. I might be telling him how important a figure he was in my life, but I was also willing to risk being rejected, which suggested that I could get along without his approval – so how important was he really? If the family divided into two parts, widowed great-aunts kept in the dark about private perversions, and powerless patriarchs presented with deviant lifestyles as facts they had to adjust to, then perhaps Dad had ended up on the wrong wing.

On 31 December when Dad had tried phoning Mum she had followed my advice and let it ring. After that, they spoke every day, as was their habit, usually last thing at night. These conversations were largely ritualized, and amounted essentially to billing and cooing, or Bill-ing and Sheila-ing perhaps. They seemed to feel the need for an exchange of endearments before bed when they were separated, as of course they often were with Dad on circuit. On occasions when I would be present at Mum's side of the conversation, I noticed the slight technical difficulties she had with making a proper kissing sound, since after her accident in 1973 medication tended to make her lips dry.

Now of course those phone calls had an extra layer of meaning to them. The Anglesey house wasn't big, and though there was an extension in the master bedroom I inhibited telephone intimacy whether I wanted to or not. Usually Dad spoke on the sitting-room phone, without seeking privacy. I imagine Mum had asked lightly, 'How are you two getting on?', for Dad to answer with an undertone of weary irony, as he did, 'We're having some very interesting discussions. He's full of surprises.'

Over the days of wrangling I hoped that Dad would at some point acknowledge that in my own way I was standing up to him, something that dominant personalities are said to admire, though not all the evidence points that way.

Bisexual Fork. One day Dad's rhetoric took a startling new tack. 'You're right, Adam,' he said. 'My generation was brought up with a very simple sense of these things. When I say I'm heterosexual, I only mean that all my past experience has been with women. There's nothing to stop me from being attracted to a man tomorrow. Wouldn't you agree?'

This was so different from his normal patterns of thought and speech that I was stupefied. Was the sly old thespian going to spring a *coup de théâtre* on me, revealing that he and his rather mousy clerk Mr Cant had been an item – lo, these many years! – that he hadn't known how to tell me and was relieved to have someone to confide in at last?

Not quite. I hesitated.

'Don't you agree?'

There seemed no way out of it. 'I suppose so . . .'

'And by the same token, when you say you are homosexual,

all you mean is that your experience to date has been homo-sexual.' He pronounced the word, as was the way with his generation, with a long first syllable – even with the sounds we produced we showed we were talking about different things. 'And just as I could have desires for a man, there's nothing to stop you having desires for a woman tomorrow, isn't that so?' And we were back in Prince Charles territory, contemplating his experiments in self-cure by rutting.

The Bisset Surprise followed directly on the Bisexual Fork. Dad told me that he knew for a fact that I responded sexually to women. His evidence for this was that when we had been watching a Truffaut film in the cinema, *Day for Night*, I had played with myself whenever Jacqueline Bisset was on the screen.

I remembered that evening, which must have been in 1972. I had seen the film already and loved it, and thought it had more than enough charm and humour to qualify as a good choice for a family outing to the cinema. The evening was not a success, I understood that. Dad was seething in some way, though it took a lot of questioning to bring his objections to light. It turned out he had thought the film obscene. Obscene? If anything I thought it was a bit timid, a bit safe. Where was the obscenity? In a gesture made by one of the actresses, looking down at her actor boyfriend as he went off to the studio in the morning. He blew her a kiss, and she made a gesture of crossing her hands demurely below her waist, to signify 'This is all yours. Yours and no-one else's.'

This gesture, according to Dad, was of a corrosive and contaminating obscenity, tainting the whole film. He gave me to understand that I had subjected the party to a measurable dose of corruption by setting up our little visit to Studio One on Oxford Street.

Now, though, he was asking me to believe that I had laid aroused hands on myself during the film, and that he hadn't made a comment at the time. *Adam, old chap, we all get carried away when there's a lovely lady on the screen – can't fault your taste, my boy, she's the most delightful creature – but next time be a bit more discreet, eh? You might give your mother a turn.* An unthinkable scenario. Of course he wasn't asking me to believe anything of the sort, he was asking himself to believe it. He was falling short of the standards of his profession, planting evidence in his own memory to substantiate something he needed to be true. He was tampering with the scene, as if he was one of those bent coppers he was known for hammering.

'Dad . . . do you really think something like that could happen? With Mum sitting next to me and you saying nothing?'

Stiffly, troubled, he said, 'That's what I remember.' Perhaps thinking he had revealed more of his own admiration for the sublime Bisset than was really necessary.

It made sense that the surprises shouldn't only be on one side. I had another one myself that I was keeping in reserve, not knowing when would be the best time to disclose it. I was in a relationship. I realized that this would in itself be bad news from Dad's point of view. Me being in a relationship would make it harder for him to maintain that I was going through some sort of phase. Naturally that was why I wanted him to know, so that he could stop clinging to invented doubts and accept my life as it was – as it was and as it was going to be. At the same time, it seemed obvious that any partner of mine would come in for an extreme intensity of scrutiny, exceeding anything that would be appropriate for high-level military security or access to international secrets. No character, however exemplary, would wring from my father an assent that would cost him so much. In fact anything that made my lover seem likeable, decent, solid, automatically became suspect and intolerable for that very reason. Under the eyes of such a judging committee, Prince Charles himself might have struggled to score a clear round.

His name was Mike Larson, an American student of architecture attached to (Gonville and) Caius College, though like every other student he had quickly learned to use the short form of its name and to pronounce it *Keys*. In those days, lacking clairvoyance, my friends and I would sit around in earnest shock discussing the oppressive madness of the American educational system, thanks to which Mike would finish his education thirty thousand dollars in debt. My generation had inherited a fear of debt from the previous one, though the arrival of credit cards in a few years' time would sweep it away.

Mike was unhysterical about his financial future. If a great architect like Louis Kahn could die deeply in debt, who was he to be solvent?

Mike was in his early thirties, nearly ten years older than me, and had a background both provincial and cosmopolitan. His home town was Watsonville, California, which I seem to remember him describing as the artichoke capital of America, but this was either a pious fib or else a title that has since been snatched by Castroville. He had joined the Marines at eighteen and fought in Vietnam, though this was relatively early in the war. The film shown on board ship the night before his platoon landed was *Dr Strangelove*. The crew, who wouldn't be going ashore, laughed less anxiously than the Marines, who would. His experience of combat was strongly charged with emotion. Love was part of that experience, though never described as such by the parties involved. Someone important to him was turned into a red mist under mortar fire. I think the name was Dennis Kovacs. Away from Vietnam, Mike was baffled that his old buddies seemed to dissociate themselves so easily from that fellowship of fear and intimacy.

Afterwards he had studied at Harvard, where the climate was uncongenial to a native Californian and (as he said) 'it snowed . . . *on my body.*' I think it was at Harvard that he learned the word 'charrette', meaning a last-minute burst (usually involving sleepless nights) to finish a piece of work. The phrase derives from the École des Beaux Arts in Paris, where the charrette was a little wagon pulled through a classroom at the last minute to be filled with students' submissions. Anyone who failed to get his work in the cart didn't get marked, and plenty were working up to the last minute, virtually sitting in the cart to add the final touches.

Then he moved back to San Francisco. Mike had spent plenty of time in a metropolitan sexual culture, and it can't have occurred to him, as he checked out a meeting at a pub on Rose Crescent, still jet-lagged, that he was more or less exhausting the gay scene in Cambridge with a single swig of warm beer. If it wasn't the A to Z of gay life in the town it was certainly the A to E. I don't imagine that he would have hooked up with me, which he did not quite on a whim but more out of curiosity and good nature than anything else, if he had known it would be hard to avoid me thereafter without rudeness, in such a small world.

Was he good-looking? I think so, though he wasn't so fiercely beautiful that I couldn't make the first move. He had a slight stammer that prevented him from being intimidating. When a word wouldn't come his head bobbed up and down. Did he look like a film star? Not quite, though if he had a vague likeness to anyone in that category it would have to be Harrison Ford, clean-cut and a little grumpy.

He had a trick of starting a sentence with 'You see . . .', but dropping the first word, so that a mild presentation of opinion became insistent, even abrasive, without him seeming to notice. 'It turns out' (or 'Turns out . . .') was another typical opening, slightly less dogmatic.

He spent the night in my tiny room on Trinity Street, but

it was hardly big enough for one. Caius had housed him on Grange Road, in a house of American students, something that irritated him since he didn't want to be insulated from the locals. If he'd wanted an American social life he would have stayed in America – though this was one of the few premises with effective central heating. I stayed there once or twice, but mainly we slept in our own beds. Somehow he conned me into being part of his fitness regime, which meant that I would jog over to his place at seven in the morning and then we would run round Grantchester before breakfast. Often he wasn't ready when I arrived (he couldn't be expected to take exercise without the first cigarette of the day) so fairly often I would do the Grantchester circuit on my own. I was slow to realize that Mike's fitness regime, which I took so much more seriously than he did, was in itself a mild Adam-repellent, a shared activity that we didn't do together.

One thing Mike owed to his Marine training was the efficiency of his mornings, and the ability to 'shit, shower and shave' in ten minutes. We would meet later for breakfast in Caius and dawdle over coffee afterwards in a café called, winsomely, the Whim. During the first term of his year in Cambridge Mike hardly attended a lecture, and we spent most of the day together talking. Sometimes in the afternoons he would work out at Fenners on Gresham Road, the University sports facility that included a weight room, though I felt he attended more for the view than the health benefits.

He was a reader, of Isherwood, of Vidal, of John Fowles and Henry James. His copies of *Down There on a Visit* and *Burr* were copiously annotated in his architect's energized small capitals. Only with his signature did he let out a little swooping expressiveness. This script with its implication of load-bearing capacity, compressive strength, was part of his overwhelming difference from anyone I'd met before.

In the evenings we often saw films. It may be that I make the connection with Harrison Ford partly because Mike had seen the first showing of *Star Wars* in San Francisco, unaffected by the gathering storm of hype, and had loved it. He couldn't wait for it to arrive in Cambridge (which took a few months) so he could hear what I made of it. Hmm. Not all that much. It was my first inkling that there was a big-kid side to this travelled, lightly traumatized man. I had seen George Lucas's first film, the rather formalist dystopia *THX 1138*, which I much admired, and then in due course *American Graffiti*, which seemed likeable pap. This was pap again, but glossier and not so likeable.

It was fun to wrangle about our divergent tastes. We had strong opinions and stubbornness in common, though they were expressed in different styles. Scorsese was someone we both admired, though Mike had a mental block about his name (and quite a few others) so that it always came out as 'Sacuzzi'. Mike was the first person I had met who cared about the Oscars and the first to use the phrase 'the economy' in casual conversation.

In architecture, naturally enough, his tastes were adventurous. He admired Peter Eisenman's House VI, with the upside-down staircase formally balancing the functional one, and the obstruction preventing the occupants (the mere clients) from installing a double bed. In fact there were multiple reasons for sleepless nights. House VI bankrupted the couple who commissioned it, so that the boot of debt was on the other foot for once.

Mike also knew every lyric from *A Chorus Line*, but that didn't come high on the list of qualities that would appeal to Dad. Military service to his country, crew cut, combat experience, aspiring professional status – a warm light should be played on these attributes to bring out all their sparkle. Love of show tunes was a different story, to be kept in the dark as much as possible. Easier to imagine Dad and Frank Zappa singing doo-wop on the back step than Dad and Mike duetting on 'One Hand, One Heart' from *West Side Story*.

If Dad knew what part Mike played in my life, a thousand individual blind spots would join up into a single massive refusal to acknowledge his merits. It made sense to introduce the person first and add the label afterwards. A good first impression might stand up to the revision required by his ideology. So I had asked Mike to stay in the Anglesey house earlier in the holiday.

I had no way of judging our viability as a couple, never having been part of one before. I could measure the success of one day against another, but not the vitality of the whole. We didn't seem to be a very vibrant combination, but how was I to know?

Just as his hesitation in speech took the edge off what might otherwise have been an over-insistent manner, so there were little complications in his world view which saved him from dismissing other people's altogether. He was a thoroughgoing atheist, for instance, who had had a mystical experience. It hadn't overturned his assumptions, but he was too honest to pretend it hadn't happened.

It was when he was seventeen, doing farm work one summer. The job involved fetching water from a well, and one day the water in the bucket mysteriously became alive as he carried it. He became aware, gradually at first, then overwhelmingly, of the water in its entangled essence. This was a drug experience without benefit of drugs. It lasted less than a full hour but more than half of one, and all that time he was aware of the water as an activity rather than a substance. He was carrying a bucket of particles in motion. He wasn't just a spectator of the molecular traffic, he was fully involved in its tingle. And after that, he couldn't in all honesty rule out the possibility of a transcendent reality, though he was no keener on the idea than he had been before.

Mike didn't seem to want to touch me or sleep with me, but still there was some strong connection. He told me that if I wanted sex I should just say so. It was no big deal. He used the phrase 'goodnight handshake' for such friendly helping out. He was always telling me that I had a moral backbone, that I was a person of integrity. These rather alienating compliments seemed to confirm that I was someone who would not be asking for a goodnight handshake any time soon.

It made sense that we started from different assumptions. Mike came from a strongly sexualized milieu. At a time when the Castro area of San Francisco was many gay men's spiritual home, it was actually his normal address. He worked out in a 'clothing-optional' gym – a nude gym. His normal place to see films was the Castro Cinema, where straight people fell into the category of tourists, sightseers as much as moviegoers. It was routine for him to start the day at a breakfast place called *Welcome Home*, where the coffee-pot was toted and the order for steak and eggs taken by a slightly sulky cowboy, whose reflex of raunchy backchat was only the local dialect of wait-staff banter worldwide. Mike was either past the stage of wanting a boyfriend, or not yet ready for it.

Our relationship meant different things to us, which usually means that the relationship doesn't actually exist. If two people have divergent ideas about the part they play in each other's lives then they are in two asymmetrical relationships rather than a single one. They overlap in a space they don't share. The axioms of an emotional logic are not held in common.

There was plenty of goodwill involved, though, and I hope Mike didn't regard the responsibility of presenting himself to the family as my partner to be oppressive. There was a Christmas meal planned by his Cambridge housemates, but perhaps he enjoyed having made other connections and being in demand. They might be insular but he was not.

I was helping him out financially, too, till he could get money matters arranged, since at that time it wasn't easy for non-citizens to set up bank accounts. Obviously he was good for his debts, but he may have felt that he was in some way defraying the imaginary interest on my little loans by accepting the role of designated boyfriend in the family drama. A walk-on who might well be booed, but with luck only after he had left the stage. Mike would be back in Cambridge by the time Dad read the small print in the programme ('and introducing Mike Larson as the surprise love interest . . .').

This was the man in my corner when I entered the ring to slug it out with Dad. Positive images and role models, though, didn't really do the trick in his case. When liberal commentators set out to break the link between homosexuality and degradation the laugh was on them, really. The link was too strong in his mind, not to be casually broken. When Penelope Gilliatt, John Schlesinger and Peter Finch (with help from Glenda Jackson, Murray Head and let's not forget Bessie Love as the answering service lady) got together to make *Sunday Bloody Sunday* in 1971, showing how ordinary, not to mention unthreatening and pitiable, the life of a gay doctor in London really was – and this was years after Ronald Waterhouse had tried to tell Dad that he had a bee in his bonnet on precisely this subject – well, really they might just as well not have bothered. Dad missed the point without even trying. He was shocked by the film (as he told me while we were driving round the equestrian statue by Holborn Viaduct) and its sordid load of prejudice. The nastiness he detected lay in the film's suggestion that a Jewish doctor could be a homosexual. This was plain anti-Semitism, as he saw it, possibly also a libel on the standing of the medical profession, though it was the religious slur that preoccupied him.

Well-meaning cultural intervention could not raise the status of homosexuality in his eyes any more than an anvil could take to the air with the help of a few party balloons.

Mike had obvious merits as a house guest, from Mum and Dad's point of view. He didn't stammer noticeably more or less in their company than he did in mine. It was natural to his generation of Americans to address their seniors as 'Sir' and 'Ma'am', forms of speech that would have seemed self-abasing or actively satirical on the lips of their British equivalents.

That suited Dad, who didn't at all mind being truckled to. He was even indulgent towards over-truckling, seeing it as a fault in the right direction, a badge of good-heartedness, not to be penalized. It was under-truckling he didn't care for, any sort of reverence shortfall.

Mum wasn't so certain, since she always suspected deferential manners of insincerity or secret mockery. She seemed to be straining to detect an element of the sardonic in his use of 'Ma'am'. Had this complicated stranger, perhaps slightly too good to be true, mistaken her for the Queen?

Mothers are apt to be sceptical about a son's choice of partner. Perhaps she could see nude gym written all over him.

There were less harmonious aspects to his manner. Mike responded to quite small surprises in conversation with the exclamation 'Jesus!', a mannerism which drew a flinch and a blink from Dad the first time it happened, and a frown whenever it was repeated.

Mum and Dad weren't hopelessly provincial. They knew that if a dinner guest cut his food up methodically, then transferred the fork to his right hand for the purpose of conveying nourishment to his mouth, there was no cause for alarm. These were standard American manners, deeply embodied aspects of culture.

Mike, though, may have been slightly thrown by grace before meals said in Welsh. There was the 'long Welsh grace', itself very short, and the 'short Welsh grace', lasting barely five seconds and in favour when food was late or appetites keen. Mike will have been exposed to strings of exotic sound, timeless Celtic phonemes reaching his eardrums as either '*Dee olch itty, dirion Da, um der dunneer, rothion ra, row innee er wen ai thlon, ara boo-id sith ger-ein bron. Amen*' or else '*Ben deeth yan boo-id, oth yew. Amen*'. The only bits he could reasonably be expected to join in were those 'Amens'.

Family meals could be a bit of a minefield – for all of us – and Mike had the disadvantage of not having been issued with a map. For instance, Tim might choose to steer the conversation towards the subject of punk rock, not just to get Dad's goat but as part of a more multifarious agenda, hinting at the 'sex pistol' primed and ready to fire. He enjoyed setting up a complex conversational turbulence, while I tried to steer the talk towards calmer water, or (in emergencies) bailed the bilges frantically and hid my fear of being swamped by the forces I had set in motion.

There was no hiding from Mike that Anglesey in winter bore no resemblance to California at any season. The Irish Sea was not a marine body double for the Pacific, not even if you half-closed your eyes to help it out. The village of Rhosneigr could boast the Premier Garage and the Bali-Hi Fish Bar but was not twinned with San Francisco. What did we have to offer that the Bay Area couldn't match? Perhaps Barclodiad y Gawres, the ancient monument on the next headland along, towards Aberffraw, a Neolithic burial chamber (technically a cruciform passage grave), if he felt like peering through railings at decorated stones, their zigzags, spirals and chevrons latent in the gloom. The interior was a little more accessible than the holy of holies in Kafka's parable 'Before the Law', being open two whole days a year. (The name means 'apronful of the giantess', though Dad always translated it as 'breadcrumbs' instead — but then he admitted that his Welsh got rusty from his conversing in it so little, and he found it mortifying to make mistakes in the hearing of more eloquent users of his mother tongue.) Or we could walk round the Maelog Lake, at least most of the way round, while Mike huddled incredulous in his windbreaker, until brambles and mud made the going too difficult.

Tim and Mike clashed enjoyably over architecture, playing the game of Lloyd Wright / Le Corbusier / Mies van der Rohe, rituals of ranking that can seem to outsiders so much like rounds of rock-paper-scissors.

Mike used a number of Americanisms that I sensed were already obsolescent, calling things not only 'cute' but 'neat'. It was refreshing, even intoxicating, to be told that, say, 'C-corb' had designed 'a bunch of stuff' that was 'just gorgeous'. It seems a safe bet that Tim, who didn't have many people with whom to discuss architecture, found Mike both stimulating and baffling in his lack of intellectual airs.

Mike's verdict on Tim, meanwhile, was 'I don't know whether to fight him or fuck him', which suggested that the holiday wasn't a complete failure from his point of view.

Mike's word for the men he found attractive was 'Munchkin', though the beings by that name in *The Wizard of Oz* weren't in fact, as I discovered when I saw the film at last, young and beefy. I had imagined a sort of junior league of bodybuilders. In the coffee shops of Cambridge Mike would point out casualties of British self-sabotage, handsome undergraduates hunching in apology for their good looks. America would have encouraged them to revel in their studliness. It wasn't too late, even now, if they played their cards right.

There were some exceptions to his typecasting – the elderly Einstein sticking out his tongue in a famous photograph somehow qualified as a Munchkin – but I certainly wasn't a Munchkin, and Tim didn't come significantly closer to that ideal.

It occurs to me now that Mike, as an admirer of Iris Murdoch's fiction, may have felt that her deepest intuitions about British life were being confirmed in this welcoming environment laced with threat. In theory my father was the target of the machinations – but would Mike really have been surprised if my elegant, quietly anxious mother had entered the guest bedroom one morning bearing not a cup of tea but a samurai sword, like Honor Klein in *A Severed Head* (his favourite Murdoch novel, and his favourite moment in it), to banish all obliqueness of dealing and force a resolution of some kind? Perhaps not.

It made sense of a Murdochian sort, the warrior being offered as a sacrificial victim, exposed to danger and enchantment beyond anything the Viet Cong could devise (though his tour of duty pre-dated the worst of the war) by the shores of a bleak sea.

Even without weaponry, Mum can't have been an entirely relaxing hostess. Part of her concern was to do with whether the two of us were well matched – and if so, whether it even mattered, bearing in mind that Mike was returning in a matter of months to his city and his career, his real life outside the parenthesis of Cambridge. She was also bound to be anticipating the impact on her family of the little piece of psychodrama I had set in motion.

So after I had made my sexual declaration to Dad as best I could (having so little to declare), I told him about Mike. He put on a fair show of neutrality, not exploding at the deceit and immorality involved in smuggling my bit of fluff (a very sturdy bit of fluff, admittedly) into the family home. He played the waiting game, knowing that sooner or later I would have to ask him for his verdict on Mike. I had given him back some power, I suppose, by showing that I cared what he thought.

Eventually he produced his assessment. 'Small beer,' he said.

I felt we were making progress here. Who would have thought that Dad was capable of dismissing the same-sex partner of one of his sons with such a light touch? No reference to the Bible or the vileness of physical acts. It was never on the cards that he would say, 'You two seem to be good together,' and I wouldn't have believed him if he had, since it didn't seem particularly true. But it had to be encouraging that Dad huffed the threat of Mike away like so much thistledown.

As Dad understood homosexuality, there was always an abusive seduction at the root of it. A person of power or glamour cast a spell on an insecure male, then turned fascination into sordid exploitation. In a strange way, the earlier in life this atrocity was perpetrated the better, since then there could be no question of meaningful consent, let alone desire. Ideally, from his point of view, I would have been turned, even sexually assaulted, by a scoutmaster in full make-up. This Vietnam-vet-architect scenario was far less easily rewritten as pathology. Still, if Dad had wanted me to be corrupted over mugs of cocoa round a campfire, he might at least have sent me to Scouts.

Male bonding had hardly begun to work its magic on the culture in those early days of 1978, and a father–son sojourn had an artificial, self-conscious feel even when there were urgent matters of sexual dissidence to be thrashed out. In the aftermath of all those disputes over princes, great-aunts and actresses we were probably both relieved when it was time to go back to London, with a more or less satisfactory deadlock in place. In the car Dad expressed a lowered tension by sucking – then wolfishly crunching – Tunes, his preferred courtroom lozenge and vocal lubricant, rather than the gnawed twin stems of his disused pipe.

It's standard practice when dealing with people implacably opposed to homosexuality to propose that they are themselves in denial. It always seems a cheap manoeuvre, not just cheap but dull, to insist that homophobes are sitting on top of a volcano of disavowed desire. If Dad had a man-loving component it was easily bought off, with male social company (endlessly on tap in Gray's Inn) and the ritual worship given to Welsh rugby players, colossal of thigh.

Dad summed up the whole of homosexual life with the phrase 'wallowing in faeces', and I wonder what made him think in those terms – what made his disgust take that particular form. I'm not saying Dad had more knowledge of anal intercourse than I did, but he can't have had less, since I had none.

With Mike I was embarrassed about my defective sexual experience, almost as embarrassed as I was of never having seen *The Wizard of Oz*. I lived in my body very approximately. Sensuality was one more thing I experienced mainly through books.

My childish body was strangely tuned. I remember soothing myself to sleep (aged four? five?) by playing with my right nipple, an action that transmitted a high feathery tickling to the roof of my mouth, referred pleasure like referred pain, experienced in a different place from where it was generated. This was the high-water mark of my self-awareness before latency dragged me back down into the dark.

As for my awareness of other bodies, I had known from an

early age that I was different from my brothers. This wasn't existential angst but statement of fact. They made wee-wee from a different thing. They did a stream but I did a spray and sometimes I felt sore. My part was different from theirs, looked different, *was* different. (How I made the comparison I don't exactly remember, but bathtime was the obvious opportunity for playing spot-the-difference.) When I was transfixed by an infantile erection aged six or seven I went down on my knees, my plump and dimpled knees, to give thanks to the God who had clearly intervened with a miracle to correct the anomaly, but my willy looked no different afterwards.

Our parents hadn't had a policy about circumcision but asked for professional advice as each son was born. The experts at the Welbeck Nursing Home, where we were all brought into being, gave their opinion. A 'snip' was felt to be necessary for Tim and then for Matthew, but not for me. No thought had been given to the possibility that a cavalier among roundheads (to use a jaunty slang I know only from books) might feel disagreeably set apart.

Technically I was intact while they had been wounded, but being the odd man out has in itself some of the quality of a wound. Then persistent infections of the foreskin showed that medical advice wasn't infallible, and I was circumcised at the age of eight or nine. I got a proper wound of my own, and riding my bicycle was something of a penance for a time. Memory tells me that it was actually a sort of tractor-tricycle with a bucket seat and satisfying deep treads on the tyres, but I'm hoping memory has got it wrong. Poorly co-ordinated or not, I was old enough to be riding a bike and a bike it shall be.

A year or two later I learned the facts of life from a Latin play – a statement that makes me seem even more the tragic casualty of an expensive education than I feel the evidence supports. Westminster School had a tradition (recent, I dare say, and probably emulating another school) of putting on a Latin play in the original, not every year but at regular intervals, usually with one gimmicky touch, such as a character arriving in a car – a Mini driven through the Abbey cloisters. When I was still at the Under School, and so perhaps eleven or twelve, I attended a performance. The transition between the Under School and what we called the Great School was smooth. In Latin lessons at the Under School, Mr Young (pink and white colouring, wet of lip, Bill Haley cowlick innocent of any pop-culture reference) would wince at blunders and say, 'Don't let Mr Moylan catch you doing that.' In turn Mr Moylan, when he took over (a being without moisture, fastidious, invariably making a dog-leg across Little Dean's Yard to avoid exposing his leather soles to the wear-factor of gravel), would say, 'I hate to think what Mr Young would say about that.'

The play was Terence's *Eunuchus*. I imagine female roles were played by girls borrowed from other schools, Westminster being single-sex then. However backward in such matters, I feel sure I would have noticed if the women were boys cross-dressed.

The plot isn't what anyone, even Frankie Howerd, could call sophisticated. A young man obsessed with a beautiful woman poses as a eunuch so that he can be taken on as part of her domestic staff, presenting no danger because he lacks the wherewithal to take advantage of her. Once alone with his mistress (though offstage) he brandishes the wherewithal and takes advantage. Coming onstage after the act, he's exhilarated and grins all over his face. *Good heavens*, I thought – *it's supposed to be fun!* This had not been mentioned in the sex talk given by the headmaster of the Under School, Mr Kelly, whose admirably brisk opening words had been 'The penis is a splendid dual-purpose instrument.' I recoiled from such frankness. As far as I was concerned, one purpose was more than enough.

I got my sex education where I could. The later novels of Kurt Vonnegut wouldn't normally qualify for instructive status in this area, being so droll and sardonic, but my need for education was great. I read his *Breakfast of Champions* soon after it came out (which was in 1973, so I was nineteen or so), and was intrigued by one of the crude drawings, the author's own work, which illustrated an 'asshole' – the body part rather than the term of abuse. The drawing was essentially of an asterisk. I asked myself if the anus could possibly look like that, and the answer was that I had no idea. I knew my digestive system ended at a certain point, and I was willing to accept as a technicality of physical life that I possessed an anus, or I would have exploded long ago. But I had no visual information on the subject. Did it seem likely that my anus resembled a piece of punctuation? No it didn't, but I had no counter-theory with which to contest it.

I'm reminded of the very touching moment in Tarkovsky's *Solaris* (perhaps it goes back to Stanislaw Lem's source novel) when the hero is reunited with his dead wife, Hari, on a space station, thanks to the intervention of the sentient planet below him. They start foreplay, and he tries to take her dress off, going round the back to unfasten it. There's no zip. There are no buttons. The dress is impossible to take off, just as it was impossible to put on. This new Hari has been made directly out of his memories, and though he remembered the dress he didn't have a specific memory of the back of the dress and how it fastened. He has to get some scissors to help with the task of undressing her. Tenderly he vandalizes the dress he remembered only as a mystical whole.

At the age of around twenty I lived in a thinly imagined replica of my own body, and the orifice Dad took for granted as the central focus of homosexual desire was like the zip on Hari's dress. It wasn't on my map. I had to crouch and use a mirror to inform myself of the accuracy of Kurt Vonnegut's drawing, showing a little more diligence than Dad did when checking the underside of his Audi estate for explosive devices. It did look rather like an asterisk! I couldn't have been more surprised if the folds of this unimagined tissue had formed an ampersand or a treble clef.

If Dad ever blamed Mum for the way I had turned out, he was sensible enough to do it out of my hearing. The surprising thing was how little changed. My role as family peacemaker and lightning-rod was intact. It hadn't been displaced by revelation of my apostasy, and there were still altogether too many late-night conversations started by Dad with the formal opening, 'I'm very worried about Tim / Matthew . . .' Where is he going, what is he doing with his life?

It would fall to me to set out the case for the defence, in front of a presiding judge who would often simply set aside the evidence and give me his ruling on the facts of the case. We were all failing to live up to Dad's expectations, and logically my own falling short should have secured me some sort of exemption from generational-spokesman duties. I wouldn't have minded a sick note that excused me from going in to bat for the brotherhood, but I was returning to Gray's Inn from Cambridge on a regular basis, and the others were based elsewhere, so perhaps it was partly how I paid the rent.

My Cambridge rhythms with Mike altered after Christmas, though not (I don't think) because of the stresses and strains of his stalking-horse duties. He was starting to work. The Mike Larson I had known in his first term had hardly attended a lecture, spending most of the day with me in coffee shops or cinemas. He claimed that this was his real Cambridge education, and though I take flattery well it may also be that he thought the architecture faculty a little underpowered, compared with what he was used to. Now he buckled down, and mighty were the charrettes. Architecture even gave him an indirect way of describing our relationship. This was the 'creative use of interstitial space'. The phrase made sense, since he was just passing through Cambridge on his way to a life and a career, though it didn't make my heart leap.

The subject Mike chose for his dissertation was 'James Stirling and the Art of Rudeness'. It anatomised Stirling's famous V-shaped History Faculty building, which Mike saw as a V-sign offered to the university and its traditions. He asked me to help him with spelling and grammar, which I did very happily. It didn't occur to me that he might be dyslexic, though the way he ran at language was all his own. In those days dyslexia was an all-or-nothing category, and Mike could clearly make his way in the world of the written, though there was still a certain amount that I could tidy up.

By June his money had come through at last. He paid his debts, and even took me and Mum out to dinner and a show, Tom Stoppard's *Every Good Boy Deserves Favour* at the Mermaid Theatre.

He had a farewell gift for me too, an inscribed hardback of John Fowles's *Daniel Martin*. The inscription compared me to Henry James's Maria Gostrey and speculated that one day I might try a novel about an Englishman and an American. I have to admit that I didn't get very far with *Daniel Martin*. Come to that, I've never read *The Ambassadors*, though I know that Maria Gostrey introduces Lambert Strether to the Louvre and the Comédie Française and is generally a civilizing force.

Another memento he left with me was an item of clothing, which I had always liked on him, a cotton sweater of multicoloured stripes. Just as British body language can seem unmasculine to the American eye, particularly the habit of sitting with the legs crossed and the knees close together, closing up the crotch (a posture known in some US circles as

227

'gin and tonic'), so this item of clothing stood out as rather too-too in a society not yet indoctrinated with the dress code known as 'preppy'. Perhaps Mike left it with me because it had fallen short of the desired effect when he had worn it in Cambridge. A raised eyebrow can do a lot of damage.

In one of our first conversations post-Christmas I had let slip Dad's verdict on him – the passing comment (*obiter dictum* is the technical term, when a judge's casual remarks, not binding in law, are being referred to) about his being 'small beer'. *Let slip* gives the wrong impression. I passed on the information without hesitation, confident that Mike would find Dad's blindness as comical as I did. It never occurred to me that this well-defended man might want to be approved of, even by people who didn't matter to him in any real way. He was mortified, and in all the years of intermittent contact since then the phrase has never been properly exorcised.

By this time I had decided that spending time in America would do me good. I applied for a Harkness Fellowship, a sort of contraflow Rhodes scholarship enabling British students to attach themselves to American academic institutions. The protocol was for applicants to approach their university of choice directly to arrange possible admission, and the obvious place to go was the University of Virginia, where Alderman Library had a major collection of Faulkneriana, Faulkner being the subject of my supposed PhD.

Geography is hardly my strong suit, but I realized that Virginia was not close to California and to Mike. Obviously I hoped to see him again. I also felt that exposure to a more energetic set of manners would be good for me.

The Harkness selectors turned me down, I imagine because my proposal was rather feeble. American Literature was a paper I had done well on at Cambridge (where it had only recently been introduced), perhaps because it was a literature, at least in the nineteenth century, unconfident about its relationship with the English canon. As a refugee from Classics, lacking an English A-level, I shared that unconfidence. Faulkner was not by a long chalk my favourite American writer, but at least his output wasn't conclusively ranked, as Melville's and Hawthorne's were, with *Moby-Dick* and *The Scarlet Letter* making their other work seem inconsequential. There was work to be done. How was I to know that at the time more American PhDs were undertaken on Faulkner than on Shakespeare?

My acceptance letter from U. Va arrived weeks after my rejection from Harkness. I showed it to Dad in a spirit of wry amusement, but he told me I should take it up anyway. He would supplement the little stipend I was given by the Department of Education and Science. I tried to make clear that this acceptance was not the accolade he assumed, what with American universities being businesses in a way alien to our domestic assumptions, but he repeated his offer. And I accepted it.

I don't think for a moment that he was treating me as a remittance man, to use the traditional word for the unrespectable family member who is paid to keep a suitable distance from those he might embarrass. I was a functional part of the Gray's Inn household, someone he could rely on to be cheerful company for Mum while he was away on circuit, as he so often was.

Virginia was the first place where I was able to present myself as gay from the outset. Charlottesville was symmetrically Anglophilic and homophobic (Alcoholic Beverages Commission statutes made it illegal for gay people and other prohibited groups to be served alcohol), so some people had a silly prejudice in my favour and others had a silly prejudice against me. I made women friends, which was intoxicating, and much easier with any ambiguity dispelled. I involved myself in the Gay Student Union but didn't have a sex life to speak of. Gay students tended to drive to D.C. at the weekend for their pleasures, and the bicycle was my only means of transport. There was an underworld, but I didn't explore it. I remember a graduate student saying, after the sauna at the University gym was destroyed in a fire, that on the whole he would rather that the Parthenon had fallen down. I knew nothing of that.

I went to Alderman Library, which unlike the University Library at Cambridge had open stacks – meaning that you could find things you didn't know you wanted. I read Martin Amis, Ian McEwan, Craig Raine, Michel Tournier, Mario Mieli's *Elementi di Critica Omosessuale*, and other books in the same run of shelves such as *Tearoom Trade* and *Nos ancêtres les pervers*. I never even entered the room where the Faulkneriana was stored. Instead I Xeroxed *The Times* crossword from the copies of the paper which arrived in batches every few weeks, and solved the puzzle over a bottomless cup of coffee (meaning it would be refilled as often as you wanted) in the Virginian restaurant 'on the corner' – the designation of a particular stretch of street facing the university. At the bookshop on the corner I bought *The World According to Garp*, *Gay American History* and C. A. Tripp's *The Homosexual Matrix*. I 'audited' a creative writing class, meaning that I attended without being assessed, since I wasn't studying for an American degree. My surroundings suited me, and I managed to get a little writing fellowship (the Hoyns) for the next year, and taught writing at the modest 250 level in the year after that. By then I had a contract with Faber for *Lantern Lecture*, and Dad's attitude towards me changed decisively. No doubt I had changed too. Meeting me after my first year in the States, Tim thought I had grown taller – unlikely – and much louder, which was certainly true, since I had learned to hold my own in a more raucous conversational tradition than the one I had been used to. Americans used to say that Brits weren't 'self-starting', that they waited with pretended diffidence for the invitation to shine. I was now officially self-starting.

It took Mike a little longer to get his career started. His big break was winning the design competition for California's Vietnam War Memorial. This was a major enterprise, since one casualty in ten came from the state, the largest single loss. Partly for this reason there were issues of cultural politics involved in the project.

Maya Ying Lin's National Monument in Washington had been controversial from the moment her name was announced as responsible for the winning design. She was of Chinese descent, and she was female. She was also still an undergraduate at the time. (The competition was judged blind, with entries identified only by number, and she stood out in a field of more than a thousand.) Her outsider status might be an advantage in some quarters, but grief is territorial. Did she have a right to voice the national pain?

Her design was un-heroic, even anti-heroic. Names of the dead were etched on walls of black granite, in chronological order of casualty, without any additional information – rank, unit, decorations. Visitors would see themselves reflected in the polished stone as they searched the roll-call for their loved ones. Remembrance of the conflict as a whole took priority over any individual combatant, so that if you wanted to find one particular name you had to consult a printed directory on the site, to cross-reference person with date of death and so find the right place in the chronological list. The visitor to the memorial, as Maya Lin has arranged things, goes down to a lower level to find a name, in some small way visiting the underworld.

She chose not to represent human figures in the monument. This isn't unprecedented (think of the Cenotaph) but was certainly the aspect of the design most strongly contested by veterans of the war. To resolve the deadlock, one of the competition runners-up was commissioned to design a statue of three soldiers in a group, though Maya Lin, realizing the danger that this might become the focal point of the monument, fought successfully to have it installed some distance away from her wall.

Even so, the bareness of the memorial was hard to take for the visiting public, and objects began to be left behind to soften its edges (objects amounting to several thousand a year), not just flags and flowers but teddy bears and even a motorcycle bearing the licence plate HERO. A separate display of medals was installed in the 1990s to recalibrate the all-important balance between grief and pride.

Any sensible entrant in the competition for the California design would take note of these debates. It was unlikely that the judges would reward a confrontational approach. Including the human figure was a sensible decision, though it might be going too far to restore it to its place high above the visitor, as in the more self-confident nineteenth-century tradition. Doubt, fear, loneliness, all these could be acknowledged.

Mike's design solution was to devise a shrine-like space, in the shape of two half-circles, so as to offer visitors a sense of being shielded, though the memorial is open to the sky. On one side the gap between the half-circles is interrupted by columns taller than the walls, not supporting anything but providing the visual rhetoric of a gateway, flanked by free-standing decorative buttresses. There's a central flagpole. The panels listing the dead, in alphabetical order of home town but also giving their ages and the relevant branch of the service, are hung on the outside walls.

The outside of the memorial gives you the statistics, and the inside tries to render the experience. Reliefs on the curved inside walls show servicemen in combat and off duty, as well as planes, ships and aircraft carriers. There are five bronze figures on the site, four of them attached to the walls. The fifth is of a young soldier sitting at the foot of the flagpole. The intention is to produce a double-take effect on someone visiting the memorial alone, and thinking for a moment that there is someone already there. This fifth serviceman is bare-armed. He rests his rifle (an M16) against his leg, holding it steady with his left hand, while in the other he holds a handwritten letter from his parents. You can read it over his shoulder.

The judges of the competition must have been overjoyed when they found that the winning design was actually submitted by a veteran. It was a gift in terms of public relations. Mike had certainly paid his dues, seeing *Apocalypse Now* again and again during its first run, gravitating towards his fellow vets where they had established themselves at the back of the movie theatre with their booze and their joints, hunkering down in the foxhole of shared dope and shared damage.

In time Mike was frustrated by the bureaucratic aspects of realizing his memorial design, particularly when corners were cut. He had specified an infinitesimal gradient for the floor of the memorial, to make sure that water ran off. This was omitted, as a cost-cutting measure, and on the grounds that it never rained in Sacramento (in whose State Capitol Park it was erected). Mike knew better, and realized that in some seasons there would be puddling. He didn't attend the opening and has never visited, as far as I know, though he does have the consolation of being able to see it in the background of the local TV news every Veterans Day.

There's a debate that never seems to die down about whether there's such a thing as a gay sensibility. If being a veteran presumably affected Mike's ideas for the memorial, did his being gay also make a contribution? It's hard to come up with a definite answer. Is there gay input in his memorial? Just possibly. If you reach inside the young soldier's flak jacket (not that you would), you'll find that his nipples have been moulded.

After three years spent very happily in Virginia, and with a book soon to be published, I had the benefit of a new interpretation of my personality by Dad, but I was still living at home. Why not? I was two hundred yards from a Tube station, but Gray's Inn was quiet in the evenings and more or less deserted at weekends. I could walk to the West End on a Monday evening and get tickets to see a play. What were the advantages of setting up on my own, even if I could afford it on the £600 advance *Lantern Lecture* brought me? I was ahead of my time. Nowadays it's standard for people to wait a good long time before they can get established on the property ladder, but in those days the lower rungs were pretty accessible and it took some fancy rhetorical manoeuvring to make my choices look anything other than lazy and infantilized. Snow might fall on my bed, thanks to the rusty skylight, but I doubt if anyone was really fooled by my charade of starving-writer-in-a-garret. I wasn't even sure I was a writer. I had convinced a few other people but not myself. *Lantern Lecture* was 'well received' but I had no idea what to do next.

I had written my first book review, of Edmund White's *States of Desire*, while still in Charlottesville, for Craig Raine's *Quarto* – I remember sitting in the Howard Johnson's on West Main Street to write and rewrite my piece. Happy days! It would take me about five years of literary journalism in print and on the radio to start earning a living. My lowly status was partly disguised by my being so conveniently located, only a short walk from the *Sunday Times* on Gray's Inn Road, where Claire Tomalin would let me root through the book cupboard for lateral assignments, and from the *TLS* in Clerkenwell. Physical proximity was much more important in those days before e-mail.

It was only the anomaly of a new and serious-minded broadsheet newspaper (the *Independent*) being set up, with an arts editor, Tom Sutcliffe, whose address book was full of radio names rather than hacks as such, that edged me into solvency. It was an unlikely combination of events, a shower of frogs coinciding with a blue moon.

In the meantime I was an adult with an eccentric portfolio of privileges and restrictions. If Dad had been a bed and breakfast, he would certainly not have advertised himself as gay-friendly. Limits to behaviour weren't spelled out, and of course there was more potential leeway when Dad was on circuit. Even so, it was clear that a new face wouldn't be welcome at breakfast, unless possibly it belonged to Camilla Parker-Bowles. Now there's a lady who can wear a hyphen!

However little time Dad and I actually spent in the flat together, it's perfectly obvious that one of us (at least) was compromising his principles, and naturally I'd rather think it was him.

Did I want to invite someone into the flat for the purposes of pleasure, someone who might murder my mother or make off with the Investiture chairs? Well of course I did. Yet the situation suited me well, even in the aspects that seemed to chafe the most. I imagined I was looking for a relationship but didn't actually establish one. Certainly the partners I pursued were self-disqualifying by reason of unavailability. If they weren't ruled out by reason of a previous commitment then it was a matter of distance, whether geographically or emotionally expressed.

I wasn't a fully paid-up non-committer. I was really just stringing committophobia along. I kept it dangling, never quite saying in so many words that I didn't see us having a future.

As far as I could see, my brothers weren't in any great rush to settle down either, and perhaps I can hide my particular pathology behind wider patterns in the family.

I remember one idyllic picnic on the flat roof of the Gray's Inn flat, where Mum used to sunbathe. I hauled food, plates and cutlery for a romantic lunch up the vertical metal ladder which provided access, using the carrier-bag-on-a-rope system she had devised to convey her sun cream and chosen book. From this distance it seems jarring to be calling her 'Mum', but it can't really be avoided, Mum being what I called her at the time.

At the end of our rooftop meal, my date delivered what may have been the tenderest, warmest speech of romantic severance ever made. He had been having a very nice time, he said, and there were many ways in which I was wonderful, but he was looking for a lover of his own age.

It took a moment for this to sink in. 'Tony,' I asked, 'how old do you think I am?' The age difference between us was about eighteen months. Even in a highly competitive gay market I didn't qualify as a dinosaur or even a coelacanth, the 'living fossil' that turned up to everyone's surprise in a fisherman's net in 1938.

I told myself that being a Published Author conferred a gravitas which might be mistaken for seniority of the flesh, and so this comment wasn't the vote of no confidence in my grooming regime it might seem to be. I've never tired of reminding Tony of his micro-gaffe, not when Keith and I attended the party to celebrate his civil ceremony with George, nor when the two of them came to celebrate ours in 2008.

I suppose it was forgiving of me to use this new-fangled legal procedure, since I had declared in the *London Review of Books* in the mid-1990s that marriage was too central an institution of heterosexuality, too well defended, to be made to yield even a junior mechanism for the benefit of same-sex couples. I suggested instead, following up a remark of

Foucault's, a modification of the adoption process as the most practical way of securing legal rights for loved ones. Since then a Labour administration had introduced new legislation, as if determined to show me up as a poor prophet of social developments, but there was no sense in bearing a grudge.

The dynamics between homophobic judge and publicly gay writer son, tolerating each other at least to the extent of sharing a roof, are probably not standard. I dare say each of us tried to avoid confrontation while also steeling ourselves against compromise. It was my impression that the slow, slow melting came from his side of the glaciated valley, but perhaps he would have said the same thing.

Along the way there was a series of small breakthroughs and setbacks. A timeline of sorts can be established.

Even before I left for the States in 1978, when I was still based in Cambridge, there was a postscript to the protracted New Year seaside debate about sexual identity. Dad sent me a letter in which he told me that remarkable results had been obtained from testosterone treatment on homosexuals. There were references to medical journals.

I found this fairly insulting even before I consulted the journals. The articles concerned testosterone levels rather than treatment, and the homosexuals on whom the tests had been carried out were female. I wrote Dad a curt note pointing this out, saying sourly that he should do more homework before accusing his sons of lesbianism.

The most painful thing about the episode, though, was that the references to medical journals were not in Dad's handwriting, but his clerk John Cant's. There had been delegation. Dad couldn't be bothered to do his own skimpy bigoted research. I felt very let down. We'd had our difficulties in the past, but I had always been able to rely on the stamina of his prejudice, and I missed the personal touch.

Back in residence after my time in the States, I didn't willingly expose Dad to details of my 'private life', but that didn't make me culpably discreet. Sometime in late 1981 an estranged sexual partner stuck a wounding letter through the letterbox of the flat. Seeing me flinch as I opened the envelope, Dad said hoarsely, 'Is it . . . blackmail?' He was playing a very straight bat to the googlies that the queered pitch of life with a gay son was going to send his way. Even so, it wasn't clear in his scenario quite how the proposed extortion was to be managed. Presumably the blackmailer was threatening to expose my secret life. But to whom?

Dad and I were basing our assumptions on different historical periods, or perhaps different trends in the theatre. He was giving a performance of pained dignity out of Rattigan, while I had overshot even the kitchen sink brigade, ending up on the far fringe, where the Lord Chamberlain would hardly have dared to tread. For those few hours my personal drama edged into Orton territory, black farce rather than liberal-leaning problem play.

In 1983 Dad asked me if I was responsible for editing *The Penguin Book of Homosexual Verse*, which had recently been published. I was offended that he could ask such a question. Wasn't it perfectly obvious that if I took on a project of such a sort I would do it under my own name? If I did decide to use a pseudonym, I would try to do better than the name on the book's cover, Stephen Coote.

I did on the other hand edit *Mae West Is Dead* that same year, an anthology of gay fiction published by Faber, providing a mildly militant introduction, and I don't remember anything being said about that. I imagine Mum kept the peace between us to a considerable extent, and warned Dad off unsafe subjects. It was kid gloves all round, some of them elbow-length, in the debutante or drag-queen manner.

In the introduction to the anthology I made passing reference to Aids, which was just beginning to make headlines in this country, as a domestic threat rather than an exotic catastrophe. Of course I hedged my bets, in the journalistic manner, trying to come up with a politically robust statement that nevertheless wouldn't embarrass me if a cure was found by the time the book was published – a sort of rhetorical ice sculpture designed to melt discreetly away if conditions improved.

There was no thaw. The Terrence Higgins Trust, the UK's pioneer Aids organization, held its first meeting in 1983, at Conway Hall, just round the corner from Gray's Inn. I wasn't based in London at the time, since I had a little temporary post as a creative writing teacher attached to the University of East Anglia, but the event seemed important enough for me to return to London that weekend.

I don't know what I wanted from the meeting, some sort of action plan, I suppose. There was a guest appearance by Mel Rosen, a member of the New York organization Gay Men's Health Crisis, whose emotive style of public speaking grated on me. When he said that he had cried more in the last six months than he had in his whole life, I'm afraid I thought, so what? The link between epidemic and emotional growth seemed so tenuous and uninteresting. What were we going to *do*?

Mel Rosen died in 1992, aged forty-one. I'm ashamed that I was so unresponsive when he spoke about the changes in his life. At the time the consensus was that only a small proportion of people exposed to what we assumed must be a virus (the organism was years away from being identified) would go on to develop symptoms, and that not all of those would progress to the full diagnosis, fatal in those days, but that's no excuse. I had made a decision to be disappointed by the Trust's lack of dynamism. Volunteering at this point would be a waste of energy. I probably wanted an excuse not to give my time to committee meetings. I was big on gestures of solidarity and points of principle (train fare from Norwich be damned), not so hot on personal involvement. I felt about Aids activism, at least in its disorganized state then, what Oscar Wilde is supposed to have said on the subject of socialism. About it taking too many evenings.

Two years of headlines and editorials eroded my sense of entitlement to distance. I volunteered to be a Buddy for the Trust, doing chores for sick men and providing a basic level of companionship. The training was rudimentary, no more than a one-day course made up of medical generalities and counselling tips. We were packed in a dark and airless room, with many of us sitting on the floor. I remember one fellow inductee seeming unable to take his eyes off my trousers, which sounds flattering until I explain that he was gazing at ankle rather than groin level. The trousers had been bought in a sale and had unfinished hems. They weren't quite long enough to be taken up for neatness.

As if to drive home the point that Aids was not an issue I could legitimately dodge, the headquarters of the Terrence Higgins Trust at the time was in Panther House, light industrial premises with an address in Mount Pleasant but geographically closer to Gray's Inn Road. I was the nearest volunteer by some way, in what was not much of a residential district. From my parents' front door to the Trust's front line was a three-minute walk.

Or a ninety-second dash in an emergency. On one occasion, there was an executive panic about what was going on with the phone line at Panther House. News was coming in that an Aids patient had tried to discharge himself from hospital against medical advice, and had been arrested to stop him leaving the premises. This was obviously an alarming precedent and there was intensive interest from the press. The Trust hadn't had time to come up with any kind of official statement. The fear was that a volunteer whose job was only to provide basic medical advice to the worried, to refer them to more expert sources, might be reacting off the cuff from Panther House. It seemed ominous that the number had been engaged for hours.

Someone was needed to get there fast, to pass on the required message: Say nothing – tell them to call the press officer. I must have been at the top of the list. From Gray's Inn Square I could have shouted out of the window and had a fair chance of being heard.

I raced to Panther House and shouted incoherently through the entryphone. It took a little while to persuade those within the fortress that I wasn't some hectoring anti-gay passer-by, and when I was let in everyone was rather nonplussed. Arrest? What arrest? Phone calls, what phone calls? Eventually someone thought to check the phone. It turned out that the last person to hang up had returned the receiver to its cradle on the slant, putting the line out of service. People had been sitting around with cups of tea, making the most of the opportunity for undisturbed workplace smoking (in those bad old days), wondering vaguely why everything had gone so quiet.

When the Trust changed address, it was to come even closer, not letting me off the hook. The new premises on Gray's Inn Road were barely a hundred yards from where I lived. If there was another emergency of the same type – providing I was at home and the Gray's Inn Road gate from the Square was open, as was normal during business hours – reaction time could significantly be whittled down.

I had no thought, when I volunteered as a Buddy, that I would be gaining experience exploitable in writing. It was partly that I hadn't written fiction for quite a few years at that point – I was generally assumed to be suffering from writer's block, something

I only fully realized when I was tactfully asked to review a book on the subject for the *Independent on Sunday*, as Susan Sontag might have been assigned a book on cancer or Gorbachev one on birthmarks.

In any case I didn't see how Aids could be adequately fictionalized. Over time I changed my mind, and began to feel that the word itself, with its then conventional 'full caps', was the main obstacle, a visual shout that was likely to drown out with its repetitions any story in which it featured. Once I had realized it was possible to write an arresting opening sentence while replacing the syndrome with the euphemism 'Slim', in a character's plausible register, the rest of the story more or less wrote itself.

I showed my story to the person I was buddying at the time, Philip Lloyd-Bostock, wanting his blessing although as far as I knew I hadn't used any of his personal details. It was still somehow an abstract invasion of privacy. He raised no objection, though it must have been disheartening to read an outsider's recasting of his desperate situation, when he himself was trying to finish an autobiographical novel. It was published after his death as *The Centre of the Labyrinth*.

I thought the story ('Slim') would be effective on radio, where the withholding of the trigger-word might even ensnare listeners with no desire to empathize. Radio 4 took an interest, Martin Jarvis recorded it, and it was scheduled for broadcast late on a weekday evening.

I became restless several days in advance. I certainly didn't want to listen to my story while it was broadcast, but it seemed silly to stay in and not listen to it. The logic was, then, that I would go out and be in some sanctioned public place when my story went out on its mission to galvanize lazy perceptions of illness.

I was in need of that quaint commodity 'gay space'. When I looked at *Time Out*'s gay listings for that evening, the only possible venue was the Market Tavern in Vauxhall, where there was a Body Positive evening. (It had to be a club rather than a pub because of the restrictions then in force about opening hours.) Body Positive was the support group for people who were HIV-positive. The ironical appropriateness of the venue was surplus to my requirements, but it was that or nothing. I would be in a room with a bunch of gay men who knew a lot more than I did about the reality of being unwell at the time my momentous little story was transmitted.

With the sort of neatness that I try to avoid when writing fiction, I met a man at the Body Positive evening, in what must have been the most stubbornly unatmospheric venue in London, who quietly dismantled the bachelor persona that didn't suit me, though I didn't myself know how to shed it.

Michael Jelicich was twenty-three and from New Zealand. He was tall (6'4") and dark, with elongated hands and feet that made him look like an El Greco. His ancestry was half Yugoslav – in those days we hadn't learned to subdivide that national identity. I'm reminded of him when I see photographs of Goran Ivanišević, who is Croatian, though Ivanišević was still playing tennis as an amateur when I met Michael. He had been diagnosed as positive shortly before he left Auckland for London. The trip was long planned and he went through with it.

I must have made some impression on him that night at the Market Tavern, but he went home with someone else, Bill McLoughlin, who became a friend of us both. We pronounced his name differently to distinguish him from other Bills we knew, calling him Beel because of his fluency in Spanish. He had spent a lot of time in South America.

He had been in Peru at a time of great unrest, thanks to the Shining Path group. Once Beel was sitting in a café when a tear-gas grenade was lobbed through the doorway. Hardly even thinking, he threw it out again into the street.

Shortly afterwards a military policeman made an entrance, demanding to know who had thrown the gas grenade back. Beel raised his hand. 'Why did you do that?' he shouted.

'Those things really kill the froth on a cappuccino,' said Beel.

There was a moment's incredulous pause, then the policeman grinned. 'Yes, they do that, don't they?' he said. A Hemingway story, really, with a tiny added element of campiness, but when Beel was doing the telling I believed it. I can still almost believe it, on the basis that Beel's Spanish, extremely good but English-accented, indicated someone it might be a mistake to brutalize.

I'm a bit vague about when Beel died, though he made it through a good stretch of the 1990s. Michael went home with him because Beel had only recently been diagnosed and thought he would never be able to hold someone close again, let alone have sex. I assume there was desire on Michael's part as well as concern – the impulses can overlap. Michael was matter-of-fact about his own needs as well as other people's. The exotic surname Jel-ic-ich was pronounced Jealous Itch, but that was just a handy mnemonic. It was the opposite of a character sketch.

Michael's health broke down rather rapidly, given his youth and generally healthy lifestyle – he didn't drink or smoke, and vegetarianism had been his preference for years. He had HIV-positive friends who swore by a macrobiotic diet to keep them healthy, and he went along with that experimentally, but his basic feeling was that it didn't make sense to add extra difficulties to the business of feeding yourself when you had no energy and hardly ever felt hungry anyway. He reasoned that if he wasn't going to be able to eat more than a few mouthfuls he should eat food with concentrated sustaining power, and if M&S Chicken Kiev wasn't macrobiotic then that was just too bad. When I started to cook for him he asked me not to consult him about what we were having. He had so little appetite that it seemed wise to hold it back for the actual food, not waste it on menus.

I remember, though, that he read some testimony about the HIV-curative properties of hydrogen peroxide, and we thought we'd give it a try. For a while we added it to drinking water, starting with just a few drops then building up to a dose that would scour the virus from his blood. I drank it too, to keep him company – but then he would get sick and our H_2O_2 regime stopped being a priority. The bottle from Boots and the medicine dropper lost their importance. I worried at first that we were drinking hair bleach, but he knew perfectly well that what was loosely called 'peroxide' was mixed with ammonium hydroxide. If I ever saw him adding ammonia NH_3 to his glass I should intervene at once.

While he was well enough he worked at a little salon called Ficarazzi on High Holborn, and later at the branch of the Hebe chain on the Strand. Both premises were in easy walking distance of Gray's Inn, and I would often bring him lunch there. It was only when I read him a story based on a weekend we had spent in Brighton that he realized I was embarrassed by my lover being a hairdresser. Was he disappointed in me? I don't see how he could have been anything else.

He was very much at ease with himself. His small vocabulary of adjectives – 'stunning' his favourite positive, 'tragic' its negative counterpart – was up to the task of conveying his subtle responses. If there was an element of cliché in his character he would embrace it, or find a way of setting it off. Liking Simple Minds, Talk Talk and U2 might not be the most maverick choices available, but who was he to resist the classics?

He bought *The Joshua Tree* when it came out and played it constantly on the Ficarazzi sound system. He did his best haircuts ever that week. Coincidence? You decide.

When I took to riding a motorbike (certainly to my own surprise and perhaps to other people's), he said that personally he preferred mopeds, and planned to choose a purple one for himself, one whose motor resembled a hairdryer as closely as possible. He loved it when people didn't notice his jokes, and never made my mistake of repeating them as often as it took for them to be acknowledged, if not necessarily enjoyed.

For a while he lived on New North Road in nether Islington, and then, after a hospital stay, in Acton, where his non-rent-charging landlord was a volunteer he had met while he was there, an altruistic set-up with its own set of complications. The only place we could be properly private was a flat in Surrey Quays that he was lent towards the end of 1987, where the price of privacy was cold and damp. Michael had never seen snow falling until he came to London the previous year, and had loved it, but didn't enjoy cold in its less ornamental aspects.

Of course, living in Gray's Inn meant I couldn't offer Michael any sort of home. He wasn't exactly welcome as a visitor while Dad was on the premises, but that was perfectly consistent. Welcome was not something he claimed to offer when it came to that side of my life. Mum's stiffness in his presence was more of a surprise to me. I had expected her to see right away that Michael, without being a needy personality in the slightest, was a person in need, and that was a category to which she had always responded.

I reasoned that she was so easily intimidated herself she didn't realize that her manner could be off-putting in its own right. Surely she could see that Michael didn't even know what to call her? Using her first name without invitation was taking a liberty, but being expected to say 'Lady Mars-Jones' was a joke. She herself disliked having a grand title, one that only meant she was married to a man who had a certain job, but if she didn't see how alienating it was to someone without status and from another part of the world then she might as well have been glorying in it.

It can't have been like that, from her side of things. I was busy sending out on all frequencies the message that it was quite impossible for me to acquire HIV, jamming the family's listening apparatus with a blanketing reassurance, while also expecting my mind to be read and my intentions clear. And from Sheila's point of view, I imagine, Michael's sweet droll presence was just the mask a virus wore when it entered her house with intent to bereave. He personified death, and not just a general death – his own, of course, but mine too.

Naturally she fought against being on first-name terms with that. As a debilitated young man far from home, with nothing to rely on except the small surprises he could spring with his scissors (for as long as he was still well enough to ply them) he also represented absolute vulnerability. Perhaps she was sending out some jamming signals of her own, to prevent unbearable possibilities from tracking her down.

Eventually I said, 'Do you mind asking Michael to call you "Sheila"? "Lady Mars-Jones" is a bit of a mouthful.' And she said, 'Of course. Silly of me not to think of it.'

Even 'Sheila' he found a bit of a mouthful, perhaps because of its antipodean usage (even if Australian rather than New Zealand) to mean *woman* generically. In conversation with me he styled her 'Shee', this being what Bobby Grant on *Brookside*, as played by Ricky Tomlinson, called his wife, Sheila (Sue Johnston). Michael preferred grim British soap operas to sunny Australian ones, and *EastEnders* made *Neighbours* look pretty silly. *Brookside* was sometimes so wonderfully gloomy that it made his problems seem quite minor.

He was in the UK on a two-year visa. Unlike (as it seemed) all his friends Michael didn't have 'patriality', the right of residence that Kiwis enjoy as long as they have had the forethought to equip themselves with at least one British grandparent. It wasn't legal for him to make his home here, and of course there was no mechanism, no civil partnership nor extended Foucauldian form of adoption, that would let me top him up conveniently with the rights he lacked.

The only form in which I could show commitment was to buy a flat for us to live in, for however short a time. HIV was doing what no other agency had achieved, by making me set up on my own. The timing wasn't great – the summer of 1988 was the last time that two earners could claim tax relief on a single mortgage, so yuppy couples on a deadline were blocking the doors of estate agents' premises. My insecure freelance income was outclassed, required to compete against mature salaries hunting in pairs.

Brought up in WC1, and in an august enclave to boot, I wasn't particularly realistic about where I could afford to live. An early Terrence Higgins Trust meeting had been held in a basement on Highbury Fields, and I was duly impressed with the amenities of the area. I could afford a three-bedroomed flat in Finsbury Park or a two-bedroomed one in Highbury. Journeys from Highbury were shorter, to the West End to see films, to Gray's Inn by number 19 bus, and it was hard to make out that I needed a third bedroom when soon enough I would be living alone.

It was August when we moved in. 'Shee' gave us a cast-iron cooking-pot, still in service in the second decade of the twenty-first century, and Michael's mother, Beverley (who had visited that summer), gave us a chopping-board made of a distinctive New Zealand hardwood. It cracked and then split a good long time ago, losing the inset metal handle, but I'll go on using it as long as there's enough square-inch-age left intact to accommodate a spring onion.

Michael had his own bedroom, and mainly slept on the

futon there. He put pin-ups on the wall with Blu-tack, large-format photos from the gay free-sheets, innocuous furry nudes. I must have looked dismayed at this revelation of preference, for him to spell out so clearly the obvious truth: if he had wanted a lover covered in coconut matting he would have found one. There were applicants.

He spent a lot of time knitting at a modest level of craft, making what he called 'peggy squares', alternately black and brightly coloured, to be sewn together into a patchwork quilt. He explained that knitting was only half an activity, and so was watching television, but between them they made up a state of satisfaction. He would sit on the sofa knitting with his long right leg crossed over, bobbing his bed-socked size twelve foot in slow tempo, keeping time with something I couldn't hear.

We weren't entirely swallowed up by domesticity. Through Edmund White, with whom I'd written a book of HIV-related stories, I was put in touch with Kitty Mrosovsky who lived near us, in Arsenal near the stadium (before it moved away). She had recently been diagnosed as positive, and needed someone to talk to. Michael came along to meet her once, and was touchingly protective of her, considering an age gap of perhaps fifteen years and a great difference of character – Kitty was academic and temperamentally nervous, a pianist and writer whose first novel had been published by a firm that had instantly gone bust, so that her career as a fiction writer was launched and sunk almost simultaneously. On the way home Michael said that he thought the stage Kitty was going through, when you know your health is being secretly ruined but nothing definite has yet happened, was the hardest of the lot to deal with. In HIV terms, he felt like her older brother.

He was scheduled to leave in early January of 1989. In December he suggested that we hire a video camera to record highlights of the Christmas period. This felt quite adventurous – the equipment was expensive and no-one we knew owned one. It was all very futuristic. I was impressed that the shop where we hired it not only took a deposit but a frame capture from its CCTV system as evidence of what we looked like.

As always with Michael, there was a lot of good sense behind the idea. He and I had been saying goodbye almost from the moment we met. There was no need to make a meal of the actual parting. The video camera would keep us looking outwards rather than in, and would have a usefulness to a wider circle. Tim's son, Ebn, was three and a half, and we saw quite a lot of him (Michael cut his hair). It seemed a good idea to get plenty of footage of this beguiling boy on separate cassettes, so that one could be given to Tim and his partner Pam, and one to my parents documenting their first grandchild. Another tape was for Michael to pass on to his family as a record of his London life. He always said he had been happier in London with Aids than in Auckland without. Another tape was designated as my souvenir of him.

Naturally enough this was the most intimate. Lying exhausted on his futon, Michael still managed to give a guided tour of his gallery of hunks on the wall, the commentary including not just names (of course there was a Brad, but also a Petey and a Wilf) but their professions and the cars they drove. In another sequence he is lying against the naked chest (hairy, as it happens) of one of our friends. He strokes it and comments on the difference from what he's used to. He says he could never have a lover after me. I should know by now that there's nothing more characteristic of Michael than to make me relax, to get me completely defenceless, and then say something just ever so slightly edged. He says, 'It took me two years to get you trained. I couldn't go through all that again.' The camera shakes because my shoulders are laughing.

It's true, though, in its way, that he trained me. He made me something I wasn't before, not *lovable* (cuddly toy) but *love-able*. Capable of responding without reservations.

In the last section that we filmed he describes Henderson, the Auckland suburb where he grew up: the orchards, the primary school, the mountain range. When Beverley can't see the mountains, rain is on the way and it's time to get the washing in off the line. He falls peaceably silent. The camera, going for an arty effect far beyond my actual competence as a video operator, focusses on the slow bounce of his foot in its bedsock.

In 1989 people thought of the world as being well connected by its media, but the time difference between London and Auckland made phone calls impractical, and we relied on the postal service almost as much as people had in the nineteenth century. To start with I wrote letters, but Michael talked me into trying his own preferred medium, the tape cassette. Thrifty and unsentimental, he would listen to my voice on a tape, then record over it and send it back. His style was loose and free-ranging – he might go on chatting to me while blood was being taken, then say afterwards that the stocky male nurse who had done the procedure was 'very you'. There came a time when he had radiotherapy on a Kaposi's sarcoma lesion in his mouth, which made his beard fall out in a geometrically square patch. He sent me a photograph of the damage, perhaps to prepare me in the event of our seeing each other before it could grow back, though he always discouraged me from making the trip, saying he only wanted to see me if he could show me around and have some fun himself. Perhaps he just sent me the mortifying photo because, unsentimental again, he had to deal with it, so why shouldn't I?

When Michael's family phoned me at the beginning of May to say that he was dying, there were still a couple of his tapes in the post. It was too much for me to listen to them when they arrived, and I never have, which feels like the right decision. I like the feeling that there are unexplored bits of Michael left over, which I could in theory dip into at any time, and so I will never run out.

The most painful moment in my whole relationship with Dad came the day after Michael's death. Mum phoned me in Highbury to express her condolences. Then she pronounced a formula I had always hated, without being able to find an effective way to expose it in all its awfulness.

Dad would like a word.

It wasn't quite that a grown man was using his wife as a switchboard operator, to place a call for him. That would just be inconsiderate and patronizing. It was so much worse: he was using her as an unacknowledged warm-up act, to guarantee a reception he couldn't rely on without her help.

Oi, mate! Earn your own intimacy. Intimacy is not transferable. No piggyback, no hitch-hiking. On your bike, your honour. There's no Plus One.

Question: how is it different for a son to use his mother as a conduit of information to the patriarch ('Oh by the way, *Mae West is Dead* comes out next week, there will probably be some reviews', 'Mario died last night, while I was there. I'm fine') and for a father to use his wife to establish contact with a son without being expected to beg . . . ?

Not now! There'll be plenty of time for questions later. Can't you see I'm getting up a good old head of steam?

There seems to have been something in the nature of the Mars-Jones family that preferred to go the long way round, avoiding the obvious communicative route in favour of letting information filter through indirectly. Might this be characteristic of British families in general? Anglo-Welsh families? Families with three sons in them? Do strings of rhetorical questions advertise a wish to change the subject?

There was also the possibility that Mum had told him that he couldn't get out of saying something to me, so that in a moment of assertiveness she was more or less frogmarching him all the way to the receiver. There is always the possibility of this sort of ramification: that it was for her benefit that he was going to say something for my benefit.

When Dad came on the line I braced myself for evasiveness. I hardly dared think what status he was going to accord Michael's death, how he would square the circle, in terms of offering condolence without granting approval.

'I just wanted to say,' he said, 'that I was sorry to hear about Michael. You've been a good friend to him – as you've been to so many others . . .'

This was worse than anything I could have expected. I could have Dad's sympathy as long as my lover's death was reclassified as a negative outcome of social work. Did I go on holiday to Skye with Mario Dubsky? Had I bought a flat to live in with Philip Lloyd-Bostock? It was hard to see that I was being supported, when the underlying message was that I mustn't expect him to look squarely at me and my life. I could have a pat on the back as long as I let him keep his blinkers on.

Part of me would have enjoyed getting angry, telling him that this was not just meaningless but cruel. I didn't have the strength. I couldn't afford any expenditure of rage at a time when my whole emotional economy was taking a battering.

I found I couldn't let it pass either. I spoke, and I contested Dad's version, but I went the long way round. Doggedly I listed everything that Michael's family had done to include me, when it must have seemed to them in their agony that I was essentially an outsider, not much more than a passer-by. I was mentioned, for instance, in the death notice they put in the Auckland newspapers. Dad didn't respond.

Needling the righteous isn't a noble sport. Dad made no special claim to virtue, though he took it for granted that God was on his side, and outreach wasn't really his thing. The only impressive pattern of behaviour he ever referred to in his own rather daunting father was the principled hiring, on the farm and in the post office, of those who had once betrayed trust. Dad's father (my 'Taid') understood that there must be a mechanism running counter to disgrace, or else the traffic is all one way, but Dad was comfortable with a fixed boundary between the clean and the unclean. As a judge, in fact, he tended to process the clean across the border into uncleanness. If there was a return journey possible – rehabilitation or redemption – he didn't play a part in the process.

One of the festivals of Gray's Inn is the Mulligan Sermon, delivered by a visiting preacher on the same text each year. 'Who is my neighbour?' That's the text. There is a festive lunch afterwards.

It pleases me to think that the originating Mulligan was laying a moderately obvious trap for the good people of Gray's Inn, in their parish of plenty, when he provided funds by the terms of his will for the preaching of this particular sermon. How long would it take the listeners in their pews, the lunchers in Hall, to realize that he was mocking them for their empty assent to the idea of reaching out to alleviate distress?

Communion in Gray's Inn Chapel was always a hierarchical event. Benchers and their wives approached to receive the elements in strict order of seniority. Of course there were polite yieldings of precedence, nods and smiles. Nevertheless communicants knelt at the altar rail with their sense of worldly positioning sharpened rather than laid to rest.

James Mulligan, who was the Treasurer of Gray's Inn in 1896 and provided the endowment for 'The Mulligan Sermon', directed that the sermon should concentrate on 'the interview between Our Lord and the Lawyer, as recorded in the twenty-second chapter of the First Gospel, and at greater length in the tenth chapter of the Third Gospel'. Luke 10:25 does indeed describe 'a certain lawyer' standing up and tempting Jesus with trick questions. No lawyer is mentioned in Matthew 22, but the chapter swarms with Pharisees and Sadducees, and perhaps the Sermon really was meant to puncture the institutional smugness it seems to promote.

There was nothing I could do immediately to repay Michael's family for the way they included me, but a while later I wrote a character sketch of him for the *Independent*'s 'My Hero' column, and sent a bale of copies of the magazine out to New Zealand. By the standards of public life Michael, dying at twenty-six after years of illness, could lay no claim on an obituary, but I made the most of the opportunity I had to write something loving and to have it printed.

In a small way Michael's death made a difference to my dealings with my mother. From then on *Shee* became my regular form of address for her. She seemed to like it, and I didn't mention the low Channel 4 provenance of the abbreviation. Calling your parents by their first names is a stilted little intimacy, most obviously so when it is a new practice, before it beds down as a reflex, self-consciously undertaken to make clear that you are no longer bound by the contracts of childhood (and who wants to be a pensioner calling a centenarian 'Mum'?). Calling Sheila 'Shee' was a way of keeping alive Michael's warm teasing, and so of keeping him dimly alive too. One evening, eating out at Joe Allen's off the Strand, I recognized Sue Johnston, the actress who had played Sheila Grant, and offered her a glass of champagne in recognition of the walk-on part she had played in my halting emotional development.

Dad wouldn't have enjoyed being 'Bill' to his sons, nor was it a style of address that appealed to me. Now that I think about it, I might have enjoyed calling him 'Lloyd', the name harking back to remote Denbighshire and a pre-hyphenated innocent, teenager with ukelele.

The conversation about how good I had been to Michael was certainly the low point of our relationship. After that, Dad slowly lost his horror of my sexual identity, though he never got as far as acknowledging a partner of mine. Long before a genuine mild dementia made him forgetful of the lovely Nimat, though she came every day to help him shower, he had perfected a frown of absent puzzlement (who could this be?) to use when not-quite-greeting Keith.

The slow relaxing process may partly have been due to the collapse of two of his arguments. I didn't seem to be especially held back in terms of career by my sexual preference, though that had only ever been a high-sounding justification for existing prejudice. As for his sorrow on my behalf at my exclusion from the joys of family life, that argument was torpedoed, sent to Davy Jones's locker without much of a splash, by the arrival of Holly in 1991. My parents saw more of Holly than their other grandchildren, who lived further away. Gray's Inn Walks were as well suited for children's play as they had been a generation earlier, even if children were much less a feature of the Inn's life than they had been, with assured shorthold tenancies being the only option for incomers.

As an Inn child I had resented the ban on dogs in the Walks. Lobbying strongly for a pet, I had overcome the first objection (noise) by finding in my *Observer Book of Dogs* a breed that didn't bark but emitted a sort of yodel (the basenji). The basenji came with the bonus of a looped-over tail like a pig's, only hairy. Then I was brought up short by the impossibility of exercising the proposed animal, which was bred in the Central African bush for the hunt, and possibly not well suited to WC1 anyway, yodelling madly down Chancery Lane in search of eland. As an adult supervising childish play I was grateful for wide stretches of lawn free of fouling, banks that could be rolled down without fear of any contamination worse than grass stains.

It was certainly true that Dad wanted the joys of family life for me, but he also wanted for himself the possibility of a conventional family portrait on the mantlepiece. Our new family grouping looked more standard than it was, and I could hardly blame Dad for setting store by its air of normality. Now he could talk about me in terms that didn't contest any other information that might be circulating. He could paint a picture that was just as true, however incompatible it seemed with the official version.

Useless to pretend that I didn't notice, and occasionally exploit, my new status as a man with a baby. I had served some sort of apprenticeship while looking after my nephew, Ebn, when he was little, and had noticed how obliging everyone became at a normally unwelcoming West End gay bar called Brief Encounter when I turned up with a small beaming child strapped to my chest, lamenting that I wasn't allowed to take him inside, and wondering if anyone would be so kind as to bring me out a Guinness. Child care was certainly good for you, if you were an unspectacular gay man on the street carrying a cheerful baby.

So when Holly was about a year old, and I was queuing to pay at the Brixton Marks & Spencer's, I wasn't too shocked to find myself being attentively considered by a man standing by the racks of socks. It seemed unlikely he was having trouble making up his mind between competing products – it's a dressy man who dithers over socks, and this man was not dressy. It was always possible that he was impersonally pleased to witness solo fathering (still then something of a novelty), seeing it as socially progressive, but that was a risk I was willing to take. I approached him and said, 'I'm Adam and this is Holly, and we would like your telephone number.' Written down, this seems as manipulative as any Disney film ever made, but perhaps casting and chemistry improved on the script.

I had also given out my own number. When the man phoned after a day or two, I was much less sure of myself. Sheila had once remarked that she thought she understood the basics of how my world worked, but she didn't know how I had the nerve to make the first move, something she had never been able to do. It's true that the first move hasn't usually been a problem for me. It's the second move that gives the real trouble. Still, Keith had begun his leisurely transformation from shopper who can't decide about socks into leading man.

The balance between father and son at this point seemed approximately equal enough to be durable. I was the misguided pervert who had nevertheless been polite enough to reproduce. He was the hectoring brute who had kept his home open to me. As Holly grew, though, Dad seemed to notice that our arrangement, however visually soothing, diverged from the standard pattern. 'How's the little family?' he would always ask, and started to see it as a brave experiment in some way.

This was welcome but unduly flattering, at least as it applied to me. Brave for Holly's mother, Lisa, to trust an arrangement that though not necessarily ramshackle, and as full of good intentions as any other, lacked any formal or informal guarantees. Not so brave for a man to sign up to fatherhood on something like a freelance basis, with an enviable freedom to pick and choose. Not sharing a roof with my daughter, I experienced a minimum of disturbed nights.

Dad's change of heart, so long delayed, went further. Seeing me with Holly, he said he regretted his own failure to touch his children when they were small, blaming it on a foolish fear of homosexuality, the terror of breeding sissies. It was unheard of for him to own up to a fault no-one had even accused him of. It seemed entirely genuine, but somehow genuine in the wrong way and thereby deeply fishy. I thought about it a moment and told him that he had touched us often but in his own style, which was horseplay rather than tenderness as such.

He would hold our hands when we were small, facing us, and encourage us to walk up his legs, then he would flip us over and return us fizzing to the ground. He didn't do hugs but he did aeroplanes. Mum didn't do aeroplanes.

I wonder where it had come from, Dad's little moment of artificial apology? By this stage he didn't stray much from the flat, otherwise I might suspect him of dropping in to a men's support group, though I don't know where he would have found such a thing. Holborn Central Library, perhaps? Or at the Mary Ward Centre in Queen Square? Over towards Bloomsbury any cultic practice might find a home. Or perhaps he had been watching some tearful family drama on the box, one long orgy of confrontations and breakthroughs, and I should be blaming television.

I was more at home with the Dad who only gave ground when he knew he was about to lose, who tracked the shift of an argument on a pre-verbal, almost olfactory level. Every now and then Dad would sniff the wind and realize he was about to be defeated in argument, and then he immediately stood down his troops. In the aftermath you could have a relatively low-key conversation.

In family conflict these moments felt like breakthroughs, but it was never possible to tap back into that mood of truce without going through a fresh round of exhausting confrontations. I remember that in about 1980 Dad gave me a hard time about the ridiculous baggy jeans I was wearing. What a stupid waste of cloth! I had nothing to fall back on but appeals to their fashionability, a poor line of defence since it reproduced his line of attack (you're only wearing them because you've been brainwashed).

Those baggy jeans had always been controversial items. When I was wearing them on East Main Street in Charlottesville, Virginia, an elderly black stranger did a double-take and then shouted after me, 'You're wearing girl pants!', divining a transgressive element in my style statement of which I was unaware. His tone was pure astonishment rather than hostility.

Dad, then, was not my first critic. Luckily I remembered seeing a photograph of him as a young man walking jauntily along the front at Colwyn Bay with his aunts Bessie and Minnie, and wearing a pair of trousers so wide they could have given shelter to a pack of hunting dogs under their hems. He wore them with a tight jacket and a tie tucked in between the buttons of his shirt. With a little delving in his study I unearthed this incriminating image.

Now I couldn't wait for him to slander my jeans again, and to produce the evidence of double standards. But there must have been a change in my body chemistry, a pheromone that made him realize I had somehow acquired a trump card. He wouldn't be drawn into repeating his indictment of my dress sense. I could have worn those baggy jeans to a funeral and still he would have said nothing, somehow knowing that I had the goods on him. Suddenly he was unprovokable, and when I lost patience and drew the photo out of its envelope at last it wasn't any sort of ambush but a meeting of old friends. He reminisced fondly about the thirty-six-inch bottoms of those Oxford bags, and after that my baggy jeans were exempted from stricture. Of course they continued to look ridiculous, but that had never been the linch-pin of the argument.

When I had been expelled from the Inn, and more to the point after I had written my article for *The Times* denouncing the hypocrisy of the governing body, I had guaranteed my status as *persona non grata*, high on the list of the Inn's Least Wanted. I might visit family friends still living there, but it would have been silly to expect an actual welcome. Nevertheless an invitation came from the Treasurer, the next year, to dine as his guest in Hall. The new Treasurer was Tony Butcher, who as the Dean of the Chapel had been one of the three polite Cerberoid heads guarding the organ from molestation by unauthorized fingers and feet. He was also someone whom I had invited to breakfast once or twice after the early communion I didn't attend.

Breakfast was being repaid, with interest, in the form of dinner, and this was a personal rather than an institutional gesture. It wasn't quite a matter of the Inn saying, in effect, just because we chucked you out doesn't mean we can't be friends. Nor was my accepting the invitation a way of saying: just because I told you to fuck off in print, making hay with the hypocrisy of your homey *Domus* motto, it doesn't mean I won't come to eat your food and drink your wine.

The motto on the Gray's Inn badge is actually *Integra Lex Aequi Custos Rectique Magistra Non Habet Affectus Sed Causas Gubernat* but that's a bit of a mouthful, particularly late on in a bibulous evening, and *Domus* is the standard, very self-congratulatory toast. Yes, badge, not coat of arms. The Inn only lays claim to a badge, or else Bluemantle Pursuivant would be after them for misprision of blazonry.

The revelation of that evening in Gray's Inn was the drink. Normally when I'm nervous in company I abstain from alcohol, but on this occasion I was too nervous to stick to that decision. There was champagne before the meal, or a good imitation, then white wine, Sauternes, red wine and port. After the meal, in one of the Combination Rooms, there was brandy or champagne again for those who preferred it. By this time most of the benchers were developing a distinct lean to one side or the other, some supporting themselves on the furniture.

I don't remember a great deal of the evening myself. If we drank a toast to '*Domus*' I hope that at the least I made a face. Another guest was Stanley Prothero, a family friend of Dad's generation, who was invited at least partly, I feel sure, to give me a familiar face to talk to. Stanley had been one of the guests at my parents' golden wedding celebration in 1997, held at Browns restaurant on St Martin's Lane. It's a chain that specializes in refurbishing grand premises, and this particular branch had been the home of Westminster County Court, over which Stanley had presided for many years as Registrar. He seemed entirely unfazed by the way his workplace had been turned into a sort of theme park, with courtrooms for hire and all the appropriate regalia provided. I wondered how Dad would cope with reality-melt on a similar scale, but Protheros are built to last.

Stanley's brother Arthur (born 1905) was also present at that golden wedding celebration, spryly taking photographs of the gathering, bending his knees to capture the shot he wanted. Those knees seemed unaware that they were entitled to go on strike, after ninety-odd years of work. They're the knees everyone wants to have, the ones with the extended warranty. At dinner in Gray's Inn Hall I asked after Arthur, and Stanley put on a bit of a show, entertaining the company with one of his brother's moments in the spotlight.

Solicitors like Arthur, being backroom boys, don't normally become well-known by association with famous cases, as barristers do, but Arthur gained some notoriety when he represented the accused in the Towpath Murders in 1953. Arthur had been paid out of public funds, and the case, though apparently open-and-shut, took up a lot of court time. The junior barrister he instructed (Peter Rawlinson) interviewed a police officer with what at the time amounted to great and sustained hostility, strongly implying that the confession obtained from Alfred Charles Whiteway was a work of fiction. There were no bent coppers in the national awareness, so hammering them could hardly be seen as a virtuous activity. Whiteway was convicted and hanged, but Arthur didn't take it personally (perhaps another difference between solicitors and barristers), describing Whiteway as an ideal client, regretting only that they worked together just the once.

General laughter. One of the occasions when a lawyer mocking the system that has filled his pockets gets an appreciative hearing from his fellows. Did I contribute a chestnut of my own to the game of anecdote-conkers, by trotting out the old story of Dad's client with Ménière's disease? It seems horribly likely.

If Dad and I can't help tracing the alteration of attitudes to sexuality, exhibits in a museum of social history, then the same is true of the Prothero family. Chief Inspector John Prothero of Scotland Yard, the father of Arthur and Stanley, was the only witness to be called in the successful 1928 prosecution of *The Well of Loneliness* for obscenity, after a typically temperate campaign against the book by the *Sunday Express*, whose editor recommended that healthy boys and girls be given prussic acid – cyanide – rather than be allowed to read it. The Chief Inspector testified that the very theme of the novel was offensive, since it dealt with physical passion, a passion that was described by the presiding magistrate as abnormal. There was no need to establish any culpable explicitness of expression for the book to be condemned (and destroyed). Theme did the trick unaided.

Chief Inspector Prothero's marked-up copy of the book was inherited by Arthur, but not the accompanying attitudes. Arthur agreed to represent Peter Wildeblood in a landmark case of 1954, a time when a bargepole's length was the minimum recommended distance between a reputable solicitor and a sexual scandal. Wildeblood was accused (with two others) of inciting young men to commit indecent acts, and was one of the first to acknowledge his homosexuality in public. He remarks in his memoir *Against the Law* that 'there is some truth in the saying that a man's best friend is his solicitor' – Arthur was concerned that his client was feeling the cold (it was March), and lent him a pair of long johns to make sure he didn't shiver in the witness box. He served time just the same.

I wish I could discover what happened to that marked-up copy of *The Well of Loneliness*. Stanley doesn't know. The British Library would receive a treasure like that with tears of joy.

I've attended social occasions where drink has flowed freely, but nothing to compare with Gray's Inn Hall in terms of the efficient delivery of alcohol. It was a revelation of what Dad's social life must have been like, not every night of the week, to be sure, but fairly often. When drink was so plentiful, when it took sustained effort to beat back the tides, sobriety became merely quixotic, a pose and a false economy.

I made the decision to keep close watch on my glass, to be sure that I noticed any sly replenishment. No-one came near, yet the next time I looked the level of wine in my glass had definitely risen. I began to see that Gray's Inn catering was run on a sort of Harry Potter system, dispensing with human agency. Our glasses were table-top Artesian wells, so that wine bubbled up through enchanted channels in the stems of our glasses every time we set them down.

As I lurched towards the 19 bus that would take me back

to Highbury, I was sure that I would wake up with the mother and father of hangovers. Or the Lord Chief Justice, with a severe sentence to pass on my lack of self-control. I woke fresh as a daisy, unaccountably reprieved from the hangover I had earned with honest toil. It certainly seemed that the cellar-masters of Gray's Inn were wizards of alcoholic immunity. They knew how to conjure congeners (those mysterious toxins) into cancelling themselves out, if congeners even exist. If only they'd been able to make the breakthrough in time for Dad to glide through those mornings when his unconfrontational wife told him some home truths.

The slow upheaval in Dad's thinking about sexual orientation made me feel that our intensive Anglesey session, Prince Charles, Jacqueline Bisset, old Aunty Mary Cobley and all, had been productive, sowing the seeds of enlightenment however long it took them to sprout. Then of course Dad had to go too far. Towards the end of his life he started being grieved by discrimination against gay people, shaking his head over the sheer unfairness of individuals being penalized for a harmless variation they hadn't even chosen.

I was exasperated. There's a difference between revising your attitudes and rewriting history. How could he be shocked by dilute expressions of a prejudice that had once been his most heart-felt credo? He was cheating by granting himself an amnesty, even a retrospective amnesia, and obliterating one of the strongest convictions he had ever had, now that it no longer suited him. If pressed, I could come up with more flattering descriptions than 'cheating' of Dad's ideological Great Leap Forward, but to say that he was refusing his own complexity seems to overshoot the target in the other direction.

One of the plays performed most successfully at my school had been N. F. Simpson's farce *One Way Pendulum*, which struck me as the funniest thing I had ever seen. I'm sure the mockery of legal language and process, Dad's moral and professional world, was part of what made *One Way Pendulum* such a hit with me. In the course of a surrealistic courtroom scene, Simpson's Judge says: '. . . you remained loyal to your masochism just so long as it suited you . . . The moment it was no longer useful to you you abandoned it without the slightest compunction. I can find no possible shred of excuse for behaviour of this kind . . .'

That was how I felt about Dad's reformed attitudes of the 1990s, with 'homophobia' standing in for 'masochism'. Dad was being disloyal to his perversion. It wasn't like being lucky enough to skip a hangover after a binge. He had been addicted to those toxins for half a century and more, yet that side of his personality and his history could apparently just fall away.

Horror of homosexuality was an integral part of his identity as a small-town Congregationalist, born in Wales near the beginning of the First World War. It was as much part of his heritage as the leek and the harp, no more optional than barabrith and *How Green Was My Valley*. It deserved better than to be thrown over when fashions changed. Doesn't seasoned bigotry have a proper and permanent claim to make on the bigoted party? It has built up rights over time, so it can be made redundant (with agreed compensation) but not just melt away without a word said on either side.

Barnacles don't just slip off the hull. They have to be chipped away at, and Dad's personality barnacles certainly clung, keeping themselves glued in place year after year. Actual barnacles have things called cement glands. I don't know what Dad used instead.

And then they were gone, and everything had been sanded down around and repainted where they had been, to leave a vessel spick and span, seaworthy for another pattern of tides.

It's possible that what I really wanted was not an encounter between Dad and his complexity but a soap-opera resolution between the two of us, with him begging to be forgiven for his blindness. That's not something I can rule out, however often I state as a fact that closure is for bin-bags not for people. It's even true that Dad had made some progress with his apology technique since my teenage years. He had learned that it was possible to own up to a fault almost without being put under pressure. Admitting to an imperfection could be a strong rhetorical move.

Making an apology needn't be like walking the plank. It might be more like a rope bridge. The moment of vulnerability could be cut short, and Dad find himself safe on the other side. Admission of weakness might even be redefined as the key to strength.

One example was what he said when I got a good degree in English, after dropping Classics against his advice. 'Well, boy,' he said, 'you were right and I was wrong . . .' – rope bridge, dangerously teetering – '. . . and I hope I'm a big enough man to admit it when I've made a mistake.' Back on solid personality rock.

So he could certainly have found a way to turn his change of attitude into a virtue. 'Well, boy,' he might have said, 'your poor old Dad may have been saddled with a lot of backward ideas by the time and place he was brought up, but no-one can say he didn't struggle against his conditioning. How many men of my generation have come so far from where they started?' That might have been a good thing to hear, but I'd have settled for him remembering Keith's name once in a while. Or perhaps I should just shut up and agree to receive what was on offer. Perhaps it was perverse to be refusing of him at a time when he was finally, and in his own fashion, accepting of me, the 'me' that he had found so hard to live with.

Of the two carers who made things easier for Dad in the last stretch of his life, it was Nimat I would have liked to see again, but though we had a couple of phone conversations neither of us suggested a meeting. She had stopped working for the care agency and was studying for a qualification in social work.

I had more extensive dealings with Bamie, though he didn't contact me directly. It was a solicitor who phoned to ask if I would testify on his behalf in court. Why? What was the matter? He was up on a charge, and my testimony could make a difference to the verdict.

What was the charge? It was rape. Bamie was being charged with the rape of his wife's cousin. My knowledge of legal procedure was and is rudimentary, but it seemed unlikely that I could give evidence in any useful way. The only way I could help Bamie's case was by proving that he was with me at the time of the alleged assault, and that wasn't on the cards.

I asked the solicitor if anything I said in court could possibly make a difference. He said it could do no harm.

Bamie's defence was that he had been having an affair with his wife's cousin at an earlier stage, when she had been living under their roof, and that there had been no coercion either then or when they resumed their relations.

There must have been a time when Bamie explained to his wife about the falseness of the accusation made against him and how it was to be combated. I was glad not to have been present at the conversation when he had given her the good news.

She had moved out, taking their son with her, and was now living in a hostel. Further misfortune had rained down on this family fragment in limbo. The little boy, exploring in an unfamiliar kitchen, had pulled a pan of boiling water onto himself and been scalded.

I gave an undertaking in principle that I would testify on Bamie's behalf, though I admit I was hoping not to be called on. I could certainly be a character witness, but how was that relevant? Rape is not something on the level of a character flaw.

It was months before the case came to trial, and then it was announced for a day when I was away on holiday – not on the far side of the earth, it's true (Devon), but far enough away to make my heart sink still further. It had to be done though, in conscience, and I took a train from Totnes with my praise for Bamie thoroughly rehearsed, ready to emerge in solid sentences. I still had the feeling that what I had to say was meaningless in this context, and if Bamie was relying on my testimony then things did not look good for him. A young female relative by marriage and an elderly stranger he looked after for pay were obviously in different categories. Ideally he would have mild and tender dealings with both, but it was faintly mad to look to one of these styles of behaviour for evidence about the other.

I didn't stay long after doing my turn in court, and returned to pick up the threads of my holiday. Later I heard that Bamie had indeed been acquitted, I imagine on firmer grounds than someone being appreciative of his skills as a carer.

Years later, when I had moved to South-East London and was waiting for a bus on Denmark Hill, I was startled by a car on the other side of the road doing a drastic U-turn, so as to end up in the bus lane next to me. A man leaped out of the driver's seat and came towards me. I have to admit that I recoiled until I saw it was Bamie, transmitting intense goodwill on a wavelength bang next door to the one usually reserved for aggression.

He told me that life was much better for him than it had been the last time we had met, though he admitted that it had been touch and go for a while. His religion had been sorely tested, and he had come close to losing his faith. He grasped my hands and said he would never forget the help I gave when he needed it.

There were so many reasons for cutting the conversation short. A 468 bus was heading our way – my bus – and even if I didn't want to board it Bamie's car was blocking the bus lane. He needed to jump back in and do another U-turn to carry on towards Camberwell. I didn't even have time to ask whether he and his wife were back together. In fact I wasn't sure I wanted to know, and I certainly didn't want to hear him talking about his recent history in terms of a test of faith, some sort of religious trial.

This was a reading of painful family events that seemed guaranteed to yield no insight, besides being unappealing to believers and unbelievers alike. The Book of Job would have exercised a lot less fascination down the millennia if its starting-point had been Job having sex with his wife's cousin.

Before I moved to South London I was unaware of religious diversity, in terms of the day to day. The beliefs on offer seemed to be variations on white-bread, meat-and-potatoes faith. Only Edith Wellwood had an unorthodox background, having been brought up in the Catholic Apostolic Church, a millenarian denomination inspired by Edward Irving. He's commemorated with a plaque on Amwell Street. The church was somehow both high and low, with a hierarchical ministry (angels, priests and deacons) but also talking in tongues, or 'speaking in the unknown tongue' as it was called in the church. As a girl Edith had been told to pray for the Lord to return in her lifetime, which she did, though adding under her breath, 'But not before I get my Matric.' The church died out like a self-limiting virus. Established in the first place to await the imminent end of the world, its constitution wasn't built for endurance. When the last Apostle died, in 1901, there was no mechanism for creating clergy, and when the last minister died there was no more church.

Living in Herne Hill I found there was an explosion of spiritual cuisine more or less on my doorstep, with many local varieties and no doubt the occasional attempt at fusion. I go most days to catch a bus or a train at Loughborough Junction, where there are such exotic spiritual blooms, though they are housed by and large in battered commercial premises, as the Power of Faith Continual Miracle Church, the Celestial Church of Christ (Clapham Parish) and the Light of God Evangelical Ministry (A Palace of Breakthroughs). There's a Vessels of Treasure Sisterhood that holds regular meetings. The Light of God Evangelical Ministry offers a monthly Night to Repossess Your Possessions, which I must admit intrigues me. Repossession has an ominous overtone, but I'm sure it's not meant to. How does the magic work? Do you bring along the possessions in question, or is a list enough?

The Miracle Times slips through my letter-box in multiple copies, with a list of preparations available that includes Court Anointing Oil ('tip the scales of justice in your favour'). I never thought lawyers would need to fear competition from aromatherapists, but that day is here. The front page is given over to testimony about the virtues of Bishop Climate Irungu's Fire Service. A woman's life was being made hell by her neighbours ('It was like this family's mission was to destroy my life, just because I'm alive and breathing'). She was building an unauthorized extension ('I like to pride myself in my home and personal belongings') when a lady came from the council to inspect the works, tipped off by neighbours offended by the noise. This lady recommended more ambitious construction, saying 'Why didn't you build more? You could have used more space!', so she went on building and the neighbours went on complaining.

Finally she put the family's name on a list and put it in the fire at a Kingdom Church service ('If we put someone's name who is innocent then God will spare them, but if they are guilty God will revenge for us'). It wasn't long before God got to work – 'people were saying, "Did you hear what happened to Geoffrey? His burial is next week!"' Yet still her troubles weren't over. Another neighbour 'was always scrutinizing my property, making my life a living hell'. Another list, another fire service, and 'the neighbour's wife is bedridden so that they need carers and expensive hospital trips. I've finally been left alone. Now there is peace in my life!' Loving your neighbour isn't the whole story down our way. For the benefit of those unable to attend Fire Services, Bishop Climate's 'prayer warriors' are waiting by the phones. Do they have the authority to accept donations, the means to process them? I feel sure that they do.

Of course I don't know if Bamie's God was of that sort or of another stripe. But whatever his denomination and whatever his attitudes, Bamie had a right to have the evidence I gave on his behalf, however soggy it was forensically. The tenderness of his duty towards Dad had been extraordinary.

While the general pattern was to treat Dad as if he was less *compos mentis* than he was (or might be), Bamie behaved as if Dad had full possession of himself, and full knowledge of his own preferences. What this meant in practice was asking Dad from time to time if he wanted to move from his chair in the bedroom to his chair in the sitting-room, or the other way round. I had more or less stopped making these suggestions myself, since Dad tended to say Yes to anything that was put to him, whether out of politeness or a spirit of adventure. Once he had been helped to move between rooms, I was careful to leave a lapse of time before suggesting that he move back, for fear of making the whole little expedition seem point-less, and the whole ritual of consultation futile from the first.

Bamie never acquired this little bit of strategy, and I have to say that I approved on general principles, however much work he was making for himself. When I returned to the flat late in the evening, he would say that he had enjoyed talking with Dad. Talking with, or talking to? He seemed confident that there had been communication.

Several times in a shift Bamie would ask Dad if he wanted to go to bed, and if the answer was Yes would change him from sweatpants and jogging top into his pyjamas, even if he found Dad horizontal but open-eyed a few minutes later, ready to give the idea of getting up again his obliging endorsement.

When Dad wet himself, I changed his pyjama bottoms. Well of course I did! But Bamie would change his pyjama top too. In some strange way, he had the higher notion of Dad's dignity and what it demanded. I didn't feel that Dad in mismatched pyjamas amounted to some sort of violation of the order of things. It wasn't something Dad was bothered by, and I didn't have another yardstick. That was good enough for me. Bamie's concern was professional, but it was more than professional. This, though paid (and indeed part-time), was devotion, uncomplicated by the turbulence of family feeling.

I'm not going for a big finish here, more of a syncopated-coda effect.

Some acknowledgement was necessary after Dad died, and inviting Bamie to the interment of ashes in Llansannan, though well-intentioned and certainly the right gesture to make, was probably from his point of view as much a test of endurance as the accolade and act of recognition it was meant to be.

The undertaking to testify in his favour was a better salute to excellence. No-one would choose to be accused of a criminal offence for the pleasure of hearing himself celebrated, but there was a latent appropriateness about my turning up at an address that could stand in for Dad's workplace, the environment of his daily life for so many years, and giving praise to Bamie for high standards in his own profession. High standards, and even something beyond high standards.

Come to that, I was testifying almost in the religious sense of the word, not really contributing to the substance of the case but giving vent to low-key middle-class whoops of acclamation and thanksgiving. Bless you, Bamie! Though whether that sort of thing went on at his home church I don't even know. Still, one way or another, it was probably an unusual thing to take place at Snaresbrook Crown Court, and even if it wasn't unusual it was a proper settling of accounts between two rather different personalities, very far from brothers, who called the same man Dad.